The Why of The Barkley
(and pretty much everything else)

Rich "Barkley scRitch" Limacher

The Why of The Barkley
(and pretty much everything else)

Copyright © 2019 Rich Limacher

Available for purchase at:
www.amazon.com

ISBN: 9781798132661

The front cover is the author's dubious depiction of the infamous "Limacher Hilton," which is what started this mess. The original spot is unknown, as he just barely remembers it at all. So he re-created these accommodations in a secure undisclosed location, snapped a pic, and made it *artsy* via the Prisma Photo Editor application of Prisma Labs, Inc. The back cover is the even more infamous RatJaw, also author-photographed and converted to dubious art by the appist making good use of his app.

Author Contacts:

Barkley scRitch
c/o C. C. WRITERS
www.ccwriters.net
P.O. Box 963
Matteson, Illinois 60443 USA
Ph.# [the box is too small for the phone]
E-mail [not in the mail box either]
Rich@Troubadoings.com

Dedication

In memory of Stuart M. Gleman, Ph.D.,
who literally hollered at me to write this book, but whose untimely passing prevented him from seeing the result of all his *encouragings*.

Acknowledgments

The author owes many thanks to folks who have been so encouraging (maybe even unwittingly) to his amateur professional career (oxymoron intended). Thanks to Frozen Ed Furtaw (for his first, and most excellent, book on the subject at hand) and to Cathy Henn (for all her books on the subject at hand and for kindly agreeing to read this manuscript) and to Julie Metzger Palmer (for beating this writer into print with her first, and very inspiring, book). Also thanks to Keith Knipling for his photo.

Considerable gratitude is owed to friends who have been particularly effective communicators—including Mike Bur, David Hughes, Leonard Martin, Keith Dunn, and Mike Dobies—and who have also successfully found various books that had been scattered around the "library" of Hiram Rogers. Special thanks is due to several extremely important "Barkers" (now deceased)—including Kerry Trammell, Chip Tuthill, and Stu Gleman—who worked magnificently to save the race from permanent banishment by one state department; and thanks to the entire Legislature of the State of Tennessee that in 2006 passed a Joint Resolution to keep the race going. To the Rev. Dr. Martin Luther King, Jr., heartfelt appreciation is owed for his universal inspiration. And perhaps something like "thanks a lot" is due to his convicted assassin James Earl Ray, whose 1977 escape from prison most directly impacted the founding of the Barkley Marathons®.

On a more personal (also perhaps amateur) level, the author owes incredible thanks to his wife Beth (the longsuffering Mrs. Troubadour) and to his closest friends, relatives, and pseudo-relatives (they know who they are) who tolerated his absences of both person and attention; and to a few kind and patient runners—like Herb Hedgecock, Sarah Tynes, and the late Norm Carlson—who basically kept him alive while "out there" at least once.

Finally, appreciation is felt for how Karl Henn and Barry Barkley support the event, but the vast preponderance of gratitude (perhaps with a little tongue-in-cheek) is due to Gary Cantrell for inventing this crazy race in the first place.

Fore Words

The Race That Eats Its Young
(and pukes its old)

In some vague way, this entire treatise might be an extension of the last chapter of my friend Frozen Ed Furtaw's definitive early history of the Barkley Marathons® that he partially titled *Tales From* Out There*. In his book the last chapter (#30) is called "Barkley Philosophy." Or maybe this treatise is more of a "rejoinder to" than "extension of." In any case, my foreword title here is only a play on words.

So if you, dear reader, have picked up and started reading my book, I would respectfully ask that you put it down and first go read his. Frozen Ed clues you in to what's happening here. Our particular subject matter *isn't* epic world-shaking saga, nor does it offer much fresh information about cannibalism, questionable nutrition, or bulimia. No. All that *this* is, is much ado about a footrace. And it isn't even part of the Olympics.

This footrace, as Frozen would tell you, is some unmeasured presumed 100-miler that takes place annually somewhere among the mountains and backwoods of Tennessee. Not only is the course not even precisely measured, but it's also entirely unmarked. The whole thing is one "loopy" unclear course of supposedly 20 miles per loop (there's a lot of us who believe it's closer to 25 miles) that is run five successive times *continuously* and in basically alternating directions within a *very* strict time limit. That's it! And if you can accomplish that, your reward according to the Official Entry Form *isn't* a half-million dollars, your pic in the papers, and a gigantic gold trophy. No, it's "you don't have to go back out" (for a sixth loop).

---

*Edwin J. Furtaw, Jr. *Tales From* Out There*: The Barkley Marathons, The World's Toughest Trail Race*. Pagosa Springs, CO: CreateSpace now Amazon.com, 2010.

But beyond these simplified basics… *ah, that's where the drama begins!* That's where you get all the rules and instructions and maps and tales and history and records and controversies and arguments and bragging rights and the entire "toughest" phenomenon with worldwide appeal and even a major, award winning, documentary motion picture** and on top of all that: you now get this crappy philosophy. ("This" meaning mine. Ed's is pretty sound.)

So the whole shtick about philosophy is "why." Why in heaven would *any* human on earth want to run some sort of footrace that's impossible? Why indeed.

First of all, I'm not kidding about the "run" part. You can't run in a jungle, can you? Through trees and weeds and woods and thickets and briars and rivers and mud-out-the-ying/yang and over-under-sideways-and-around huge gigantic hills (nah, they're mountains) both *straight-the-hell UP* and *straight-the-hell DOWN* and at night and in every kind of weather ever experienced on the planet! Haven't humans as a species *learned anything?* Don't we "get it" yet that certain jungle is impenetrable? Certain exercise undoable? Unsustainable? And some feats are mythical? Some efforts are futile? And anything like *this* is impossible? Hey, get it through your heads, humans: *You* can't fly!

And yet, here you are. You're reading about questions and nonsense and futility and "meaningless suffering without a point." You might even be thinking of attempting the race, let alone tackling all this verbiage. Well then, how about this: If The Barkley were myth, you would be Sisyphus. Hell, we'd all be! Which brings us right back to Frozen Ed.

In *his* philosophy chapter, Frozen compares the futility of a Barkley finish to the myth of Sisyphus, who was this ancient mortal Greek dude that somehow pissed off the gods enough to condemn him in Hades to pushing a boulder up a mountain all day, only to have the mega *rock roll* back down when he'd get to the top, and then he'd have to boogie up all over again from the bottom—for all eternity—which pretty much defines "meaningless suffering without a point." The philosopher Albert Camus (whom Frozen quotes) concludes that we must imagine Sisyphus is "happy." (*Huh?*) Apparently because at each new push up the hill, this

---

**Annika Iltis and Timothy Kane, Producers and Directors. *The Barkley Marathons: The Race That Eats Its Young*, documentary film. Barkley Movie, LLC: *www.barkleymovie.com*, 2015.

Greek dude keeps hoping he'll make it—*an' his rock won't roll no mo'.* Hence the internal uplifting *uh* joy. And thus Frozen Ed's Barkley philosophy is that happiness is found in the effort, not in the result, which pretty much explains away all the abysmal failure and keeps all the happy campers happy.

These two wizened sages, I should imagine, might agree with the old adage that fulfillment is found in the journey, not the destination. I would also imagine, regarding all the runners, that Barkley Race Management deliberately *keeps* the race "out there"—through constant course tweaking—at the limits of human possibility, or impossibility, so as to give 'em their money's worth and thus keep 'em all happy despite all their failure. Today's Barkley Sisyphus is no sissy. His (sadly no woman has finished yet) internal hope of joy is perhaps best illustrated by several now-finishers-but-then-failures who kept coming back year after year to start over. And if this Sisyphusian logic suggests anything, it's that those rare Barkers who have finished are no happier after their conquest than they were during their failure. This might be further proven by the even rarer finishers who come back to try finishing *again!*

All of that, however, sets up the Barkley philosophy in terms of failure. It argues that, in general, die-hard Barkers keep pushing on until they fail; and then happily tramp back to camp to laugh and joke and feel fulfilled—until the next year, when their happy fulfillment-seeking cycle kicks in again. This is all well and good, but it doesn't account for quitting. Sometimes you're just so goddamned miserable *out there* that you just cannot wait to goddamn *stop*—especially if you still have time to continue. Happiness and self-fulfillment never even enter the picture. As the star of the show says in that wonderful documentary movie: "And for some people, just to get back to camp alive is all they want in the world."

So that's what I mean by this treatise beginning where Frozen Ed's leaves off. He speaks of happiness in the *effort* to avoid failure. What I want to talk about is just flat picking up your pack and balls and going home. Sometimes ya just want mommy, *ya know?*

Oh yes, and there's fodder enough here for several shots at other people's canons (of belief, or disbelief). For example, why does The Barkley even exist? And if it didn't, would it be necessary to invent it? And why in the world is it so damn popular, and seemingly growing in popularity all over the universe?

And *is* it a footrace? Isn't it more like all that silly "reality TV"? Shows where, for example, naked people try to survive in the jungle someplace? [Of course they'll survive. There are camera crews and gofers and helicopters!] At The Barkley, you know, your basic survival is *not* guaranteed. And that could be part of the allure, too. Humans like to take chances, *eh?* Feats of derring-do and Las Vegas are built on that premise. "Free soloing" (climbing cliffs without safety ropes) and "going all in" at the poker table are two examples where your taking of chances could kill you—literally and, well, financially, which could then prompt your suicide. Of course, so far, not a single chance-taker at The Barkley has killed him- or herself. But it's exciting, isn't it? Hey, there's even rattlesnakes out there!

In my view, for all of the high-mindedness and nobility and glorification of what hundreds of years ago was termed "the noble savage" (watch that Barkley movie; you'll see savages), the invention of this footrace wasn't done as some expression of philosophy. No. It was conjured by a certain personality type finding itself ass-deep in some long-lost woods. It was created during a time when running and racing was all about *speed*. During the 1980s, for example, world records at ultra-distances were set that haven't been bested since. The prevailing mindset was "how fast can you go" and not "how much can you endure (without dying)?" So in my view, the creation of The Barkley came from a backwoods hiker who had been beaten in *a helluva lotta* footraces. There must've been a certain amount of chip on the shoulder.

The race's inventor told me himself that, after James Earl Ray escaped from prison and in several days could only bushwhack his way for a very few miles, he and his lifelong friend wanted to go there and see that terrain for themselves. After hiking awhile blindly—using their feet to "feel for" the actual mapped trail because it was so densely overgrown—the one turned to the other and said, "What a kick-ass place for a race!"

So that's how it started. As to *why* it started, we might have to psychoanalyze the shoulder chip. I like to imagine a frustrated ultramarathon racer wishing a certain "revenge" on all those fast-asses who couldn't find their way out of the woods if their lives depended on it. But put 'em on asphalt in good shoes with 100 kilometers in front, and say "go!" Then *zoom!* They go. [One hundred kilometers in roughly six hours—*or less?* You gotta be kidding me! I can't hardly drive that fast.]

So put 'em in the jungle for a *real* test of stamina! Yes? Well, then you have The Barkley, and then none of *them* show up. Nor would they ever want to. "Ultramarathoning is for speed racing, not jungle trudging!" And there you have it. That helps to explain why it took so long (decades even) for The Barkley to catch on.

But I get ahead of myself. These kinds of philosophical inquiries happen later (after I've had my coffee). For now, let the following suffice:

Running and racing, I like to say, is like recess for adults. And during recess there is always some squirrely individual who wants to "dare" people. And so, well over a half-century later, I have come to chalk-mark The Barkley as just one more "double-dog-dare-you" on the playground of life. I (and you too) have been thoroughly, tortuously, agonizingly, no-sleeping-all-night *taunted* by that bad kid in the class.

"I double-dog-dare-you to finish my Barkley!"

But what the hell? Today, right now, I just double-dog-dare-you to finish my book.

Table of Contents

DEDICATION iii
ACKNOWLEDGMENTS v
FORE WORDS vii
IDEAL CONTENTS (of your backpack) xiii
    This is typically the full course setout. If you are to finish, you must collect your correct page from *all* of the following:

For Loop 1:
    BOOK 1 Clockwise (your first objective) 1
    BOOK 2 Clockwise (your second objective) 7
    BOOK 3 Clockwise (your third objective) 15
    BOOK 4 Clockwise (your fourth objective) 19
    BOOK 5 Clockwise (your fifth objective) 25
    BOOK 6 Clockwise (your sixth objective) 33
    BOOK 7 Clockwise (your seventh objective) 39
    BOOK 8 Clockwise (your eighth objective) 45
    BOOK 9 Clockwise (your ninth objective) 51
    BOOK 10 Clockwise (your tenth objective) 59
    BOOK 11 Clockwise (your eleventh objective) 67
    BOOK 12 Clockwise (your twelfth objective) 71
    BOOK 13 Clockwise (your thirteenth objective) 79

For Loop 2:
    BOOK 13 Counterclockwise (your fourteenth objective) 87
    BOOK 12 Counterclockwise (your fifteenth objective) 91
    BOOK 11 Counterclockwise (your sixteenth objective) 97
    BOOK 10 Counterclockwise (your seventeenth objective) 103
    BOOK 9 Counterclockwise (your eighteenth objective) 107
    BOOK 8 Counterclockwise (your nineteenth objective) 113
    BOOK 7 Counterclockwise (your twentieth objective) 119
    BOOK 6 Counterclockwise (your twenty-first objective) 125
    BOOK 5 Counterclockwise (your twenty-second objective) 131
    BOOK 4 Counterclockwise (your twenty-third objective) 137
    BOOK 3 Counterclockwise (your twenty-fourth objective) 141
    BOOK 2 Counterclockwise (your twenty-fifth objective) 145
    BOOK 1 Counterclockwise (your twenty-sixth objective) 155

xiv   Table of Contents

For Loop 3:
    BOOK 13 Counterclockwise (your twenty-seventh objective) . . . 165
    BOOK 12 Counterclockwise (your twenty-eighth objective) 171
    BOOK 11 Counterclockwise (your twenty-ninth objective) 177
    BOOK 10 Counterclockwise (your thirtieth objective) 181
    BOOK 9 Counterclockwise (your thirty-first objective) 185
    BOOK 8 Counterclockwise (your thirty-second objective) 191
    BOOK 7 Counterclockwise (your thirty-third objective) 197
    BOOK 6 Counterclockwise (your thirty-fourth objective) 207
    BOOK 5 Counterclockwise (your thirty-fifth objective) . . . .
    BOOK 4 Counterclockwise (your thirty-sixth objective). . . . .
    BOOK 3 Counterclockwise (your thirty-seventh objective) . . . .
    BOOK 2 Counterclockwise (your thirty-eighth objective) . . . .
    BOOK 1 Counterclockwise (your thirty-ninth objective) . . . .

For Loop 4:
    BOOK 1 Clockwise (your fortieth objective). . . . .
    BOOK 2 Clockwise (your forty-first objective). . . . .
    BOOK 3 Clockwise (your forty-second objective) . . . .
    BOOK 4 Clockwise (your forty-third objective) . . . .
    BOOK 5 Clockwise (your forty-fourth objective) . . . .
    BOOK 6 Clockwise (your forty-fifth objective) . . . .
    BOOK 7 Clockwise (your forty-sixth objective) . . . .
    BOOK 8 Clockwise (your forty-seventh objective). . . . .
    BOOK 9 Clockwise (your forty-eighth objective). . . . .
    BOOK 10 Clockwise (your forty-ninth objective). . . . .
    BOOK 11 Clockwise (your fiftieth objective) . . . .
    BOOK 12 Clockwise (your fifty-first objective) . . . .
    BOOK 13 Clockwise (your fifty-second objective). . . . .

For Loop 5:
    BOOK 1 Clockwise or BOOK 13 Counterclockwise (your 53rd obj.) .
    BOOK 2 Clockwise or BOOK 12 Counterclockwise (your 54th obj.) .
    BOOK 3 Clockwise or BOOK 11 Counterclockwise (your 55th obj.) .
    BOOK 4 Clockwise or BOOK 10 Counterclockwise (your 56th obj.) .
    BOOK 5 Clockwise or BOOK 9 Counterclockwise (your 57th obj.). . .
    BOOK 6 Clockwise or BOOK 8 Counterclockwise (your 58th obj.). . .
    BOOK 7 Clockwise or BOOK 7 Counterclockwise (your 59th obj.). . .
    BOOK 8 Clockwise or BOOK 6 Counterclockwise (your 60th obj.). . .
    BOOK 9 Clockwise or BOOK 5 Counterclockwise (your 61st obj.) . . .
    BOOK 10 Clockwise or BOOK 4 Counterclockwise (your 62nd obj.) .
    BOOK 11 Clockwise or BOOK 3 Counterclockwise (your 63rd obj.) .

BOOK 12 Clockwise or BOOK 2 Counterclockwise (your 64th obj.)..
BOOK 13 Clockwise or BOOK 1 Counterclockwise (your 65th obj.)..
BACK WORDS 211
APPEND DICK'S (Official Entry Form for 2016—filled in) 217

BOOK 1 – Clockwise
Another Bullshit Night in Suck City (by Nick Flynn) or later
Defiled by Chickens (by G. Alexander Trebek)
(Your First Objective)

There is nothing more persuasive than the urge to quit. This happens with pretty much everything in life, especially when you're lost, hopeless, weak, lacking energy, facing humanly impossible challenges, gawking up at monstrously impossible climbs, and you are officially entered in some idiotic 100-mile footrace and the race has just started.

Welcome to the Barkley Marathons, a marathon so wonderful they make you do five of them. The Barkley tries mightily to contravene every basic truth and bit of sound advice hitherto known to man—and woman. Women especially. For instance, in the real world the sound advice (as Will Rogers first advised) is: "When you find yourself in a hole, the first thing to do is stop digging." But at The Barkley, the first thing to do is *keep* digging. Otherwise, of course, you'll want to quit.

The reason I called out women there is because women generally have better sense. They don't do the digging to begin with. They get some thick muscle-mind mensch to do it. They also have better sense than to enter impossible footraces, and quitting *anything* that men won't just isn't applicable. They're women. Women have better sense. With women, there is no machismo humiliated by shame. Women are the first to recognize impossibility, and so they quietly stop and move on. Men feel the *need* to keep digging.

Women are among the first to recognize the swelling on the side of the head when all it's doing is banging itself against the wall. They *see* the wall. Men don't. Men would keep head-banging and hole-digging *ad infinitum* if women weren't there to argue that it's all right to stop. Just quit! All this is changing, however, as you will see even during the present footrace.

What I'm on is called Loop 1. Like as if: I am soon (or ever) to be chugging along and grinding out a Loop 5. Ain't happening. I'm quitting first.

Isn't that odd? To be already knowing of The Big Quit before the end of a race that has just started. Almost every race I (and probably you too) have entered was all about the ending. The finish. As in, "How long do you think this will take?" "When do you expect to finish?" And "Are you going for a PR?" [Personal Record—which means: your fastest ever finishing time for that particular distance.] All races are about time. *Finishing* time. I have never in my entire "racing life" heard this asked before the start: "How long do you think you'll last before you quit?"

Until this one, that is. This one is an anomaly. An ugly, wicked, mean, and nasty mentally twisted afterthought. A freak of nature. Hell, a freak even of non-nature. Preternature. The supernatural? This Barkley Marathons thing isn't about setting PRs. It's about *how long will you last before you blow up?* And quit.

It's inevitable.

Certainly for all but the *supermen*. And for *all* the women, super or not. Because—from its very first running back in 1986 and right on down to this very day [at this writing]—not one woman has finished the Barkley Marathons. It's because they have more sense. But that may be changing. Keep on readin'.

So, what you automatically first know—at the very start of this race, and even beforehand—is that you're somehow stopping before the finish. Does this give comfort? Maybe. But what it gives more so is allure. Magnetic attraction. Enticement. Bravado. Machismo. The totally irresponsible illogic of men. Men think they're *gonna* beat this thing. Women want to "test it," see what it's all about, challenge the very pig-headed notion of men that women *can't* do this. *Women are too weak.* It tells you that in the very paperwork you need to fill out to apply for this goofy race.

If I were a woman, I would take umbrage. How dare any man say what is or isn't possible for a woman to do! Do men bear children? How is it even possible for man-unkind to pronounce universal pronouncements for womankind? In this day and age of gender equality (and, hey, at some 10,000 years in the making, I'd say *it's about time*), nevertheless it is a fact—so far—that women have never finished The Barkley. When estrogen has toed the line here, so far in history it has failed. When testosterone has toed the line, it has *almost* always failed as well. Except for the supermen, we *all* fail.

It seems to me that, in order for all this equality to become fairer (or at least more equal) at The Barkley, there needs to be a better commingling of these two hormones. The first woman to succeed here might actually have equal amounts of estrogen and testosterone. The vast majority of everybody else has varying mixtures. Throw in the hormone of chickenshittedness, and there you have it. Fewer than a score of supermen have—indeed, amazingly, somehow—finished. Everybody else (and I do mean *every single body*) has quit.

So, the obvious takeaway here is The Excuse. For this race, you will need some *excuse*. Some goofy silly-ass reason for, you know, just stopping! You will be pressed to give one, as you bedraggle your pitiful mortal coil towards the Yellow Gate and, sure, touch it in total futility. You are asked, "Why? *Why* did you quit?"

The best answer possible, I suppose, is that you died out there. But then, of course, you're dead; and so some other body will have to answer for you. I think of my very first time here, and the very real possibility that I might well have been that "other body." The gentleman I happened to be with... well, I hoped very, very fervently that he would *not* die, thereby forcing me into a moral or mortal quandary, thinking: *I'm lost. So what in the hell do I do if he dies? If I wait until morning and go off—where?—in search of help, how the hell will I be able to guide that helping individual back to where my partner is?* The better choice would have had to have been: *Pick up the corpse and carry it.* To where? I hadn't a clue. I was lost. And he and I had already quit. But when you quit at The Barkley, you still have to get back to camp. And *that* was the whole problem, right there.

I think about all this now as I look at: my watch, my compass, my map, and my copy of the "Official Instructions." None of this makes any sense. We're supposed to cross over the Pillars of Doom and "shortly after" see a little peak to the north and then turn right and go over the top of it. Right. Define please: "shortly after." And while you're at it: "the Pillars of Doom."

Let's say, would it be asking too much of the creator and writer of these cornpone, backcountry, hillbilly-type instructions to, you know, *instruct?* Using such useful terms as *feet*—or yards or meters or furlongs or football fields or counties or states or countries or continents or hemispheres or planets or solar systems or galaxies or light-years. *Give us something we can use!* I scream inwardly. For there is no screaming outwardly. I'm with Winter. Winter is *the* veteran Barkley pathfinder scientist, astrophysicist, and philosopher all rolled into one. You don't fuck around with Winter. He is omniscient. The Way, the Truth, and the Flashlight. You do not question our beloved Winter.

"It's over here," he says.

"The peak?" I ask.

"And just beyond that is Fanghorn Forest." He ignores me completely. Usually does. But I follow him willingly. He is, after all, The Wise Man. The Wisest of the Wise Men. *The Wisest of Even All Impossibly Wiser Men!* And he's old enough. He might well have carried gold or frankincense or myrrh to the Babe in the Manger. Except he's an atheist. And besides, he too has always quit. So during the ancient first-Xmas days, "Winter" might have made it to "spring," but not to Bethlehem. Jesus would then have had to grow up without coin under the mattress, hippie incense, or whatever the hell myrrh is. Hey, myrrh is probably the correct, exactly needed mixture of estrogen and testosterone!

But we're on a hill in the jungle, I'm with Winter, and he, as he says, "keeps climbin'."

And then he "keeps descendin'."

It's what you do in this godforsaken race.

Is it a footrace, or the human race?

Well, it has long been called "the race that eats its young," so I'm thinking the metaphor could go both ways. On the one hand, the athletic event is so damned difficult that *all* "newbies" are just chewed up—and either eaten and digested or spat out so nobody dies. No newbie has ever finished either—no, that's not true. There have been spectacular exceptions.

On the other hand, the bigger metaphor is this vile and wicked *human race* we're all in. And the case could well be made that people on this planet—once they've gotten theirs—do not want others to get *any*. It's *the law of the jungle*, the "me first" mentality. "If I can get mine, I don't care if you get yours." It's winner take all. The first monster to grow up gets to squelch all the little monsters. Or, figuratively, eat them.

We are the race that eats its young. We pretty much gobble up everything today, so that there really isn't much left over for the kids tomorrow. I'm telling this to myself, while Winter, who is several years older than me, is hollering that *that* should be the title of my book: *The Race That Eats Its Young*. Or maybe, with my edit, *The Race That Eats Its Young and Pukes Its Old*. Quickly I decide to scrap the whole thing and just watch where I'm going. This is Fanghorn Forest; it's wet and rainy and cold and miserable, and we are still trying to find BOOK 1.

It is, of course, in the last place we look. At the end of some long spur or spear or ridge or outcropping or *clearing* surrounded by a clump of trees, and under some gigantic goddamn rock—which takes both of us to lift—we find this ungodly moldy stinking plastic-bagged paperback book entitled: *Another Bullshit Night in Suck City*. Its author is some dude named Nick Flynn.

We look at each other. I go, "Exactamundo!"

We argue a minute about the appropriateness of that particular book's placement here, but we agree that its message of bovine defecation applies excellently well to *this* mud-sucking "metropolis of misery" that we haplessly now happen to find ourselves in.

There's another different book inside the plastic baggie that we've just unearthed, but the one in Winter's hands is magic-markered: "USE FIRST." It's all just another bullshit joke from the cosmic head librarian of hell itself, the race director of this ungodly crappy monstrous-suck footrace that *eats its young*.

We check our bib numbers, locate pages in the book that match them, and rip the sons of bitches right out from the binding. My bib/page is 65, and I don't know or care what his is. I think up a joke but say nothing. If only I were older than him, I'd skewer this mouthy brash Asperger's syndromic genius over a campfire and then *eat him*—while waiting for help that never comes.

For indeed, we happen to be the very last "geniuses," young or old, in the race; so if we don't get moving, *we* might get eaten.

BOOK 2 – Clockwise
Ten Stupid Things Men Do to Mess Up Their Lives
(by Laura Schlessinger) or later
Good Luck, Sucker (by Richard Telfair)
(Your Second Objective)

It's probably too soon to think about quitting, *ya think?* We've only just now found the very first book, and for this particular edition of the race, "The Official Barkley Marathons Instructions" tell us there's thirteen of them. And probably this is a good time to mention how that too is fiction, because really there's twenty-six. How does *that* work?

Well, as I'm thinking in my head in my early delirium, the reason might possibly be due to *my* very own "invention." I now hereby take credit for the whole bib-number-matched-to-page-number concept. When I first showed up at this godawful event, runners were instructed only to "tear out a page" (*i.e.*, any page) of each book found. So generally this meant tearing out pages at the beginning of the book. And by the time I'd get there, the book seemed half-empty. But I was bothered by the notion that, in many books, the first several pages are actually blank—or very minimally printed. So I reasoned, *how in the world does this prove I've been there and ripped a page out of the correct book?*

I then suggested (no doubt sometime afterward via e-mail, which was just getting started) that each runner's bib number match the page he or she is supposed to rip out. This serves a couple of functions: One, since no one's bib will say *blank* or *zero*, nobody needs bother with the first barely-printed pages of any book. And two, if ever (god forbid) any *search and rescue* operation needs be undertaken, the hunters and seekers could actually tell which book the hunted and sought last found before getting lost. If my bib is number 19, say, and I'm lost and in trouble, future rescuers will start at BOOK 1, see if page 19 has been removed and, if it has, go on to BOOK 2 and so on. Whichever book still has page 19 means I never got that far, so rescuers will concentrate their searches between the last book without a page 19 and the next book with it.

Lazarus Lake, the inestimable Race Director and Fumbling Father, liked my idea and incorporated it and now it's part of The Barkley, probably forevermore. Hah! Nothing is forever, as he himself will tell you.

But there are two problems with this procedural amendment. One, all runners' bibs must not be in strict numeral sequence. Why? Because each paper sheet in a book has two page numbers—frontside and backside. So you can't, for example, have bib number 19 for one runner and bib number 20 for another. Then you instigate eventual warfare between two runners demanding the same sheet of paper! [An interestingly wicked rule tweak might be, of course, to let the first runner who gets to the book keep the page; and the second runner, upon arriving and finding his or her page missing, then must quit the race. But also of course, that won't fly.]

No, the obvious solution is to restrict all runners' bib numbers to odd numbers only. Each book (as you've undoubtedly noticed by now) has a right and left side, and all right-side pages are odd. Their backsides are even. So, as I look again—today, right <spit> now—my bib is #65 and so is my one-and-only torn-out page. Which brings us to the second problem: More bibs are needed! Because this method requires that each runner who continues on subsequent loops must get new bib numbers, right? Because his or her current page from all the books have already been ripped out and turned in at the Yellow Gate. So on Loop 2, for example, I can no longer be bibbed with #65.

To go out on the next loop, every runner needs a new number in order to fetch a new page. Which brings up the third problem: What if his or her new bib numbers go higher than the numbers of pages in any one book on the course? [We could be talking some pretty thin volumes here, huh?] Well, this problem is solved by placing *two* books at each checkpoint, with some designation as to which one to use first. Always in Laz's fertile imagination is the *possibility* of "a mass finish." Mathematically speaking, that would require a whole lot of bib numbers and two big books at every checkpoint.

OK, that's not mathematical. But let's say, for ridiculous argument's sake, that on some mythical weekend all 40 starters will all finish all five loops. That's 40 different odd-numbered bib numbers requiring 40 different odd-numbered book pages (with their even-numbered counterparts on the backside) needed for five different times, which means: (40 x 2) x 5 = 400 pages. That's 400 pages with regular-printed numbers on them. Which means: no "front matter" (like prefaces and acknowledgements and whatnot) and Arabic numerals only. Which means: You're going to need two books at each checkpoint, unless you can come up with 13 different pretty hefty tomes of more than 400 pages each. Most of the *zingers* that Laz likes to set out do not have that many pages. And by "zingers" I mean ironic-as-hell books like *Another Bullshit Night in Suck City*.

As further proof of the paperwork quagmire, all this is assuming that each runner gets a new bib for every loop, and that his next bib will always follow numerically from the last bib issued to the last runner that started the previous loop. So if, say, your first bib issued is #1 and there are 40 runners, then (according to 1 + 3 + 5 + 7 and so on) the 40th runner will have bib #79. Sure there are 79 pages in a book. But then for Loop 2, the first runner out would get bib #81, the next runner #83, the next #85, and so on. Then the fortieth runner out would get bib #159. Repeat this for the next three loops, and you have #239, #319, and #399, respectively, for the fortieth runner to go out on Loops 3, 4, and 5. So again, there's not a hell of a lot of paperback books with 399 pages. [Including the one you're reading right now!]

So that's why there's two books per checkpoint—or theoretically should be—and sooner or later the stack of bib numbers at the Yellow Gate needs to start over with #1. Ol' Laz knows (because he and his crew set them all out on the course *long* before the race starts) just how many pages the thinnest book has. So, he administers the bib numbers accordingly. Most likely the slenderest volume would still have 159 pages, so the above *modus operandi* should be good for all runners for two loops. And generally—like today—when whoever reports first at the Yellow Gate to go out on Loop 3, Laz should have a fresh pack of bibs and safely assume that *that* runner's #1 will cause everyone then and thereafter to start using the second book at each checkpoint.

Again, even *this* assumes "a mass finish" by everybody of at least four loops. *Ain't happening.* Laz's two bundles of bibs are always quite sufficient. As long as this writer lives and breathes, there will *never* be forty finishers of Loop 4—all under cutoff, all finding all books and retrieving all pages, and all in the same race during the same year. I don't recall (I don't think) anyone *ever* needing to delve into the second book! It would mean that 40 runners are still in the race after two loops, yes? But no, that doesn't happen either. Two bundles are plenty.

I'm thinking of all this practical procedural rigmarole as we scurry, more or less, *straight-the-hell DOWN* Jaque Mate Hill. This is apparently yet another "course change *demanded* by RawDog." But what it really is, is a nearly freakin' vertical (and very, very high) hill whereon there is no path. It's just: pick your bearing and plummet right on down amidst all the trees and shrubs and blow-downs and weeds and leaves and sawbriars and *mud* and hope to hell you end up at Phillips Creek—where, by the way,

BOOK 1 used to be, before, I suppose, all these changes were "demanded by" (*i.e.*, blamed on) RawDog. It's a total bushwhack. Shoes digging, legs buckling, arms flailing out of control, we tumble *down*. Once I even dislodge a boulder and it descends (rapidly) crashing toward Winter's head, who's (always) a*head* of me. It narrowly misses.

"Jesus Christ!" he bellows. "You tryin' to kill me?"

"Sorry."

"Watch what the hell you're doing, asshole!"

"Sorry," I mutter while still struggling to either right myself or extricate from a clump of branches, underbrush, blow-downs, or sawbriars. There's *always* briars. I think of that famous old record album by Frank Zappa and the Mothers of Invention, *Weasels Ripped My Flesh*. Amen.

I think I'm bleeding. But I have no time for *that* now. We arrive at the bottom of Jaque Mate Hill completely off-course. Nowhere near Phillips Creek. So we "spread out" to look for it. After many *many* wasted minutes (or quarters of hours) thrashing about, Winter hollers he's found it. Hippity hip hop hooray.

We reconvene at that ancient cairn (think: rock pile) that marks the northwest corner of the park. It's on one boundary line (hence the North Boundary Trail) but you never see the other one: the west. No, until RawDog demands yet more total bushwhack course changes, Jaque Mate Hill is the only westerly jungle that runners ever see, and feel, taste, touch, and smell too. (*Mmmm*, fresh pine!) So we acknowledge the rock pile, within which BOOK 1 used to hide, spit on the ground, and leave. The rest of the actual North Boundary Trail is, in this day and age, fairly well defined. Of course, back in "my day," it was just more jungle.

We mosey along the NBT for *a little ways*, and then Winter urgently announces he needs *to respond to nature's call*.

"I'm going on ahead, scRitch, and off-trail a ways. Do *NOT* look—under pain of imminent death by blunt force trauma!"

"OK," I say. "I won't." And trudge again, and more slowly, somewhere *up* the North Boundary Trail. For that is indeed where we are. Somewhere. *I think*.

Basically what we're doing right now (well, I'm doing; he's squatting) is climbing Jury Ridge. Years ago, apparently, the Boy Scouts came here. In fact, they still come here. Many times I've witnessed the "caravan" of little prepubescent testoster-ones lugging backpacks bigger than they are up and down some of the park's more candy-ass trails. I have also—very late some nights in the freezing rain and fog—heard "cheering" up top from some sort of boys. That would probably be the Boy Scouts, camping at the mountain summits in specially marked backcountry camps like, for example, Mart Fields, or that one I'm familiar with in the fog near Tub Springs. There is nothing quite so bone-chilling as seeing no one but still hearing cheers very close to where you're trying to stay alive after midnight in the sleet and fog.

But that prepubescent caravan at least twice in the past had carried something *else* in their backpacks: namely, letter-burned wooden signs and stakes. They had hiked up the wrong ridge and planted one sign labeling the place "Jury Ridge." Then somewhere else they did Henry David Thoreau the favor of permanently misquoting him. The sign they planted there reads: "IN WILDERNESS IS THE PRESERVATION OF THE WORLD—HENRY DAVID THOREAU." But the correct thing that Thoreau wrote (we always say that people *said* it, while they might never have uttered the phrase aloud in their lives) is: "In wildness is the preservation of the world." Not "wilderness."

I marvel at the lexicographical carelessness of, especially, the Boy Scout Troop Master, who is of course supposed to be wiser and better educated than his charges. This is evidence of proofreading, or the lack thereof. Or it's just the complete and total breakdown of America's educational system today. Nobody's teaching boys to quote carefully anymore. Probably because none of their teachers are capable of quoting carefully anymore. It's a universal problem, or at least intergalactic. I've learned of late that literary accuracy is particularly troublesome on Mars, where, of course, boys and men are from.

You can amuse yourself with damn near anything while trudging along the North Boundary Trail in the company of an elder statesman who'd rather you weren't here. But just at the moment, *he* isn't here. But this is short-lived.

Winter suddenly catches up, and way quicker than I otherwise would've supposed. Must not have been a full loaf.

"Everything come out all right?" I ask when he achieves altitude.

"If it were any of your fucking business," he huffs, "I'd fucking tell you."

Thank you very much, Doctor Winter, I'm thinking, *for that succinct interview. We now send it back to you in the studio.*

Perhaps it is by cause-and-effect that haggling incessantly allows us to make headway. We argue (that's the cause; *any* cause) and then advance (which is the effect). We try to maintain what others have termed *relentless forward motion.* We switchback up to the ridge-top this way. *Zig-zag-zig.* Boom: in a matter of just hours, we're there.

Jury Ridge gets its name, I theorize, from the series of capstones along the top of the ridge, which look for all the world like a jury of "peers" seated in a jury box inside some imaginary courtroom. You have to have some imagination to "see" these things, certainly better than the Boy Scouts, who saw... I don't know what the hell they saw. They planted their damn sign on the wrong ridge! [Not to worry. It has since been corrected—moved off the wrong ridge and replanted on the right one. Pretty much right *here*.]

Later along the NBT, as I'm remembering, near to where the "Jury Ridge" sign used to be, there is something else (perhaps planted) that has a sign nailed right on it—high enough so no Boy Scout can tamper with it. That sign says "Legacy Tree." I have often wondered just what the legacy is. In my imagination I'm thinking maybe Daniel Boone himself planted that tree, except that I don't know how far south of Kentucky Mr. Boone ever trailblazed, nor do I have any clue exactly *how* some old trailblazer, however famous, lugs a little tree into a fucking forest already full of trees, and then plants the son of a bitch right *there*. The legacy must come from something else—where some Johnny Reb single-handedly whupped a platoon of Yankees, maybe, back in the Civil War. Hence giving rise to today's movie portrayals of Confederates bragging that "one good Reb can lick a dozen damn Yankees!" Maybe one did! Right where the Legacy Tree is.

New this year is the Vertical Smile. And credit for that, I'm musing, is probably due to the course "librarian," after whom it is named. Since The Librarian knows this course almost as well as James Earl Ray did; and because he collects what's left of all the ruined books after the race is over, he has occasionally been given opportunities to alter the course. Either that, or Laz simply blames The Librarian—just like he blames his friend RawDog—whenever it suits him after *he* decides some course change is necessary, usually each and every year after someone finishes. *Why?* To make the course tougher, and thereby increase the likelihood that *nobody* will finish the next year.

This new Vertical Smile is some goofy point along the North Boundary Trail where you're supposed to find the point, make a sharp right, and then plummet boucou hundred feet *straight-the-hell down*. The Official Instructions are specific. We read: "It is very steep at first, and then it gets worse." And BOOK 2 isn't even at the bottom! No. We're supposed to boogie along some stupid creek confluence, or other, or both;

then find the base of the correct ridge we later need to climb to *get-the-hell up* this Smile; and then consult our Instructions: "At the Base of that ridge, behind the draw between the two creeks, are two trees about 20 feet apart. Each one is hollow at the bottom. Behind the one on the right (West) are two large rocks leaned together. **BOOK 2** is in the crack between those two rocks."

We marvel. "Do you know the calculus," I ask Winter, "for computing the correct number of trillions of trees in this forest that are 'about 20 feet apart'?"

"Incalculable," he snorts. "But we're looking for the base of a ridge and a draw between two creeks. You asshole. At that exact spot, you'll see the two trees."

"Oh," I snort back. "Then that clarifies everything."

We keep descendin'.

We reach bottom, then hike and look for water, creeks, confluence, ridges, bases, trees, and whatever else. It takes for fucking *ever*. Winter finally hollers in the distance. "I found it!" And I cover the distance in a hurry, lest he leave in a hurry and I'm abandoned and then *I* can't find it.

When I get there, the "two large rocks" are no longer leaning together. Of course not. What is it about The Barkley that might give you any clue that those runners who are ahead of you will want to take care of you? That they'll preserve rocks and baggies and books exactly as they found them so that you, too, can find them? It's "the race that eats its young," remember. Those who have gone before you want only to eat you alive. You should study that dictum. Memorize it. It'll be on the test.

The book we need that was in the baggie on the ground—no longer between any *leaning* rocks—is now in Winter's hands. He shows me the title: *Ten Stupid Things Men Do to Mess Up Their Lives*. It's written by a woman, Laura Schlessinger, whose life presumably *isn't* messed up. We sort of grunt.

"It figures," he says.

"Are we to assume that running The Barkley is number one?" I ask.

"No," he argues (of course).

"No?"

"No. It's all ten."

"You mean, the 10 stupidest things we can do are *all* here? We do them all *during this race?*"

"You understand!"

Winter has told me this before. It's how, in fact, we met back in the day, and became great enemies. We were seated with a group of Barkers in some good old grandmother's diner having breakfast during the week leading up to raceday, and he was expostulating about—hell, I don't know—nuclear physics, space travel, atheism, whatever. He asked a question and I apparently answered it to his liking.

"You understand, scRitch!" he exclaimed at the time. And I felt myself privileged in that, incongruously, I might be in the presence of others who didn't understand. Ever since then, of course, the goodly doctor of philosophy and rocket scientist has done his level best to prove to me that I *don't* understand.

We rip out our pages like the Instructions instruct, and then we gawk *straight-the-hell back up* again at this ridge we're supposed to climb. The muddy cliff-like mountainside is in fact very nearly vertical. But nobody's smiling.

BOOK 3 – Clockwise
How to Stay Alive in the Woods (by Bradford Angier) or later
I Should Have Stayed Home (by Horace McCoy)
(Your Third Objective)

I'm pretty used to Winter's manner (or manners, or lack thereof) due to fairly frequently finding myself in his company. And the reason for that is simple: we're both older than mud, and slower than the entire geological process of rain beating rock into mud. We've been attempting this crazy race for years, and we have succeeded in quitting every single time.

Generally, Winter utters his traditional curse against the guy in charge (which could also include God, any god, or the god he does not believe in). The exasperation is more generally directed at the race director, who himself "blames" all these course changes on RawDog, which everyone who knows him just *knows* isn't true. Laz is a funny guy. He goes through life having fun—good naturedly of course—usually at the expense of someone else he can pin something on. In my case, it's that damn Hilton. In this case, it's new course changes; but in this particular case, it's Winter blaming Laz; but Laz will claim he's had nothing to do with it—it was RawDog—when actually none of the above applies. Supposedly. This time *this* course change is being pinned on The Librarian and labeled his Vertical Smile.

So, being pissed and uttering curse words all the way, we two start climbin'. The Instructions tell us to look up at this impossible ridge we need to climb to get the next book at Bald Knob. "It doesn't look so bad, huh?" Laz, the creative writer of instructions, writes. And then: "Don't worry, it gets worse."

Soon we find the "worse." We arrive at what the Instructions call "a highwall." It's this, like, *sheer fucking cliff!* Winter stops still, gawks up, and utters the following profundity in a pretty loud voice: "He's gone too far this time. Somebody's gonna die out here!"

Obviously, this "he" refers to our beloved Laz.

But there's an *out!* Laz permits us to go around this highwall—via several hundred yards of detour—and find a somewhat easier slope up. And there in those Instructions we find yet another "typical Laz." Obviously, you can go either of two ways—right or left—to skirt around a highwall. Laz writes: "If you go in the wrong direction, you will come to a place where further progress is impossible. Don't go that way."

That's it! *That's all he tells you!* No other clue! No way to know whether the "impossible" path is to the left or right. (But of course the correct path is straight-the-hell *up*.) I defer to my genius companion.

He defers right back.

"Which way do *you* suggest, scRitch?"

"Let's try left."

"No." Of course he's contrary. "Let's go right."

It figures. *Why the hell even ask me?* I think.

But also of course: his way proves to be right. OK, correct. But I reason that this is only due to the fact that he knows this territory like nuclear physics. And also, of course, he's a phenomenally good guesser.

Isn't that what genius is? Great guesswork? More than half the time his hypotheses are spot-on? I wouldn't know. Most of my 50-50 chances in life have gone the other way.

Never mind. *Finally*, we do eventually climb to arrive on the actual "knob" atop Bald Knob. Of course, it's not at all bald. (One supposes "bald" means no trees or anything.) Of course not. The frickin' thing is as overgrown with trees and weeds and shrubs and sawbriars as anywhere else on this miserable course. One rather supposes (knowing this park less well, like me) that the mound became bald after all the lumberjacks stripped the area bare, once upon a time. "Clear cutting" is the term. It's the same as "strip mining." It means, if you're a lumber company, you come into a woods and annihilate it. If you're a coal mining company, you come to a mountain and level it. If you're a politician, you're serving your constituency—bettering the economy and providing more jobs. If you're an environmentalist, you are utterly destroying Planet Earth.

But if you're me, you're lost on Bald Knob—which, after all that, was probably bald-looking since the beginning of time because of the capstone. Capstones lie atop many or most of the mountains in Icehouse Delirium State Park (our nickname for it). Capstones are these gigantic rocks about the size of half a basketball court which sit across summits. But in the case of Bald Knob, that capstone crumbled asunder eons ago. "Only the fragmentary remnants . . . survive," the Instructions reveal. So, over the eons this greenery has grown. And that is why you would never know where in the hell the "bald" knob is.

That old tribe of the Fugawe comes to mind. As in, *"We'r th' Fugawe?"*

I ask that of Winter. He says, "Be still and learn." And then: "Behold. *There's* that fucking rock!" Apparently, what we're looking for is "a big rock."

Indeed, he's just found yet another in an endless tour of BIG rocks. It is, as our beloved Instructions tell us, about 10 feet from a big tree which is just a little northeast of center at the very summit of Bald Knob. Right. So. *Where the Fugg Are We?*

Again, it takes us both to lift it. And there underneath, and decidedly outside its weather-protective plastic baggie, lies BOOK 3. The one marked for our first use is: *How to Stay Alive in the Woods*, by Bradford Angier.

Apparently, I think, *this old Bald Knob capstone never read Mr. Angier's book.* As if, of course, capstones were ever alive to begin with.

BOOK 4 – Clockwise
Left To Die (by Lisa Jackson) or later
Corpses Ain't Smart (by Rod Callahan)
(Your Fourth Objective)

Zooming back down the boundary trail from Bald Knob and trippingly switching through the switchbacks toward Son of a Bitch Ditch, a brand-new "theory" begins to concoct. While Winter was making his biological deposit awhile back, I myself took the opportunity to find similar relief. I did Number 1—while, of course, *standing* the whole time. And isn't it about the first lesson you learn in life, that boys stand to pee while girls *have to* sit?

Why is that?

At this moment in this wilderness along this pseudo-candy-ass trail somewhere in the middle of this non-race, I can come up with no good reason.

Why in the world of human beings does one-half the population get away with standing (just think of the time-savings!) while the other half is plagued with the necessity of every single time having to stop, pull down clothing, (sometimes having to extract one leg from shorts, etc., entirely), squat, and finally pee. Then *wipe?* Their bottom? With what, leaves? Why? Men don't wipe. Why should women? And then finally having to reverse all that, get dressed again, and continue along the pseudo-candy-ass trail, being only pseudo-relieved because of all that time lost!

So? Maybe there haven't been any women finishers because they *all* have to do *all that*, and thereby fall behind without ever being able to catch back up. This refers to two things, no, three: 1) If only men have been able to finish, then only men know the way, *eh?* 2) It then behooves women to follow those men, *right?* 3) But men can pee faster and zoom on ahead. Meanwhile the first gal to have to stop—unless she can persuade the man to stop—then and there loses the way to go, while she is, in fact, *going*.

It is a well-known maxim at The Barkley that "scraping" is well known. And well practiced. The deal is: the man who knows the way will always take the first opportunity to *scrape off* any and all of his followers, generally at the very moment of pee time. And it's totally unfair. (Is there anything at all about this race that *is* fair?) And the Men Who Know *know this*. It's unfair because everyone following some man who knows the way must stop and wait whenever *he* pees, but he does not *and will not* need to stop for them. The solution? Pee only when your leader pees; but it's unfair because, if you're a woman, you will be *scraped* if you can't pee as fast.

So. Why. Can't. Women. Pee. *Standing up?*

There is no reason. None at all. And I myself have indeed witnessed that very phenomenon! I have rounded some corner along some trail in some other race and wham: just off to the side, next to a big tree which is being used by one arm as support, I'm running—eyes googley—right smack past a woman *standing* with legs wide apart and using her other arm *and fingers* to pull aside the crotch of her shorts while, yes, *peeing!*

She could only smile. I could only admire. But I learned something. She was thereby *not* losing any more time heeding nature's call than a man would.

Bingo! Ladies: take heed. You, too, might learn something. Ever since then I have always recommended to any and all the incredulous women that I might know, to: practice in the shower. Or even (weather permitting of course) while naked outdoors. Yes, practice. Your fingers can function even beyond just serving as a shorts-fabric-holder-backer. Practice! [Little boys practice. Drunken men often don't. Thus explaineth women's universal complaint about all that *wetness* on the toilet seat.] Practice! Stand there, move whatever needs moving, and *piss fer heaving's sake!*

Soon, you will *not* be splattering aimlessly. Soon you will *not* be hosing down your lower limbs. Soon you'll be peeing completely equally with men. [Gender equality, right? Well? Hop to! You *can* do this!] And then, next year at The Barkley, you won't even be able to get scraped.

So, amending any and all previous conjecture about women finishing this race, there now needs to be added to the correct mix of hormones: the correct vertical urinating posture.

And *don't* do what men do. (*Huh?*) I'm talking about: standing at the urinal and looking straight ahead at all the graffiti, pseudo-pornography, or that day's "special savings" newspaper ads (if you're standing inside, say a Walmart or Costco Men's Room). No. Look down. *Watch what you're doing!*

It also begins to dawn, farther up this pseudo-trail, that most runners—of either gender—who attempt The Barkley do *not* do it in shorts. There are, after all, evil sawbriars to contend with. Which means, if you try running this race in shorts, the skin on your legs will be sliced to ribbons.

Imagine how peeing on *those* legs might feel!

So, maybe just cut a strategic "hole" into the fabric of your running tights or pants. (All the better, *eh?* If you just splatter pant legs, no one will notice *or care!* And don't worry, you'll be waist-deep in creeks soon. It'll all wash off.)

These "theories" come naturally when your mind is numb, or you are braindead. Which is precisely how I am now. We are, non-god knows, somewhere along this not-all-that-long-ago cleared NBT. It may now be candy-ass (Laz calls it the "Interstate Highway System") but it's not *that* cleared, and we do need to pay attention. We still have to leap across Son of a Bitch Ditch, visit the Coal Ponds, and climb all the way up to The Garden Spot.

We keep climbing. Which is weird because we're supposed to be descending. But this whole race is weird. The whole thing is nothing *but* climbing and, very rarely it seems, descending. According to the Official Instructions, we're practically supposed to make a beeline—following switchbacks of course—directly down and east from Bald Knob all the way to Son of a Bitch Ditch. The awesome technical writer of all these succinct instructions tells us: "It is recommended to build up a lot of speed, so you can leap over SOBD in a single bound." And ha-ha-ha to that directive. SOBD is this downward-sloping anomaly of nature that looks more like a small canyon than a big ditch. Actually it's just a gully, a washout from some creek connected to the Emory River that once-upon-a-time overflowed and carved out this gully while descending the hill. Hell, I don't know. But I do know this: the "son of a bitch" part comes from having to figure out just *how* to cross it. And no, you cannot do it by leaping. That son of a bitch must be 30 to 40 feet wide.

Years ago some inventive hunter or poacher had pushed a small fallen tree trunk across the top, chasm lip to chasm lip. If you were daring—and *very* steady on your feet—you could literally walk across the top of SOBD and be on your way in no time. Years later that rotting log had morphed into a couple of long skinny branches that were nearly impossible to walk across. And this year? Winter and I see nothing. Now we either have to crawl down into the ditch, go across where the rushing water used to be, and scurry up the opposite side; or, as he once again reminds me, we can go completely *around* this thing by going down the hill until the chasm lips level out with the ditch bottom. But that "to the time conscious runner" is not a very good solution. Better to go through than around.

We go through.

Soon we come to the Coal Ponds, which is where active coal mining was done, oh, maybe a hundred years ago, and the small "ponds" still contain some seriously contaminated mine water. There's also some coal chunks scattered around. You can take a lump of coal, if you like, and use it next Christmas. I have done this. But I don't think Winter has. Winter to Xmas is like plutonium to Hiroshima. The "aura" alone is all you need to spread joy and happiness.

I think all this as we sidestep the ponds and approach the old hill that recent do-gooders have marked with flags to make switchbacks. It's a son of a bitch series of steep switchbacks, but eventually we do poke our noses over the highest height. There's a road there. Winter knows the correct way to turn and, after a little ways farther, we suddenly reach the Garden Spot—which is the northeast corner of the park. But whoa! This year this is *not* our checkpoint.

But it always used to be! Probably since the beginning of time. And yes, these sudden cataclysmic shifts of *modus operandi* are always jarring to the system. We re-consult our technical writing wizard's handiwork. "Continue past the corner point of the park," he writes, "and go on out to the bluff. There you will see a big rock cairn. Next to the big cairn is a small pile of rocks. BOOK 4 is interred inside the small pile of rocks."

Let me see if I've got this straight. At the edge of the park we go to the cliff. Before we go over the cliff and plummet headlong to our death, we stop at a big rockpile. Next to the big pile is a little pile, and that's our checkpoint. *Hell, Laz*, I think, *this whole fucking place is a rockpile!*

But alas, my thoughts are too hasty and too harsh. The large rockpile, the cairn, is now *somewhat officially* dedicated to Barkley's fallen comrades. The first to be so honored was Tramper, who hadn't died yet. At least not before this cairn was built, probably by some hikers who wanted to warn future generations to stop at the rockpile and not proceed over the cliff and plummet to their death. [Here I *could* be risking cosmic warpage of the space-time continuum by thinking in the present of the future of a past that hasn't happened yet. But I'll take that risk.]

This cairn was here long beforehand, and in fact it marks Tramper's favorite spot on the course, which he called "The Overlook." Tragically, at some point in time after his choosing of favorite places, Tramper died *much too soon* from an apparent heart attack, having collapsed on the floor of his house when no one else was home. After his death, his lovely wife Scamper—they might've even met here, decades ago, during this very event (or not)—came back to The Barkley and personally handed out little baggies of his ashes to some of us who knew him well, to be spread around the course. I took my little baggie to The Overlook.

That circumstance might well be worth another parenthetical pause, not to mention space-time-continuum-risk, in order to discuss something in the past tense of a future that hasn't happened yet—while I'm standing here with Winter who's as lively and agitated as ever. It turned out that the year I went to The Overlook, I was joined by two other Barkers. At that time the cairn was not yet part of the course, but we left the Garden Spot deliberately and trudged out to the rockpile and the bluff that comprises this overlook. We left the ancient rocky and rutted "thoroughfare" nicknamed Quitters Road (because it'll take you directly back to camp) and climbed up and out there. I was with Beans and Trout, just us three old fogies. We went out to The Overlook to scatter Tramper's ashes. And then, lo and behold! It turned out that Trout was himself carrying a little baggie of ashes—*those of his son!*

Beans and I were dumbfounded. What in the world do we do about *this?*

Well, we're Barkers. We do what you do whenever you seek solace in the woods. You carry on. And the solace comes.

Beans came up with an impromptu prayer, we two acolytes dispersed our sacred relics, we bowed our heads and paid our respects; and then we turned around and took Quitters Road back to camp, too overcome at The Overlook to continue our race.

Three times, so far, I have repeated this funeral ceremony. Three Barkers that I knew personally very well have passed on, and their families have asked some of us who are still here to spread their ashes around the park. Which is apparently illegal—but don't get me started about *that*! So far, Tramper, Indian Tracker, one more, and Trout's own son have had their ashes spread around the Barkley course. All you future Barkers should be mindful of this while you run here. Or rather, trudge.

The last footnote to add is the fact that ever since Tramper's demise, ol' Laz reads the (growing!) list of names of Barkers who have died, but who ought never to be forgotten. He reads their names, our bugler blows *Taps*, and then he starts the race.

[But all *that*, in Barkley Time, will come well after *this* time, today.]

Right now Winter and I suffer very little from death, since we're so lively engaged in unearthing BOOK 4. He exhumes it first, of course. We rip out our pages, and then he re-entombs the books in the bag and the bag in the rocks.

Book setout (usually done in wintertime well ahead of the race) is nothing if not designed on purpose to spread grief and irony—not to mention sardonic humor—all over this course. And so today's chief BOOK 4, mausoleumed deep inside this small stone pyramid, is: *Left To Die* by Lisa Jackson.

In yet another cosmic warp of Barkley Time, here is the *real* reason for this separate rockpile [which continues to get bigger yearly]: These rocks are collected and left by Barkers who make it this far on the course, and who choose to leave a small remembrance in honor of all their fallen comrades who are being memorialized by the big rock cairn.

In the Jewish tradition, for example, leaving a small stone atop a tombstone is testimony to having visited and honored the loved one's grave. If you visit Jewish cemeteries, you will see this.

BOOK 5 – Clockwise
The Place That Didn't Exist (by Mark Watson) or later
The Places That Scare You: A Guide to Fearlessness in Difficult Times
(by Pema Chödrön)
(Your Fifth Objective)

So after all my warpages of the space-time continuum here on The Overlook concerning fallen comrades who haven't fallen yet at the time being written about here [these cosmic clusterfucks are right up Winter's alley, which is precisely why I write them], the obvious question now is: "Where do we go from here?"—which is precisely what I ask him.
"Didn't you read your Instructions?" Winter fires back.
"I kind of skimmed 'em."
"Then you're an asshole, scRitch. You're not prepared for this race."
"But *you* are," I smile. "Which is why I follow you."
"So now you expect *me* to save your ass."
"Right!"
"What if I just abandon your worthless ass and leave you to die out here?"
"Well, Winter, that's a good idea—for you. All's ya gotta do is outrun me!"
He's not moving very fast, and he knows it. I can in fact keep up with him, and he knows that, too. Today I am *not* going to be scraped by Winter.
"I believe we go that way," he points.
My own particular "take" on the next particularly whacky instruction is: *Oh, we're off to see the Buttslide, the Bun-derful Blizzter of Azz!* I remember that not-very-emerald shit chute from years past, but I'd also thought the Buttslide was taken off the course by *The Wicked Warlock of The Least* and The Powers That Wuz in their fairly constant efforts to thwart the race, but no. Apparently now the Buttslide is back on again.
Winter starts moving and I follow.
Now might be a good time to note by a good, conscientious author that what Winter and I are doing, and have done, and will continue to do isn't *running* the Barkley course. No, we're just trudging it. But you are

not reading the words of a good, conscientious author. So I don't have to note that.

But I might possibly note this: In the Official Instructions each and every single year since time immemorial, old Laz puts right in there on the very first page in rather large print: **"Now is a good time to reinforce the prohibition of switchback cutting."** [If you're caught, you're DQ'd.]

Seeing this forever on page 1 of the Instructions is what reminds me to add a note about walking, or trudging. "Cutting switchbacks" isn't really a current problem, nor do I believe it ever was. Except maybe back when The Godfather ran—and he really did run!—the course. This guy, now famous, used to tear up this course like nobody's business. He would do almost anything to save a second or two. So (although I never saw it myself—I couldn't; I'm too slow) I'm pretty sure his antics were the cause of ol' Laz's current instructional note on switchbacks. But ever since The Godfather stopped beating himself up (as well as the course) by always trying to better his performances, I have not personally seen any evidence of cutting a switchback. (But maybe Laz has?)

By the way, what that means is "saving time" by *not* following along a trail section's full length to reach its end before it turns—usually sharply back toward itself along the same lateral climb in order to ascend or descend *gradually*—and instead making that turn abruptly in advance in order to ascend or descend *immediately*. This kind of shortcut makes a fairly ugly mess near to where a trail is normally supposed to turn. It looks for all the world like some kind of weird earthen proof of the Pythagorean Theorem. You have two legs, a base and hypotenuse, made by the trail before and after the switchback, and a connecting "altitude" made by the right-angle cuts before the corner. I'm pretty sure ol' Winter would argue with me on this, so I don't bother to say it out loud. We just trudge on, not feeling any particular time crunch that would tempt us to cut *anything*.

We're actually fairly close to what's known as "the first water drop." Race Management (*i.e.*, Laz, who likes to substitute that collective term for his individual self—although he does have *some* managerial help—probably for the same reason kings like to say "we") cannot be labeled *complete sadists* because, well, water *is* provided, and at *two* different points on the course! The first is just past the Garden Spot and very near to Coffin Springs—which is off the course. Coffin Springs is to the left, while what's known as "the green gate" is somewhere off to the right, depending, of course, on which way you're facing. Downhill and somewhat hidden from the jeep road near the gate is where Race Management dumps, oh, maybe 40 gallons of water (in their non-original containers—*heh*—plastic milk jugs rather than lakes or streams or pipes). Once we look down and find this dump, it's to hell with any switchback-cutting prohibition—*we plunge straight-the-hell-down to the jugs.*

We fill our water bottles. We have both been here when the air temperature was considerably less than 32° Fahrenheit and discovered, to our immediate chagrin, that all the jugs were *frozen solid!* (But thankfully not today.) There's only one thing to do when your water supply is frozen solid: pee into your water bottles. (It's a joke, but again I refrain from speaking it out loud. Present company is the reason.)

Actually that has happened! (Or something fairly close to that.) I remember when one of the early heroes of our race, nicknamed Maple Syrup, was "out here" during his 2nd or 3rd loop when it was *SO COLD* that—believe this or not—he tried to warm up his hands by peeing on them. It must've worked, because today he's one of The Alumni. He finished all five loops that freezing year, possibly frozen solid himself.

In fact, the other memorable tale to be told from Maple's amazing finish, despite such frigid arctic conditions, is that when he was done he apparently showered in the bathhouse and retired immediately to his tent. The campground emptied out *in a hurry.* The next morning when Mr. Syrup awoke and emerged from his tent, he was all alone. The entire place was covered in snow, he himself was still freezing, and then he discovered one *very cold* piece of chicken (also covered with snow) still on the campfire grill from the day before. And he was so hungry, he ate it.

I believe it was during that freezing race that good old Henry Speir also tried unorthodox methods for thawing his hands. Henry's "patented method" for hand-thawing in the woods when everything's frozen—including your pee—is to bang them against a tree trunk.

Maybe this helps the ice to chip off?

But today the weather gods have cooperated and the temperature of the water jugs is above freezing, *well* above. So we have liquid, as opposed to solid, refreshment. And we fill our bottles with nary a word between us. Certainly nothing that's publishable in polite society.

From this point we trudge on in our attempt to locate, actually, Buttslide's Buttslide and Bobcat Rock. Buttslide isn't just the name of some *straight-the-hell-down* geological anomaly; it's the nickname of the gentleman who bequeathed the same to the slide. The *uh* mudslide. Because after the first two or three Barkers careen wildly *straight-the-crap-downhill* in that freakish deep trough, the whole chute is nothing but mud.

28   Loop 1

Buttslide is an interesting character—thoroughly ensconced within the medical profession no less—whom no one would even suspect of having a butt wide enough to carve out a hillside trough. But apparently, if you careen wildly straight down the same mud often enough, anyone's ass can gouge the hill. When and how it got gouged out in the first place goes farther back in history than I do, or than my Barkley visits do. I only know the chute. And it's a *mother*. *Straight-the-hell DOWN* and *gawd hep ya* if you need to brake or stop.

Anyway, we need to find it, and, according to the new Instructions, we need to find Bobcat Rock first. We apparently, somehow, just follow some *road*—other than the one we just found the water jugs off of—and come to some *switchback* and *ignore* it. (*Huh? I thought switchback-cutting is prohibited!*) Then just go straight-the-hell downhill until we find some *other* road and *that road* leads us to Bobcat Rock. Either that or we fall off a *highwall* and die.

It reminds me of the old Instructions. At one point when you came to a multiple-road convergence similar to this, those Instructions told you to "take the right road." "Right" meaning *correct*, not the one on your right-hand side.

Uh-huh.

After much map study and indecipherable instructions reading, Winter now thinks he remembers the *right* way, so he starts down and I follow.

By now I'm probably getting delirious all over these hilltops and hillsides, these constant ups and downs, enmeshed in briar patches everywhere we go, and bleeding—yes, from all the thorns and briars. I'd check my wristwatch, but first I would have to wipe the blood off to tell the time.

The day's actually getting quite warm—hot even—and I assume it's well after noontime, but well before evening, and Winter and I are intensely looking for the right road (now called a *coal road*) that will lead us to Bobcat Rock. Where is it? Why is it suddenly so hard to find? It should be easy. We found it years ago.

Of course, we were able to find and do thousands of things years ago. Things that we're not able to find or do now. Like find some of these books! Like find that gigantic goofy boulder—with a narrow crack, or split, vertically dividing the thing in half—which was somehow christened "Bobcat Rock" when it no more resembles a cat than Winter does a gigantic mouse. It should've been named "Butt-Wipe Rock," on account of what I remember as that big vertical ass crack up the middle. Also, it is apparently right across the street from the Buttslide, on the same damn road.

Ah, but there's the rub. There's more than one road! This one's a coal road. There are also jeep roads, haul roads, gravel roads, dirt roads, paved roads, country roads, county roads, forest roads, fire roads, rail roads, road beds, and all manner of deer paths and game trails. Years ago, when this whole territory was being mined and stripped for its coal, these roads were built for coal-hauling purposes, and they were built into mountain- and hillsides at various elevations.

Apparently, the coal itself was found at various elevations; so, at our current location (lost as we are), rather than force loads up to the next higher road or lower the tonnage to the road below, they just built a middle road. Carts or trucks or trains could haul the coal, but that makes no difference to us. Right now we realize there's *three* roads, and Bobcat and the Buttslide could lie beside any one of them. And when I say "road," you need to think *nearly disappearing rutty muddy overgrown barely damn discernable* "path."

Also in the old days, things like altimeter watches were permitted in the race; so you could pretty well determine your elevation anywhere on the course. Today not so much. In fact: NOT! Not at all! These days not even watches themselves are permitted! Nope. Now before you start the race, your wristwatch is issued to you. Every runner receives the exact same brand and model, and all are set to the exact same time. This is to ensure that nobody has an altimeter. So today Winter and I cannot check our altitude with any fancy-ass watches like we used to do in *the good ol' days*.

In other words, we're basically screwed.

"I think we need to go back up a level," he says.

"Back *up*? I argue. "Why?"

"And isn't *that* the fundamental question of existence," comes Winter's rejoinder. "Why!"

"Right."

So I resume thinking. We are here because we're lost. Any idiot can see that. But only temporarily, because most idiots can't see. And *the reason why* they can't see that we're only temporarily lost is because they don't know our history, that we've found the right road before, and that the damn objective really *is* pretty close to where we are right now.

The other thing I think, as I ponder the thought I've just thunk, is that it contains a rhetorical error. Yes, it was none other than my old *old* friend The Grammarian who explained that "the reason why" is redundant. It's because "the reason" itself is the "why." You don't need to repeat it. So in my previous thought, I should have trimmed it to state that *the reason they can't see that ... is yadda yadda.* You don't even have to say "because" after the "is." The idiots out here, who might actually see us, won't know we are only temporarily lost, instead of permanently lost, because they really don't know shit—certainly not about *us*.

Besides, if we're permanently lost, we'll likely end up dead out here. And they (Race Management) won't want that because we would then need to be buried and they do *not* want to be stuck having to do it. Presumably they would prefer we do it ourselves.

And ain't *that* the illogic of The Barkley?

So it turns out that our original descent made it to the correct level after all. Winter suddenly recognizes it on our way back up to the next higher level, when he happens to look down and see the correct level below us; so then we have to go back down. This is complicated, but consider that Winter and I haven't had to hunt for these parts for quite a few years. Unless your memory is sharper than Winter's, you're going to make the same mistakes he's making. If your memory is a whole lot worse (mine would qualify), you're going to remember a whole lot less and the mistakes you make will number a whole lot more. Which suddenly reminds me of an axiom I invented some years ago.

It goes like this: *Before you can possibly know what's not enough, you first have to know nothing.*

It is in this spirit that I continue to traipse after Winter all around this course.

We are essentially heading south along one of the jeep roads that was built there to haul away coal from the mountain behind us, the one that Tramper's Overlook overlooks. More or less. Point being that *that* was high ground and we are *still* on high ground but we've made some major descents, even cutting a switchback or two—per the Instructions methinks—despite the prohibition. And trippingly do we *ease on down the road...* towards The Wiz? No, The Bobcat.

Winter sees it first, of course, on the left. Presumably, then, the Buttslide is on the right. But the Buttslide happens *before* the Bobcat, but you have to go all the way to the Bobcat to find the Buttslide, which, at the moment, is invisible. All I'm seeing downhill on the right is a slope going downhill—a pretty steep one at that. Somewhere down beyond this road-level assemblage of all the required briars and weeds is the top of the mudslide chute. We are told it's unmistakable. Wide enough for just one butt at a time, and slick as shit and muddy as hell and straight-the-crap damn *down!*

Years ago I remember a discarded (and crushed) green soda bottle marking the spot. So you'll never guess what. It's still here!

We turn off the road, right here, and immediately begin the horrible plunge down. We are beginning the hapless condition and circumstance of *breaking every limb on our bodies!*

It is a *loooooooong* damn way to the bottom, complete with a few almost-flat spots along the way, which are put there by the local building code. You cannot have one single uninterrupted staircase that goes for six or seven stories straight up-and-down. No. You need to install *landings*. These we notice during our downward plummet, and they damn near break our backs (in addition to our falls); but at the bottom I have to conclude that "the Buttslide is up to code."

I say this to Winter after we've both stopped plummeting, and he goes, "What the hell are you talking about, scRitch?"

"Never mind."

We stand there shaking, and then we try shaking all the mud off our pants. And shirts. And skin. And everything else that becomes mud-caked on the way down mudslides. It's not fun at all, so I deem it not best to dwell upon. But I do halfway curse Buttslide himself for having ever invented such a non-thrill "ride" in this totally non-amusement park.

One of the new "twists" this year is: When you land your butt at the bottom—and have to trudge yet another lengthy distance out-and-back to collect your next page—you then have to turn around and climb back *UP* the Buttslide! This is impossible, especially if it's raining (or has been recently), and so then your best option is death. Try to do it quietly and make sure you're not a Yankee. The Official Entry Form for this silly footrace specifically states: "No Yankees: we don't want them buried here." So maybe on second thought, you *don't* want to die on (or off) the Buttslide. Winter and I don't, of course—otherwise this narrative would have a whole different tone, *ya think?*—die, I mean.

Instead of dying, we trudge on, looking for—and eventually finding—all the waterways, confluences, juxtapositionings, flat spots, and ancient settlement ruins, just like the Instructions instruct us. Eventually we find the (yet another) huge damned stone in the correct damned corner of those ancient damned ruins, under which is our next damned book.

We lift the rock and pull out the plastic baggie and Winter pronounces: *"The Place That Didn't Exist.* Well la-de-da," he says. "It still doesn't, but we found it anyway."

Loop 1

"Let's not tell anybody," I wisecrack back. "That way this place will *stay* in its state of non-existence."

"You asshole," he says. "Who you gonna *not* tell? We're last!"

Oh, that.

BOOK 6 – Clockwise
Southern Discomfort (by Rita Mae Brown) or later
Wait for Tomorrow (by Robert Wilder)
(Your Sixth Objective)

We turn around, without further philosophy, and trudge back the way we came. We then stand—this time—at the *base* of the Buttslide. *Cheeses Aitch Crisp but it's a bloody muddy long flocking way UP!*

Winter immediately starts the climb, and I hesitatingly fall behind. Then we climb and climb and climb and climb and climb and slip and slip and slide and fall back and fall and fall and slip and try climbing again and grab weeds and briars and vines and stumps and twigs and trunks of trees that come right out of the ground in our bloody muddy hands and we dislodge boulders that come crashing down—nearly on our heads, killing us instantly, or at least inflicting major headaches—and we occasionally fall *out* of the trough and careen wildly back downward and curse, loudly and soundly, the respectfully unnamed motherfucking son-of-a-bitch that routed this goddamned miserable mud-sucking backwoods course through these horrible gut-retching jungles and mountains just to mess with us, and that goddamned miserable assassin jagoff who escaped from that filthy-assed-mountain state prison in the first place.

I am so mad at this moment I could projectile defecate. Launch nuclear poo right out my shit silo.

We, as they say, just "suck it up" and keep climbin'. Eventually we do make it to the top and pour ourselves out onto that same pissing jeep road we left so long ago. Tattered and torn and with bruised egos to match, we curse.

"Fuckin' Buttslide!" Either he says it or I do, but we both mean it. And I fully expect him to add his famous line "this time he's gone too far," but he doesn't. At least not that I can hear.

We *ease on down the road* a tad and there, on the left, is Bobcat Rock. We find the high vertical cleft which, upon much closer inspection, is actually the entrance to a cave (sort of). The Instructions instruct us that this is a good place to: 1) be out of the weather, and 2) stop and have a cigarette or a snack.

What is this guy smokin'? I think to myself. But of course I already know: *Camel Filters*, I think.

And maybe Race Management stopped here to suck down a sandwich and a cig, but Winter and I are on a mission. As these damned Instructions further instruct, we go all the way through this "cave" and climb up and out of the rock at the other entrance we are to find at the rear. And then, of course, *keep* climbin'.

In rocky geological maniacal allegorical lunacy, what we're doing (as I twistedly imagine) is "fucking" the Bobcat. We ease our way into the vagina, stay awhile, have a smoke, and then—miraculously although non-humanly—ooze out the other side: the *um* anus? Well, I know better than to voice this fantasy to Winter. He'd use every power of his argumentative arsenal to try and convince me I'm a pervert.

What if he'd be right? I think to myself.

Cumming *um* out the other side of Bobcat, we climb up some brand-new ridgeline and proceed to follow it all the way to something else brand-new: The Librarian's Pool & Spa.

Supposedly this is yet another "official resting place" (to sit, eat, and smoke?) mainly because there's a sofa. Yes, a goddamned *sofa* out in the middle of nowhere, on top of a mountain, sitting before obvious evidence of campfires, and flanked by a couple of weird flags and banners.

Actually the sofa is a truck seat. One of those dark red bench seats that was probably ripped out of a pickup truck and hauled—doubtless by the Ku Klux Klan—all the way up here for, yes, smoking and snacking and drinking and *cross burning?*

There are certainly enough empty beer cans to suggest all this. And these weird banners and flags?

But what's truly noteworthy about this so-called "pool and spa" is that I actually have been here before. In fact, one (you're not the one) might even say, "scRitch discovered it!" I can, however, take some bragging rights from the fact that years ago I happened to be in the company of Sawzall (a legend at this race) and several others while we were scouting out routes down from the mountain in order to hit just the right spot for crossing the highway. And it's a total bushwhack no matter how you slice it, or how the sawbriars slice you.

In those early days, it was permissible for Barkers to reconnoiter the course before raceday. Not in *these* perilous times though. You get caught off-trail even once today, and you're disqualified from running the race *forever!*

Don't do it. Just hike along the prescribed public park trails. It'll give you enough of a workout, and it will teach you all the convenient escape routes for when, during the race itself, *you quit*.

Back to thinking about Sawzall; sadly I have to say he *was* a legend because unfortunately he met with what most of us might consider an "untimely" or much-too-early death. And do note again my warpage of the space-time continuum. At the time I'm thinking this, Sawzall's alive; at the time I'm writing this, he has met his demise. He was, however, in his seventies, so why would anyone think he was possibly short-changed late in life? The reason is because the man was a stallion. A stud! He was too fit to die! He could—and did—outclimb, outdistance, and outrun just about everybody, yours truly included. Me at, what, three-fourths his age?

Anyway I'll never forget that day with him on our totally spontaneous hiking trip, and how a group of us drove out to the highway (it's a two-lane county road, but it *is* paved, so there is that) and parked in a "scenic pull-off" section and then bushwhacked up the mountain—Sawzall first, another camper second, then another, maybe one more, and me bringing up the rear. It was all I could do to keep them in sight! These are old men! Try not to imagine my embarrassment. I'll try not to as well.

Eventually, after a fairly circuitous route (which included discovering a Civil War cemetery, maybe), we finally came to a "place" that had obviously been visited before. My first impression? It was a mountaintop gathering place for the Ku Klux Klan. No kidding. There were weird banners and flags with suspicious symbolism. There was a campfire pit and many, many discarded beer cans. But the *pièce de résistance* was this truck seat. Just imagine all the subversion that can be planned by the Klan, surrounding a blazing fire on a mountain, guzzling beer—being careful to hit the mouth-holes in their hoods—and roasting their wienies and s'mores while sitting on a truck seat! Then unfurling their symbolic, though questionable, insignia, while caucusing for an unyielding true-blue far-right political agenda and applying parliamentary points of order to their psychotic action items. It boggles the mind!

When we found this that day, Sawzall immediately sat on the seat and posed for my picture. And it's this photograph that provided the impetus for modifying the course and making all the runners climb up here—even if for only a pause or a so-called "rest"—and calling the damned spot "The Librarian's Pool and Spa." And I guess the reason for *that* is because it was The Barkley Librarian who asked me for the photo.

Ever since then, of course, I have come to believe that the Ku Klux Klan had nothing to do with it. It was all just one more example of what Winter is fond of calling my "bullshit."

"scRitch, you asshole!" he bellows after I tell him about me and The Librarian and Sawzall. *"That's* not KKK insignia. That's the Tennessee State Flag!"

Oh.

Ouch.

And probably whatever other insignia is here, it's that of the Boy Scouts, the local chapter of the Moose or Elks or Lions or Rotary, or possibly even a hazing spot for initiating pledges into some local college fraternity. (Is there a local college with fraternities in this hidden backwoods part of the country? Methinks not.) Maybe it's where fraternities from other parts of the country get together with sororities and hold orgies? Nah, no mattresses. So it's probably just the monthly meeting place of the local Good Old Boys' hunting club. Possibly those same old boys who built a deer stand down by the Buttslide.

Winter decides to take advantage. He plants his ass right down onto that wiggly mountaintop truck seat.

"Go on without me," he snorts. "This place is like Stuckey's. It's my fuel and souvenir stop." He proceeds to pull some food out of his hip-pack.

"Nah," I say, knowing full well that I *can't* go on without him—I would be lost in twenty minutes. "I'll just join you in a sandwich."

"Sit over there!" he roars. "This fucking wobbly seat is about to fall off the mountain!"

"OK," I say as I plop on a log. "This certainly was some kind of meeting spot for somebody."

"Imagine lugging this seat up here."

"Right," I say. "It's no doubt something *you'd* make *me* do."

He shoots me an evil-eye look.

"I'm always good to you, goddamn it, scRitch. I've never gotten you lost, have I?"

This time I shoot *him* a look.

"You've never had to sleep in the woods under a goddamn space blanket, have you?" he demands.

"Only once."

"Never with *me!* I've saved you from that."

"Right."

We sit in silence for a while, just munching lunches. Then, when *he's* ready and I'm not, we get up to leave.

"Try to keep up," he growls, still being goddamn nice.

One would think—wouldn't one?—that maybe the best place to hide BOOK 6 would be right underneath that truck seat. Oh, but no. We are not dealing with any one *one* who does anything whatsoever that could possibly be construed as "best" or "obvious" or "most beneficial" or even "most appropriate." No. What we have here is nice and sweet psychosis bordering on sincere sadomasochism.

It's why Winter keeps saying: "This time he's gone too far."

But this time, miraculously, he hasn't gone too far. *We* have. We apparently strode right past all the "stuff"—the markers—and now we have to turn around and go back a ways. We're looking for all kinds of "new" stuff, like Phike's Peak Crater, a 4-wheeler track, and the Foolish Stu Trail—whatever the hell *that* is. Winter seems to have some sort of premonition, perhaps, and we keep looking in an area where we *know* we're close.

Upon our re-walk and re-search, Winter finally finds what we're looking for. There's this gigantic goddamn *stone* (again with the stone) which, as the Instructions instruct us, is about the size of a large dining room table. Does *The One* actually expect us lowly and, by now, emaciated runners *to lift that thing?* No. That one *one* has a better idea. This huge stone block is chock full of "boreholes." One of them has little stones inside. All the others have rattlesnakes. Our job is to find the book in the correct borehole under the little stones instead of under the snakes. But oh by the way, they *could* be one and the same. What's to prevent a big fat rattler from coiling up on top of the stones which are on top of the book?

The Official Instructions fail to give guidance here. Winter goes around plunging in his arm up to the elbow.

"What if you find a rattlesnake?" I inquire.

"Then we'll eat a better supper," he responds matter-of-factly. "They taste like chicken."

"Cooked or raw?"

"Strangled! Just gimme one lousy fucking rattling snake," Winter boasts, "and I'll twist the little bastard into sushi."

Thankfully, he finds the book snakeless.

Pulling out the plastic and extracting the correct copy, he intones: "*Southern Discomfort*. And ain't *that* the truth?"

"There would be a whole lot more discomfort with a rattlesnake," I suggest.

"No, scRitch," he says, "there'd be less. 'Cuz *you'd* be prepping the sushi!"

As we rip out our pages, I'm wondering if I could possibly like the taste of *any* sushi ever again. This is especially problematic since I have never liked it in the first place. I think I would pass on the raw rattlesnake chunks, and begin a diet of leafy weeds instead. If we were both *uh* "out here" starving to death, that is.

BOOK 7 – Clockwise
The Confusion of Languages (by Siobhan Fallon) or later
Maelstrom of Pee (by Roy Cohn)
(Your Seventh Objective)

From here (wherever here is)—What, the corner of Foolish Stu Trail and the 4-wheeler track? No, this gigantic granite block with the snake holes inside!—our next objective is *down the hill and across the road to grandmother's Testicle Spectacle we go.*

Grandmothers, of course, don't often have testicles, but the spectacles are *de rigueur*. Still, they don't often need to bushwhack a couple miles straight downhill and cross a nasty highway and then climb a totally nasty mountain to find them. They can generally retrieve their spectacles by reaching down on top of their gigantic breasts and grabbing the chain.

Not so with Barkers. Winter and I must now begin downwards the same bushwhack that Sawzall and I once did upwards. Our task then was to find the quickest way up (and down) this nasty Phike's Peak. Our task now is to get only down, and end up at that same pull-off where Sawzall and company parked our cars. That little parking place is right dead-center where we cross the road in order to get to the other side where all the Spectacle is. [Question: Why did the half-impotent old Barker cross the road? Answer: To find *that* Testicle, of course!]

Getting down wild and woody briar-infested perilously steep muddy slopes in the jungle is… not… easy. The descent all by itself is difficult, but adding to that the difficulty of following Laz's frickin' Instructions makes it next to impossible. We're supposed to follow tracks and ridge lines; bypass high walls; find park boundary lines and markers; find "game trails" (*what in the piss is a "game trail"?*); go down bluffs, dirt banks, and cracks in rocks; locate draws, old ruins, and even geographic features that line up with certain words printed *on the fucking park map, fer chrissakes!* You have *got* to be kidding me.

Thankfully, I remember the old ruins from my old trek with that spritely "young" man of 70 nicknamed Sawzall. Nevertheless, Winter and I emerge from the jungle probably an eighth of a mile off course. Since we're not at the pull-off parking, which way do we go along the highway to find it? Well, I go left, he goes right, and we holler when we're there.

Oh, one other "thing" about these Instructions. We also have to find some new river (not kidding, its actual name is the New River) and cross that to get to the highway. But if the raging river is too high, we're instructed to take a detour. (How many more miles does this add to our journey? We hesitate to guess. But today we don't have to. The New River's old water is down.) The detour takes us to a bridge, but the bridge is on—or right next to—some local green-teeth trigger-happy hippie-hating redneck, and thus we are emphatically warned in the Instructions: **"If you wander into that man's yard, he will probably shoot you."**

Supposedly there's "a little waterfall" on the other side of the highway that designates *the right place*. I've been here a dozen times and have never seen a damn waterfall. Instead, I know that the place to begin climbing (there is always climbing) is located very close to the county boundary line sign which is conveniently provided for whizzing-by motorists. So never mind getting shot. We are much more likely to end up splattered on the pavement as "road kill."

Winter hollers first. He sees the roadside sign first—and waterfall too no doubt—so I try hurrying along toward his voice. I know full well that if I don't get there quickly, he'll be happy to scrape me.

He's halfway up the hill on that side of the highway by the time I get there. I look up. Still no waterfall, but his butt is in much plainer evidence. So I start climbin'. We don't actually get to the *bottom* of the Testicle Spectacle until we've climbed *up* about half a mile.

In my mind I'm remembering the last time I faced this, and that I was staring up from my location at the lowest level. But, as is the case with most memory regurgitation, some of the undigested chunks don't come back up. And this time that un-upchucked chunk is how high you have to climb just to *get* to this lowest level.

But finally we're here, looking up. This is a monstrous mountain. And from the bottom you can see the whole thing, including the top, with a fairly clear and discernable path leading all the way up. And what all this is, is a "powerline." In mountainous ultramarathoning parlance, a powerline has nothing whatsoever to do with *your* power, or lack thereof. No, it's electrical power. You look above your head to see high-tension wires that were put there by the local power company. Or probably that company contracted out these installations to nearby prisons and other sources of cheap stupid manpower. Nobody in their right mind would *want* to erect huge towers carrying live wires straight-the-hell up one side of a mountain and straight-the-hell down the other side. Would they?

At Barkley, you have the convenience of a nearby prison. Actually these days, there's more than one. One for the true badasses, and others for offenders needing less constant supervision. For example, you have the briar-cutting work crews. I have come upon such folks, waved to them even, and they've waved back. Their job is to cut down all the mountainside under-tower-and-wires overgrowth. Apparently, there is some law or Department of Homeland Security edict that requires all power companies with towers and power lines running up and down hills to keep the weeds cut. And for local utilities with power lines near prisons, the job is a cinch. Just have a couple guards with shotguns monitor a stalwart crew of dudes in orange jumpsuits as they go up and down swinging scythes, sickles, and the occasional lawnmower. And when they're done, you can see—vividly!—the very impossible upward path of that which you are about to *climb*.

I tell myself, later on we'll intellectualize over all the wicked history behind forced prison labor versus hiring local work-hungry workers who expect to be *paid* for such work. Oh, there's history here all right. Books have been written about it. But probably not the one Winter and I are looking for right now.

So why *is* this powerline mountain called the "Testicle Spectacle"? I know the answer because, in fact, it was Winter who told me. Indeed it was Winter himself who *christened* it, which is ironic because it's Jewish, and is a direct result of (of all things) a so-called *Jewish Sign of the Cross*. It mocks the ancient Christians, we suppose, who would make the Jesus version of such signage just before they'd face the lions in the Coliseum, or wherever. As they would move their right hand around their face and torso, they might whisper: "In the name of the Father, and of the Son, and of the Holy Ghost, Amen." Jews, I'm told, go through the same hand motions while checking to make sure they still *have* all their stuff: specifically their "spectacles, testicles, wallet, and watch."

Wintertime (no pun intended) Barkley book setout parties also scout the woods for possible new routes and places to hide future books. During one such reconnoitering, the scouting party made bold to cross the road (this highway is also the county line) and go out of the park and directly into unseen territory. Winter stopped short at the bottom of this brand-new powerline mountain, looked up, and, terrified, made the Jewish Sign of the Cross. It was the "spectacles, testicles" part that gave the mountain its name. And by the way, the reference is to a Jewish businessman in full three-piece suit who carries his wallet in his left breast suit pocket and his pocket watch in the right pocket of his vest.

Loop 1

The shtick here, I suppose, is that it takes good eyeglasses and big balls to climb this bastard. Which, I also suppose, might put women at some disadvantage? Not to worry, however, because all the beautiful strong women I know that come here can climb this bastard with ease. I find myself—often—wishing for a sudden, though temporary, sex-change operation.

Once again, we pull out the Official Instructions. To find BOOK 7, which we are now trying to do, these directives (invectives?) tell us we need to have crossed the road (check!) and climbed up to the bottom of the TS (check!) and dropped our lower jaw. If we're in the right place and gawking up at the right powerline, then—wouldn't ya know—*we've* gone too far. In the inimitable phraseology of those indecipherable directives: "Yes, that is the Testicle Spectacle. You have gone just past **BOOK 7**."

So *WTF?* We just got here and already we missed it? Yes, and now you know more (actually less) about the indecipherable confusion of Lazarus Lake's language. Because we are now instructed: "If you look back on the south side of where you entered the powerline clearing, you will see a small sort of clearing with an old dead beech tree on the far side. If you walk towards the Beech tree, you will know if it is the right clearing. To either side of the big, dead tree, are smaller trees with hollows at the bottom. Your BOOK 7 is in the hollow under the tree on the left."

And so, of course, what's *not* stated here is that you will know if you're in the right clearing by clairvoyance. Now suddenly, in addition to being a super athlete and orienteer and having a totally understanding head full of wisdom on your shoulders, you must also be a psychic.

Uh-huh. We're supposed to look for the big *dead* beech and nearby, at the bottom of yet a different sickly skinny *hollow* tree, we'll find the book.

Check. Right. Christ. *It's winter!* The entire goddamn forest is full of nothing *but* dead trees!! Or certainly dead-looking ones. *WTF?* And *HTH?* (*What The Fuck* and *How The Hell*, for those needing a glossary. And actually, while poring over *these* goofy instructions, *I* need a glossary!)

So let's review. It's, like, end-of-March/beginning-of-April; it still gets cold even here in Tennessee; the rattlesnakes are still in their holes (and boreholes); there's not one single *live* leaf left on any branch of any tree anywhere, and especially not on *these* trees. To either side there's a whole damn forest full of dormant ones, and we're supposed to pick out the one that's dead.

"Impossible!" I shout, and give the damn stapled instructions back to Winter. "How in the fuck are we supposed to find *the* one *dead one?*"

"scRitch, you're too fucking citified. All you have to do is look for it. It's there. Hell, I can damn near see it from *here*."

Don't ask me how, but *why* we are still able to keep going along this course of insanity is because Winter has found the tree. And the book. And the book is entitled: *The Confusion of Languages*.

And here methinks is how he found it: Never mind him yakking that it's his "genius." I'm pretty sure it's because he was part of the reconnoitering group that set the book out in the first place. He just suddenly remembered *where*.

But here it is! Nestled inside its plastic baggie stuffed into some damn "hollow" of some dead tree trunk. We then recite its title in unison, with some exasperation thrown in.

I look at Winter and go, "Ya see that? He's fuckin' with us!"

"Yeah, scRitch," Winter agrees for *once*. "He certainly is."

We rip out our pages and struggle mightily—and very, very slowly—upwards toward the mighty summit of the Testicle Spectacle; or TS for short; or, in honor of that scalawag Lance Armstrong, for *T*esticular, *S*ucker, cancer!

BOOK 8 – Clockwise
The Whipping Room (by Florenz Branch) or later
Psycho Circus (by Andrew Shaw)
(Your Eighth Objective)

The grinding climb up the Testicle used to be made somewhat easier by the clear, and bare, fairly discernable ascending pathway previously described. That is, you could *see* the whole damn path as well as the fact that it was nearly completely bare of vegetation, meaning *no sawbriars*. But on this, Winter's and my umpteenth "visit," suddenly that path isn't so bare anymore. It seems to be showing its age. It's like an old man, getting older, and starting to stop shaving. The word *grizzled* comes to mind. Grizzled old men are usually thought of as unkempt, gray-headed, and with equally gray whiskers all over their face. Substitute mountain, disappearing skinny reddish-yellow color, and sawbriars sprouting all over the place—and you have today's TS.

The up-and-downness of this monstrous co-creation of Mother Nature and the electric company is just a tooth-pull. So agonizing but yet so necessary. I think of the two of us slogging forever upward—battling the thorns and briars all the way—as too damn boring to think about. Besides, our next objective is something called Raw Dog Falls down the other side, and the instructions describing *that* adventure are just too damn convoluted to contemplate. So I decide to just follow Winter and think about something else.

Like, maybe, getting my thoughts to catch up to where we're at. We're at the topic of the confusion of languages, especially whatever the hell language Laz uses.

In these so-called Instructions, we see various imaginary constructs like: "a little ways," "a short distance," and "after a little bit of a grunt." Wow. These various confusions of language are basically completely evil and ought to be banned from schoolrooms and courses in English from the first grade to the post-doctoral. What, pray tell, is the actual measurable distance of "a little ways"? Such a description to you will mean something completely different to an avid, studious, non-reader like me. "A little ways" is, what, measured in feet? In inches? *In pissing furlongs?* And how exactly damn many feet, inches, and furlongs? Personally, I can think my coffee cup is "a little ways" from my keyboard. Meanwhile you could think it's only "a little ways" from here to Wisconsin.

At The Barkley, "a little ways" is whatever Lazarus Lake thinks it is, and that could have nothing whatsoever to do with measurable reality. "A little ways" up or down the Testicle could vary from 1,000 vertical feet to the average distance between sawbriar patches. Same with "a short distance." And especially the same with "after a little bit of a grunt." Up or down this damned Spectacle, there is *always* a grunt. Many, in fact. Impossible to count, in fact! And so what exactly is the measure of a "grunt"? Is it one second? One-tenth of a second? A nanosecond? Fifteen continuously uninterrupted minutes of constant guttural exhortation? *What?*

And isn't "grunt" here used as a kind of collective noun, like plural forced into singular? "After a little bit of a grunt" fairly obviously considers *grunt* to be more than *just one* expulsion of oral (as opposed to anal) gas. (A little bit of a fart, no?) This ambiguous construct of dubious rhetoric is effectively the same as: "a bit of a feast" or "a modicum of chew" or "a shit-load of drink." The first is more than one mouthful, the second is more than one chomp of both jaws, and the third is more than one growler of beer. So it follows that "a bit of a grunt" is one long fucking trudge upwards. To do it, the average runner (no, hiker) is going to be grunting as much as, perhaps, ten thousand times.

"A little ways"? Ha! The actual distance in feet and inches is incalculable. And I recall voicing that very concern to Race Management it-or-himself. "A little ways is exactly what it says it is," he's told me more than once, "a *little* ways!" As opposed, I suppose, to a *big* ways.

These Instructions. Why even have them? This latest edition consists of 6 damned pages of *single-spaced* typing. I can easily estimate [afterwards in the comfort of my home chaos] close to 5,200 words; and damn near all of them are as ambiguous and frustrating as "a small sort of clearing with an old dead beech tree." Yo, a "clearing" is clear, no? But what exactly is a "sort of clearing"? A clearing that only sort of has no trees? Maybe there's a tree or two (or fifty!) still there? Isn't a "clearing" clear of *all* trees! And now you're looking for a dead one? In the wintertime when every damn tree in the entire fucking forest looks dead! Ambiguous and frustrating, as I've said. But let's keep going for a little ways.

Why?

Why indeed are we keeping going or why are there Instructions? We're keeping going because we haven't quit yet. [But maybe you have?

Is this book now just a little or a big ways away from your lounge chair?] Maybe these infernal Official Instructions are just part of the mystique, the shtick, the whole goofy Barkley aura that has somehow descended like a fog that now disguises almost the whole of the planet called Earth and confuses the hell out of almost all of the peeps called Earthlings.

Why?

Indeed.

Why is this so apparently so?

Why are we here?

Why is *anybody* here?

Why do these goofy peeps come to The Barkley? And *keep* coming?

Why am *I* so goofy?

Why is this damned race so popular?

Why is this damned race getting to be even *more* popular?

It's global! Maybe universal! But *why?*

And why indeed was the universe created in the first place?

I have no answers.

You, dear reader, have just wasted your hard-earned cash.

[Pause. Count what's left in your pockets.]

Maybe.

But if you think you have, then that explains the long ways away from your reading chair that this goofy book now is.

And if you think you haven't, then let's try to pick up on the thinking that lies behind the thought process of Barkley instructions-writing in the first place, at least as it pertains to present activity.

It is nothing if not goofy as hell.

First of all, most of the fairly successful Barkley runners I know do *not* read these Official Instructions. They rely on the map, their memories from previous failures, and their abilities to navigate—to do map things like "take a bearing" or count the wavy lines indicating altitude, slope, and steepness. In other words they are successful where I've been a failure, mostly because I cannot do those map things. I'm stuck trying to decipher language—this confoundedly unintelligible "hillbilly-ish" pseudo-language. This post-Civil War former-Confederate States fucking *jargon*. So there you go. I have a linguistic interest here. But not, unfortunately, very much athletic or navigational ability.

So the athletes and navigators shit-can the verbiage and focus on the landscape. They do not basically *care* what the difference is between a coal road, a log road, a haul road, a jeep road, an old road, a new one, a roadbed, or a frickin' "game trail." They learned where all the hidden books are supposed to be, and take map bearings as to the most direct routes to find them. Never mind the hillbillyspeak. They've got their eyes on the prize!

Which now brings up the whole philosophy of cheating. If your eyes are sharp and well-focused on each "prize" (these infernal books we're supposed to be finding and ripping pages out of) you could conceivably cut a whole lot of corners *off* His Nibs's amazingly picayune ("picky-yoon") literary composition-of-the-first-degree-of-obfuscation. These six stapled pages of single-spaced 10-point type that can barely be discerned in the stark blazing sunlight of day (let alone by flashlight at night) might just as well be written in mud. *Who reads this shit?*

Well, me! And Winter has passed them under his gaze and astonishment once or twice himself. And we have both scratched our heads. When the instructions say something like "that way isn't the Barkley course" and "you must turn around and go back until you find it"—I'm, like, *shurrr. We'll hike backwards for another hour-and-a-half just to get to that* other *"wash" or "draw" or "ridge" so that we can take* three *more hours to reach the next goddamn book that, we're sure, is just over yonder* here *through these trees, weeds, and briars a little ways.*

Are you kidding me? This whole race is about bushwhacking. So? Let's whack us some bush!

I stand here gazing at all these ridiculous directives on how exactly—according to Hoyle—we are to scrimmage down mountains and over waterfalls to reach a damn place that we can plainly see on the map lies about one-half inch from the highway. *So, I think, WTF's stopping anyone from strolling down the highway? Hell, running the highway! It's how to make up time, no?*

Ah, 'tis Ye First Conundrum. This whole race was realized from the get-go that it is potentially a cheater's paradise, which is precisely why books were invented. Johannes Gutenberg did not know this, of course, but his sole purpose in life was to figure out a way to mass produce enough bound stacks of paper with writing on them to allow for dozens to be scattered around Icehouse Delirium State Park every year for The Barkley Marathons.

I can fairly "see" the light bulb flashing inside someone's brain. "I know!" someone might've said. "We'll set out books and make runners tear out pages to prove they were there!"

Brilliant! Except there's just one thing: there's not enough of 'em. Per the map and these Official Instructions, we learn that this year we are to be finding thirteen books. There ought to be *thirty*.

As we read all the convoluted garbage about ridgelines and capstones and steep sections and waterfalls and climbing walls and whatever-the-hell else certain wicked minds have conjured up, the plain fact of the matter is: BOOK 7 is at the bottom of the north side of the Testicle and BOOK 8 is at the bottom of the south side and a paved frickin' highway runs in between. Up-and-over and boom! You've just saved maybe two entire hours! And if your crew has a car, you're up and over in minutes. And in the middle of the night, who's going to see you? Hell, in the middle of the blazing sun of day, who's going to see you? There are no "course marshals" and runners are scattered all throughout two counties of Tennessee!

Thus is the real critical need (IMHO, as "they say" on social media; meaning In My Humble Opinion) for many *many* more books. To prevent cheating, a book ought to be placed about every half mile and at every bloody obstacle in order to be sure all runners follow the prescribed course. Starting at the bottom of TS, for example, a book should be there, then halfway up, then all the way up, then halfway down, then over to the waterfall—both above and below—then down to the "draw" or the "ridgeline" or the "valley" or "WTF" and inside *both* the old formerly used rusted barrel *and* this newfound ugly "bog old tire." Yes, that's how these Instructions describe it. So WTF is a *bog* old tire? (A bald sixties-vintage 14-inch steel-belted radial whitewall partially sunk in a bog? Don't be confused by the 15-incher!)

Otherwise? There needs to be course marshals and, possibly, police personnel from two different counties. (OK, that might be too extreme. Forget the cops. There's no money involved here. No cash prizes and just a buck-sixty to get in.)

There are many places all over the place where "the time conscious runner" can significantly shorten his *or her* [Let's not limit the temptation to cheat to males only; remember Eve? Subway Rosie?] time out there on the course (or off it). The North Boundary Trail is paralleled by the ever-handy "quitter's road." That road can easily be taken—instead of the gnarly mountainous trail—between BOOKs 3 and 4, thereby conveniently avoiding Son of a Bitch Ditch. And there are other conveniences all over the place by the TS. There are park roads down to the highway, the county highway itself paralleling the TS, and back on the park side of the highway there's a real sweet jeep road going from Army's Gap up to the starting elevation of RatJaw; or hell (if you're *really* gutsy), take that road all the way to the top where BOOK 9 sits under the fire tower. Between BOOKs 8 and 9 are all kinds of thorny bushwhacking tortures that "the time conscious runner" can cleverly avoid if, that is, *the time-conscious runner* is hell-bent on saving time!

And cheating.

One runner once [but I'll bet there've been more over the years, racing to the finish] came to the finish line (that infamous Yellow Gate) at the end of his loop—from the totally wrong direction! How does one go clockwise, for example, and not finish clockwise? It's a damn loop *fer chrissakes!* Unless one is in fact *quitting*, how does one get turned around and try to finish a clockwise loop in the counterclockwise direction? We've been trying to figure this one out for years. Why? Why indeed, *unless* (shudder) *the runner was trying to cut off miles and* save time *near the end?*

Who among us hasn't cheated every once in a while? [This is a rhetorical question only. I *don't* expect you, for example, to research my number and start ringing my telephone until I pick up, then answer my question.] *Who* indeed?

Winter. That's who.

And I'm with him now and following blindly all over and under and around and sideways throughout all these fucking ugly tortures that Race Management has conjured up on the way to BOOK 8. It's the one inside the "bog old tire" that's *sooo* painfully close to the paved county highway that you just want to cry.

Winter finds it, we rip out our pages, and we're on our way. Its title is *The Whipping Room.*

Indeed.

BOOK 9 – Clockwise
Run Faster You Bipedal Bitch, and Other Stories
(by Damon Knight) or later
The Lost Girl (by D.H. Lawrence)
(Your Ninth Objective)

Why indeed for just about everything? *But for sure, for right now,* I think, *why do we have these cockamamie Instructions?*

To get to BOOK 9, this sheaf of ambiguities, typos, figures of speech, obfuscation, creative garble, poetic license, cornpone humor, and drawling hillbillyspeak basically tells you to climb the highest mountain in the park and look underneath the fire tower. Even the most naïve tourist knows that in big parks full of little else besides mountains and hills, something perched at the highest point is what every tourist wants to see—like a fire tower. And, conversely, even this much naïveté allows for an easy way to get there. Like, there's this jeep road. And there are gates, generally with locks on them, to keep the peeps from driving to such attractions; but to the exhausted cheatin'-hearted Barker wiseguy, jeep roads are wonderfully likeable.

So yes, Winter and I *could* take the jeep road from a place nearby along this very highway (called Army's Gap, which is gated and locked) and arrive at the fire tower in half-an-hour tops. But of course: *that's not The Barkley Way.* The Barkley Way is to follow all the ambiguities, typos, figures of speech, obfuscation, creative garble, poetic license, cornpone humor, and drawling hillbillyspeak contained in this godforsaken sheaf of incomprehensible papers in order to get to your next checkpoint in the most *in*convenient way possible.

"Let's go find that goddamned pig's head," Winter grunts.

And now, I think, *for a word from our sponsors. This next indecipherable section of your adventure into absurdity is being brought to you by the trail known as Pighead Creek.*

If you cross the highway (no, *when* you cross the highway)—unless you are at Army's Gap—you won't ever see anything like a trail. It's just jungle. ["It's a jungle out there." And thank you, Randy Newman.] But in Race Management's wishingest thinking there *is* a kind-of-a-sort-of-a "game trail" that leads up (*damn near straight up*) spear-like from the pavement into no-man's-land. But you have to be right *there* to see it. And it could be anywhere along this infernal highway, but across the road on the park side. And this is why pigs' heads were invented: to spike on a stick and mark the spot. And thank you very much, Race Management.

You can proceed for everlasting hours, hiking up and down that highway for probably miles—from the old prison to way up across the county line—and you will never (*not ever!*) find a pissant pig's head stuck on a stick staked in the ground a couple of yards into the jungle. I know; I've searched, and in the company of several of the best minds of my generation. There. Is. No. Pig. Or. Head.

Nope. But guess what there is?

A *skull*.

Yes, a bone. Some grisly roundish-type once-living container of, probably, brains. It is a fairly damn *small* skull. You and I and anyone else even halfway versed in the English (not the Tennessee) Language recognize bones when we see them, and so we call a skull a "skull"—*not* a "head." And we can seriously take it only on faith that it once belonged to a pig.

Myself and those aforementioned best minds of a generation have hiked up and down and up and down and up and down looking for some furry, snouty, nostrilly, pink-faced hairy *head* of a hog from the barnyard or of a boar from the jungle. Imagine the literary frustration!

It is a *skull*. And it is one tiny son-of-a-bitch of a bonehead about the size of your clenched fist. There's a spike ramrodded through it and it sits far enough off the roadway and into the weeds to be invisible. [But that's part of the shtick, you see? The idea is that Barkers can see it but the passing motorists cannot, thereby preserving the ghastly grubstake from theft or vandalism. Right. Got that?] So all the Barkers that don't know any better are looking for a grisly severed head set up on a spear. Everybody else and their brother can't see a damned thing, but those well-versed in hillybillyspeak spot the skull and are on their way.

Again, time for a word from our sponsor, who asks the question "Why?" And then answers it. Why *in*deed do we need these *in*sufferable, *in*conceivable, *in*decipherable, *in*credible, *in*calculable, *in*comprehensible and ultimately *in*consequential and completely *in*sane **Instructions?**

It's 'cuzza Laz.

It's because he *wants* to write. He wants to be a *great writer* (nowadays even a *great movie star*) and this official instructional shtick provides a great opportunity. And actually Lazarus *is* damned good! But he fails miserably if the art of technical writing is clarity, succinct-ness,

BOOK 9 Clockwise   53

readability, understandability, and, last but not least, the correct conveyance of information in such a way that will actually enable your readers to **do** *WTF you're fucking telling them to do!*

As it is, such writing can not. And it explains why nobody but me an' Winter ever bother to read, analyze, dissect, ponder, explain, argue about, *and recognize the genius of the thing!*

And that genius is precisely this: The writing is designed—on purpose—to have all sorts of multiple meanings. It is crafted in such a way so that, no matter what happens to you during your run and how you complain about it later, Mr. Tech Writer can always say: "But it's right there! It tells you to look for a pig's head, doesn't it? It doesn't have to have hair on it, does it? It's still a head!"

Which is also just exactly why he has always told me, after listening to *my* complaints: "But 'a little ways' is exactly what it says it is, scRitch. A little ways!"

So, yeah. It's a thing of genius all right. But it's just part of the shtick of getting thick kicks from what's stuck on sticks that some might learn quick—but me and Winter, we have trouble.

Another little genius trick to make readers of instructions pause, scratch their heads, and utter the phrase "you gotta be kidding me" is to utilize this neat rhetorical device called "used to be's." There's an example in the Instructions just as we're trying to find that damned swine's skull: "There used to be a sign for the Park Boundary just up the highway from Pighead Creek Trail. It was missing during book setout."

U-godda-be-kiddin-me. Now we're being asked to find markers *that no longer exist!* "Oh, so it USED TO BE here, huh? But it's not here now! So why am I looking for it? How will I know when I'm not standing at the spot where that sign is not, and not still have to keep looking for what's not there?"

How could I possibly miss it?

This reminds immediately of one of old Laz's own pet peeves. There is this "listserv" on the Internet, accessible via email, which is free to join and amounts to what those of us of a certain vintage used to call a "chat room." Everybody who subscribes gets a copy of every sender's submitted email. And if you reply, everybody receives what you write. [Truth be told, if you ever do intend to apply for Barkley race admittance, you need to be on this list. Although lately Facebook seems to be taking the place of listservs.] Anyway, Laz is on it. And "a little ways back" he regaled the whole cyber-assembly with wonderfully written satires about other Tennesseans who use "used-to-be's."

Loop 1

Asking for directions: *"Oh, y'all wanna gits ta Ralph's Purdy Good Grocery? Welp, furs ya gots ta go ta whar Lem's Hardware used ta be, than turn leff an' mosey down yonder ta whut dey used ta call Bridge Street—till dey changed it on accounta th' bridge bein' out—than turn raht whar Ol' Mutha Hubbard used ta live an' go down her old street ta whar the Water Deepartmint was. Go thru th' alley to whar tha Ol' Grand Hotel used ta be an' lookee leff. It used ta be thar, but now it's ta th' raht, on accounta more parkin'. But y'all won't be able ta see et unless ya parks an' walk. Y'all kin steel gits in thru th' side tho, cuz Ralph's took over th' bake'ry naigst door, an' y'all kin git in thru thar."*

Whoever that person was, giving directions, probably now serves as an editorial consultant to Laz's Official Barkley Marathons Instructions Committee. Because, you know, he used to be a schoolteacher.

Never mind how the Instructions instruct us once we find that swine-skull-stuck-on-the-stick. Suffice it to say: "gobbledygook." After a little time (ha!) Winter does indeed find it and—without hollering his discovery to me, of course; I who am still looking—he disappears upward into the jungle. I, wherever I'm at, realize his absence and hurry back down the highway to his last known spot. I needn't have worried.

I peer into the jungle and finally see the *super-tiny almost invisible* skull, and gangly dangling about 15 feet up: himself. He's completely entangled by vines, weeds, and briars; not to mention clinging to the side of some perilously steep muddy side-slope.

"We have to go up *this*?" I ask, lamely.

"Shut-up and climb!"

At this point it never even occurs to us that the sweet jeep road up from Army's Gap lies probably less than two football fields to our right. Both that road and this ungodly trail lead to the same place: something called the "Prison Mine Trail" (PMT). We just have to get there before we *really* have to start climbing.

We slog our way upward. This so-called "trail" is made excessively tough by virtue of its steepness *and* overgrowth. A climb anywhere on the Barkley course is no mean feat, mostly due, of course, to the bushwhacking. There never seems to be any *cleared* trails where you want to go. In fact, Race Management tells you that if you're on a trail, you're off the course. Sure there's ancient old roads, jeep roads, haul roads, coal roads, and roadbeds (where railroad rails *used to be*, and in some places you can even see some not-yet-completely-decomposed railroad ties); but to get from one "road" to another, you have to bushwhack. Or, whack bush. Or even whack off, like, maybe, we're doing right now.

Whacking bush up and/or down hillsides brings with it special terrors. There's steepness—that's one thing—and mud—that's another—and sawbriars, which are only too happy to rip your flesh to shreds. This is why you wear long pants, or some other kind of whole-leg covering, and why you don't wear shorts or other barelegged running outfits, like skirts or dresses or "bunhuggers." For most of the latter outfits, you probably ought to be female. But again, if you are female—and wearing some kind of a brief, barelegged running outfit—you're helping to perpetuate the misogyny, the myth, and the wrong-headed belief of Race Management that women *can't finish* The Barkley. Why? Because your legs will be sliced to the bone, and that will provide you with a somewhat legitimate reason to quit.

Wear pants or leggings and you might not. I'm wearing them, and I still might. No, will. It's never a matter of *if*; it's a matter of *when*. Winter, of course, eschews all compassionate human concern and wears shorts. Yes, what he does is goddamn *defy* the sawbriars to rip his flesh. Which they do, of course, but it makes his eventual defeat much more manly, or so he would have us believe. He *is* tough. I'll give him that, but it's an otherworldly toughness. And it's a total paradox: He must suffer the likes of us *stupid* humans (me) remaining in his company, and yet by baring his legs, he proves the stupidity. He's not finishing either.

Oh, one more caution to the potential cheaters "out there": I wouldn't, if I were you, plan on taking the aforementioned sweet jeep road all the way up to the fire tower. Why? Because of all the spectators.

Yes, spectators are a byproduct of recent years wherein Race Management—still on the lookout for lookout tower-type unreachable places in which to stash checkpoint books—nevertheless has had to concede that inside the park this fire tower is a public attraction. The park cannot suddenly declare that, on such and such a weekend, some public attraction is off-limits to the public. Spectators are public and, wow, you should see how many show up to spectate!

The thing is, is that all these members of the public—right?—can also be every runner's cheerleaders. They all have to hike up there (to the fire tower) of course, and there are quite a few free public access ways to do this. The first is another candy-ass trail (very well maintained and hikeable) that leads from the paved road inside the park practically straight up to the tower. The second is that sweet jeep road up from Army's Gap. Mostly that gate there is locked and prohibitive to vehicles, but cheerleaders have been known to park along the highway and simply go around the gate and hike up the jeep road. It's not very far. On the perfectly legal candy-ass trail, it's only a little ways longer.

There is yet a third way, and that's to hike practically the whole perimeter of the park on Quitters Road. It eventually gets to the fire tower too, but it's one hell of a big ways.

Anyway, you as a runner do *not* want to be caught hiking that sweet jeep road by all the damn spectators. You will all be using the same road! No, the wiser option for stupidly cheating is to risk taking that road only as far as the PMT, turn left on that, and go to the bottom of RatJaw. That's the name of the mountain (*oh-my-god-is-it-ever*) that you do need to climb *and in full view of the spectators*. High atop this mountain is where the fire tower sits, and all over the convenient grassy-sloped viewing area just in front of the tower is where the spectators sit. There isn't a more natural bleachers section for spectating at a spectacle in any other park in America.

So you need to climb this humungous heap called RatJaw right smack in full view of the audience. Unless of course… it's the middle of the night when most folks are *not* filling those bleachers. And if there are any peeps sitting up top there at 3-in-the-morning, they're probably your very own crew and they've been a partner to your cheating all along. Hell, they've facilitated it!

No such crew for Winter and I. In fact, since we're so far back in the pack, by the time we do scale that mammoth mountain, there's no spectators, period. We're half-to-three-quarters-dead before we even attain Army's Gap jeep road level. [Ya see? That same road passes directly in front of the bleachers.] We're also too pooped to give a shit about the lack of applause. We just wind our way around the final ascent of the road to the (basically public) parking area at the base of the tower. There's a picnic table there, containing all manner of gallon water jugs. This is "the second water drop" (remember "the first" back at Coffin Springs?) and it's also where the book is. I find the plastic baggie this time (because it's easy) lying on the tabletop surrounded by empty jugs, discarded plastic caps, and other trash. I pull out our paperback. It's called *Run Faster You Bipedal Bitch, and Other Stories* by some dude named Damon Knight.

"Right!" Winter bellows, and he's almost on the verge of laughter. But he stifles the reaction because he hurts so much. Me too.

And I pull out the Official Instructions again (in my frequent attempts to cross-reference book titles with what we're doing on the course) and I read: "Grab a drink, snatch up your page, and get moving. The course is about to turn ugly, and time's a wastin'."

Run Faster You Bitch scRitch, I think. And my very next thought immediately is: *Run? You gotta be kidding me.*

BOOK 10 – Clockwise
Ultramarathon Man (by Dean Karnazes) or later
Weirdo Haven (by J. X. Williams)
(Your Tenth Objective)

So we're at the top of this nearly 2,000-foot climb which starts at the old Prison Mine Trail which is itself nearly 2,000 feet up from the actual old prison; and the horrible, bitter, entire prospect we are now faced with is: we have to goddamn *double* what we just did.

This is new, of course. The old course (back in "my" day) totally avoided that damned old prison like housemice avoiding my poison. If you went *down there*, you could be shot. Every Barker knew this and, anyway, it was easy to avoid. It's 4,000 hellish feet all the way down there (and back up) and thus we were grateful, and then we happily trotted off along the highest ridge in the park towards our next book.

Did I mention that this is an *old* prison? This is the very one that once housed that horrible, bitter, and entire psychopath named James Earl Ray. Well, he died a long time ago [in prison, of course, of whatever "natural causes" you can die from since your victim can't murder you back] and this prison kept getting older and taxpayers were being billed and—boom!—a whole other brand-new prison got built. Indeed, but on the other side of the mountain. So what the hell? (And we *knew* this was coming.) Good Ol' Lazarus negotiates with whomever you need to negotiate with on such matters and suddenly—the next year for the next Barkley—the horrible, bitter, entire course now *includes* this old prison.

Oh yes! Now we must go down 4,000 feet from the fire tower, visit the fucking ancient penitentiary, fuck around, turn around, and *climb the same motherfucking 4,000 feet back UP the mountain!* And hah! How about this? The entire Barkley course "officially" has not increased in distance by a single damn inch! The full loop is still only 20 miles total. (Like hell it is.) And thus Race Management believes the 5-loop 100-mile mystique of the thing is preserved.

To the resounding applause of nobody, [everybody's gone; hiked back down to camp already and are doubtless feasting on "digitally prepared" chicken] Winter and I start down. And down. And down. And

60 Loop 1

down and down and down and down and down some more. It lends itself to more horrible, bitter, entirely philosophic thoughts.

I'm thinking we just climbed this mile-long bastard hill in just about an hour. Probably less than a mile, but it still took every tick of one whole hour. And so what you ultimately have here is: the blazing running speed of *one mile per hour*. Thankfully, it's quicker going down.

I think of this as I sink, slip, and slide—and slice myself to ribbons on all the sawbriar remains. [Indeed, short ugly thorny *piercing* stalks of sawbriar are what's left after the good old prisoners have mowed the mountain, which is also a powerline. Oh, and don't forget all the real thorns of all those real whips of sawbriar still lying all over the ground. Don't fall!] One-hour miles. *Hmmm*... seems about right. Doing the math, however, by determining the sheer number of steep climbs like this all over the course and then multiplying each by an hour and adding the whole thing up; well, the traditional cutoff time of 13 hours and 20 minutes per loop seems tight. *Real* tight. And as I look at my still bloody wiped-off watch, I begin to think we're over the cutoff right now!

Time to quit, yes?

I think about voicing this conjecture out loud to my also-obviously-philosophizing companion. Then, I think better of it. This guy is *bound and determined* to make a full loop—no matter what or how long it takes. Me? I could give a shit.

Thirteen hours and twenty minutes per loop. Same as it's always been. No extra free minutes for all the damn extra turf we're now expected to cover! But—ah ha!—that's *not* the allowable finishing time for the full Barkley footrace! No! Why? Well, because! Because, for one thing, there's *five* loops to the race, and if you multiply 5 times 13:20 you get something weird: like 65 hours (5 x 13) and 100 minutes (5 x 20) which is 1 hour and 40 minutes, all of which totals 66 hours and 40 minutes, and all of which is *wayyy* over the cutoff for *finishing*, which is 60 hours. Period.

So where does the 13:20 come from? That's what's allowed, and computed, by Race Management to work for 3 loops—and 3 loops only—to merit what's humorously termed a "Fun Run." For that, you can take 40 hours. Period. Because 3 times 13:20 will give you 40 hours (3 x 13 = 39 hr + 3 x 20 = 1 hr = 40 hours). Why? *Don't ask.*

Why 40 hours for the Fun Run? And/or why 60 hours for the full monty? I, your friendly neighborly huffing-and-puffing-fool-on-the-hill have no clue. You'll have to ask Race Management.

But I do have a theory. Maybe more than one. First and foremost, the whole entire reason *why* this race exists in the first place is because of the aforementioned James Earl Ray. He, the nefarious and notorious assassin of the Reverend Dr. Martin Luther King, Jr., was once incarcerated in this very prison we're presently descending to. But that's not why. The why is because he escaped! Yup. And the conventional wisdom on the matter [Frozen Ed has researched this for his book] tells us Ray was out of prison for all of about 54 hours, but he could get only around 5 miles away. That's 54 hours to run 5 lousy miles. Oh my goodness! U-godda-be-kidding-me.

It caught the immediate attention of Race Management, which, when the escape happened in 1977, was in no way familiar with the terrain. "Wow!" it allegedly exclaimed. "Why, in 54 hours *I* could run a hundred miles!"

But Race Management, being knowledgeable of running long distances within generous cutoffs, also considered two things: Either Mr. Ray was practically a cripple, or the area he escaped into was one entirely horrible madrefarting ass-whuppin' god*damned* place! And later, upon Race Management's first-ever venture to this park (which wasn't even a park yet), the latter possibility was confirmed. This ***is*** *one MF-er of a horrible ass-whuppin' place!*

And of course, as a corollary to this prison-escape discovery, Race Management immediately intoned its prophecy for the next millennia: "What a kick-ass place for a race!"

So perhaps with a vague nod to Mr. Ray's feeble attempt at "long-distance" running-for-time, Race Management initially created this race as a 50-miler with an unbelievable cutoff of 24 hours—or something less than half of old Ray's time "out there." And since there was no way of telling just what the hell Ray was *doing* all that time, or where the hell he went, Race Management did the best it could in determining the oft-considered *de rigueur* distance for a good ultramarathon: 50 miles. Certainly 50 kilometers qualifies, but in those days, we think, Race Management was simply accepting the macho attitude that *real* ultrarunners go 50 miles. [I had encountered this machismo often in "the early days." A 50K was, and still is, just a little ways more than what marathon runners run.] Conveniently, 50 miles roughly—*very roughly*—approximated three loops around what was then considered the perimeter of the "forest," which is what the whole place was before it was christened into a *bona fide* state park.

In fact, it was called "Morgan Forest," and to this day if you're off-trail far enough, you can actually pass right by an old boundary marker stone with the letters "MF" engraved and painted on it. That paint by the way, in the early years, used to be red. Those two letters by the way, in *my* early years, used to stand for *Mother Fucker*.

So, Race Management set three loops and 24 hours as *the race*. It was first held in 1986 and the most incredible thing happened: *nobody* finished. Nobody! No finishers even for a race of just 50 lousy miles! Research into this event reveals that almost all of the runners in that first edition of the race did *one* loop and stopped. My theory is that most all 50-mile ultras in both those early years as well as today give runners 12 hours to finish. A little deeper research reveals that, yes, most of the quitting runners had run that *one* loop in 12 hours or less. To them, I'm sure it felt like 50 lousy miles. (Heavy emphasis on the ***lousy***.) And yet, at 50 divided by 3, the mileage they had supposedly just covered was around 16-2/3rds—which, to an ultrarunner capable of an 8-hour 50-miler (which most of those runners were), TWELVE hours to run just that little distance must have seemed both *MF-ing* and *whup-ass*.

Yup! 'Twas. From my own early years on this course, as I think of it now as I stagger haphazardly downhill, the "biggest reason" for all that failure to finish had to have been the North Boundary Trail (NBT). In those years, the damn thing was impossible. Imagine a mountain range; the Himalayas will do for a start. Now imagine the mountains just a tad shorter, and cover them with trees. Now topple all the trees. Now cover all the gnarly toppled trees and tree trunks with vines—crawling, snaking, thick-ass vines. Now cover all the spaces in between with briars and mud. Now grow all the thorns on all the briars extra long and sharpen them into saw blades. Then imagine some silly skinny trail winding through it all that was built in the days of Daniel Boone. Now imagine that all that ax-wielding trailblazing had never seen footsteps since.

And there's your mental image of the North Boundary Trail. Upon *my* very first stepping onto that so-called "trail," I thought I was marooned on another planet. It seemed like an Edgar Rice Burroughs' novel cover. The gnarly, twisty, horrible-ass vines and briars and overturned tree trunks all seemed like Venus. All that was missing was the ugly monster and the half-naked chick. I would take five steps then slip on the mud and have to duck under something or crawl around something in order to get to somewhere else.

We're supposed to be following a trail, I thought at the time. *What trail?*

Here's an example of how the course can prove hazardous to your mental health: You think you're on "the trail"—and you are, for about fifty feet—and then you come to a huge fallen tree lying across that same trail in front of you. It is huge and horrible and gnarly and tangley and impossible to get around, or even to see around, so you plunge right *through*. You hack and climb and squeeze through gaps that *seem* to have fewer limbs and branches, but still you're smacked in the face and your feet slip and you "post-hole" with one foot down to the ground though all the branches and you invariably wrack yourself in the crotch on a limb. It is horrible-ass all right, but somehow you make it all the way through and come out on the other side and expect to see the same trail again. *Right?*

But no. This is The Barkley. That tree has fallen directly across a switchback. The trail turns left at that point. If you continue straight (which we, the unknowing, all do) you are lost. Utterly and profoundly. You then have to backtrack to that fallen tree, climb all the way back through it *again*, and this time notice the trail veering off to your right— which would have been to your left coming from the other, your original, direction. Time lost? Oh, half-an-hour easy.

Just navigating the NBT alone (during the early years) would take most of your first day. And *then*—after you're totally exhausted crawling through trees, under logs, around vines, across mudslides, and up huge-ass never-ending hills (and I mean you're encountering a whole 'nother obstacle *every fifty feet*)—you always see brand-new *gigantic* mountainsides. In the very early years, there were really only two: Hell and RatJaw. [Now there's too many to count!] So, those old exasperated 50-mile sprinters would finally *finally f-i-n-a-l-l-y* get to the end of all *that*, and Race Management tells them they need to do it **two more times!** What do you think is going to happen? I think they're going to quit.

Thus are the origins of Barkley running, and thus the arisings of the imperative to quit. Let's call it *The Quit Imperative*, for short. But no, as much as I personally would love to, Winter absolutely hollers that, "We *ain't* quittin'!"

We have to at least get down to prison level.

Of course, the Instructions clearly state that we *can't* quit at the prison, despite it being about sea level (or close) and on flat terrain with lots of parking spaces and right next to the highway. No. Rules state clearly that nobody can quit there. Apparently, all the cars in the parking areas are already too full to take on any more passengers. (I was going to think *prisoners* there, but caught myself.)

We keep thundering down.

We're on a curious tract of nature, made even more curious by an act of cartography. So why *is* this tract called "RatJaw"? Why indeed? It's inside the park all right. [As is everything else after crossing back over the highway—except for the now-empty prison which, according to the very latest news, is being developed *as a tourist attraction!* A prison!] Anyway, Barkers call this mountain RatJaw, but the park doesn't call it anything—probably because the park never expects anyone ever to be there.

Basically, just like the TS, it's this powerline going straight up and down from prison level to the highest point in the park: that fire tower. But the reason it's called RatJaw is because of the map, not because of the fears and terrors that rats are supposed to conjure up in your mind. The park sells a basic topographic map in the visitors center, which is the same map that's been sold, I should imagine, ever since the U.S. Geological Survey, or whatever, first surveyed the place. And if you look on this map below the fire tower, noting the little lines representing the PMT and other trails, and then superimpose the "official Barkley course markings" (usually done in some kind of colored highlighter) the end result will appear like the head and open mouth of a rat. The open-mouth part of that head is the "jaw," up through which this powerline takes us. Sort of.

Actually the whole thing is goofy and I've never understood it. The profile of the rat's head is facing left, as you gaze in awe and wonder at the map lying flat in its proper orientation, and the way up to the fire tower would indicate a left turn about halfway up. However, as anyone who's ever tried trudging *up* that bastard, the turn you actually make in the flesh (the briar-ripped flesh) about halfway up is to the right.

So when, as happens nowadays (which never used to be), groups of spectators gather up at the fire tower, they have a pretty cool view of the top half of the mountain that the runners come up and go down; and what they see, as they gaze in awe and wonder down the slope, are all the runners first coming into view—*waaay* down yonder—from somewhere off to the left, and then they turn right to ascend the slope. One final point to make about all those fabulous Barkley runners that all these spectators are cheering: nobody's running.

All of this, of course, is inapplicable as Winter and I pick our way *down*. The "picking our way" refers to trying, as much as possible, *not* to be strangled by sawbriars, or to have them ensnare our ankles and trip us, causing us to plunge headlong to an early death. There are seemingly quite a few places where the mowing prisoners missed.

"Wait-a-minutes," we're told, is what the natives call the tall overgrown sawbriars. They seem to grow to right about the height of your neck, then wrap around it python-like so as to strangle you to death then eat you whole—if only you could find the end of the thing. No slit-eyed head with rat-like teeth on the "pythons" of RatJaw, however. Instead, they cause you to stop—to wait a minute—while you unwrap the briar-whips from around your neck. Winter and I are *en-wrap-tured* by quite a few of these loving vegetables on our way down to the prison.

When we get there, of course, it is one huge disappointment. Whereas at the top of RatJaw we had no cheering spectators, here at the bottom (finally!) there are no prisoners. No guards with rifles with scopes—or even sidearms—with orders to "shoot to kill." No nothin'. Nobody!

We are also told that, to protect the vacant property from vandals and their ilk, one or two "security" guards have been hired, but we don't see them either. We assume they're either taking a break and guarding the nearest donut shop, or else taking a "well-deserved" nap somewhere inside. Not kidding about the well-deserved part. It's like that old joke about the kid beating a drum in the middle of some American forest. When asked why he's beating the drum, he tells the hiker: "I'm keeping all the wild elephants away." The hiker, amazed, goes: "But there aren't any wild elephants for thousands of miles!"

"Pretty effective, huh?" says the kid.

Wiseass punk. Well? So whatever these security guards are or are not doing, there's nobody here but us two exhausted Barkers; so their method of keeping away wild vandals must be pretty effective, too.

We dutifully follow the Instructions and dive into some damn under-road tunnel that's immersed in water and we sluice our way from one end to the other and then somehow manage to climb up and out the other side. The tunnel is like some kind of 19th century drainage ditch. It doesn't go directly underneath the prison (thereby affording some interesting, and very soggy, escape stories over the centuries). No, it's just a covered ditch basically, and there is absolutely no reason for us to be here. James Earl Ray never used it. He never had to. To the best I can figure, this stupid obstacle to solid running progress is just Race Management's way of forcing us to do what Race Management thinks *might* have been cool to do "back in the day." But Winter and I think no such thing. It's just another fucking impediment. It's Race Management's way of fixing things so that we won't be able to complete our loop on time.

Upon emerging and climbing up to ground level again, we do what these infernal Instructions tell us to do and look south, which is to our left. We're told that "there are some poles next to the prison wall. **BOOK 10** will be hanging between those poles." When I read that now, my weak logical mind shouts *you can't hang anything* between *more than two poles. In this case, you have to say* "among *those poles."* Between only works when there's two. We strain our bloodshot eyeballs. Ah, there are only two. We read more and see that the following priceless historical note has been added to enrich our experience: "This is almost exactly the same place James Earl Ray went over the wall & originally raised the question as to whether one could travel 100 miles here in 2.5 days. Thanks a lot, James."

But let's leave "the rest of the story" to Ted Koppel and the historical television footage from his *Nightline* program—which, by the way, is easily seen these days simply by buying or renting this wonderful movie, remembered earlier, called *The Barkley Marathons: The Race That Eats Its Young*. The whole James Earl fiasco is in there.

Screw the "over the wall" idea. Winter and I march to the place and see the rope from which used to hang our wonted book. There's still some rope, baggie, and duct tape evidence of its one-time suspension; but by the time we get there, BOOK 10 is on the ground. There's weird symbolism at work here.

The book is this once-upon-a-time supposed bestseller called *Ultramarathon Man*, written by one Dean Karnazes, with whom older traditional Barkers (*i.e.*, stuck-in-the-details curmudgeons, like Winter and me) have been at odds ever since he first burst on the scene. Some years ago, author Karnazes (a very good runner by the way) began boasting of quite a few vainglorious and *unique* feats of endurance, speed, strength, courage, and pizza-eating that were dubious at best. We questioned his fame-claims all up and down the Internet, but that's another story for another book and matters not at all to this one.

But the irony (call it *weirdness* or *symbolism* or both) is unmistakable. Here at this sawbriar mountain prison we discover (or should have, if we'd only run faster) "Deek" outside the wall, strung up on a rope, making a grim spectacle before the eyes of all the villagers, and whose very best work is being ripped to shreds.

On to the next....

BOOK 11 – Clockwise
Nice Guys Finish Dead (by Albert Conroy) or later
Get Tough! (by Major W. E. Fairbairn)
(Your Eleventh Objective)

Our wonted task right now is a total upchuck and trudge. Some might call it "parallel hell." I call it nuts. What we're supposed to do is figure out a way to climb forever, or close, which is another way to say: climb this monstrosity called The Bad Thing. What it is, is a goddamn climb right back UP the *same* damn mountain we just goddamn climbed DOWN—but in a different place. An altogether much *worse* place. At least part of RatJaw has the advantage of being trampled-down over the years and mowed occasionally by prisoners. The Bad Thing is relatively brand-new; it ascends through some of the thickest hillside frustration-forestation ever beheld by god or man, or madman; and yes, there are sawbriars—by the tens of trillions.

"Pick a bush," Winter says, "and let's whack it."

I spot a small bare spot, and we whack that. Then up… and up… and up… and, well, you catch the drift.

And the best use of one's mind while climbing is ruminating. Let's go back to that Library Pool and Spa for a second. It's a fairly goofy concept, is it not? I mean, libraries typically don't have pools (the swimming kind) or spas (the mineral baths and massages kind) and footraces don't usually have librarians. But this one does! Why? Because of all these damn books, that's why! Somebody has to lug them out here all over the park (and outside of it) before the race starts and then retrieve them afterwards, lest Race Management be guilty of littering. Race Management typically does all the book setouts, and our beloved Librarian comes later at his leisure and picks them all up. The whole process can take months.

There's a lot to this, I'm thinking, as Winter and I *keep climbin'*. First of all, all these books are placed out here in the elements and—paper being paper and not very good at surviving melting snow, pouring rain, or nasty rodents that'll eat anything—they therefore need protection from the elements. For that we have plastic baggies, Ziploc® even. And we also have duct tape. Typically there's two books per checkpoint, as explained earlier, and both books are inside the same plastic bag and that bag is wrapped *unmercifully* all around with half a roll of duct tape. Old Lazarus generally loves to tape the books to some tree or bury them under some stone, the heavier the better. There's even an instruction in the Official Instructions that says, if the stone is too heavy, you'll have to wait for the next runner to help you lift it. But sometimes, of course, Race Management takes the option of stringing up books, whose authors we might like to strangle with ropes hanging off prison walls.

Secondly, Race Management *loves* to fuck with us by means of each book's title. Perhaps you've noticed this, reader, as you've been following along. In the same baggie with that last book, describing the superhuman feats of one superdubious dude, there's a second one titled *Weirdo Haven* (found at a prison) which is fairly easy to *un*appreciate for its sardonic humor: *Of course this is* all *a Weirdo Haven! The only nutcases out here trudging for days on end would* have to be *weirdos!* We are all out here in this psycho pissing library finding books—but not to read; to rip apart! And we weirdos need to find the *right* book (which may or may not be magic-markered "use first" or "#1") and tear out the *right* page (if you forget, you need to look down at your bib and read what is surely upside-down to your perspective). You pass the book around to everyone in your "party" who happens to be there, all generally hollering at you to: *"gimme the damn book, scRitch! Quit reading it!'*

The third thing about all these books is the duct tape. Apparently, Race Management expects you to chop your way through half a roll per checkpoint. So what does Laz expect us to carry all over these mountains and woods, a machete? No, this too has been somewhat well thought out in advance. The thing is, Race Management tells you that if you intend to be first, you need to carry a pocketknife. You will need to cut through all that tape to get to your book and retrieve your page. But what if you're *not* first? Well then, your pocketknife is pretty much useless, just extra weight in your pack. And you *do* need to carry a pack. Hey, lunch! If you don't carry it, you don't eat. There is *nobody* out here—no aid stations—that will feed you the per-usual *uh* ultramarathoning smorgasbord. ("Moveable feast" is another name for aid stations.)

So, I'm thinking that carrying a pocketknife at The Barkley becomes unto itself an enviable "status symbol." It subtly proclaims to anyone who sees it (especially before the race): *"Yo. That's right. I'm badass. I'm the guy what's gonna be FIRST to every single book on the course!"* Well, hubba-hubba and more power to ya, buddy. But if I were in contention here and did not think I'd be first to every single book, I would *still* pack a pocketknife. Hey, the first guy could get lost. It's been known to happen, despite all the clarion clarity of these Official Instructions and the crystal accuracy of the traced race route on that damned map that you have to copy yourself.

It's probably a moot point, of course, because *I'm* not in contention. All's I have to pack is a sandwich. No, make that my dinner entre and appetizers as well. And other essentials, like maybe a snakebite kit.

And the fourth thing is: Now that you have your page, how do you carry it? How do you preserve the damned thin sheet of flimsy paper all the sweaty way to the end of your loop so Race Management can look at it? For some people, this page-preservation process can take *days*. But by then, of course, they're useless. Race Management doesn't want to see them. You are then and there out of the race, and that's the reason for the campfire: Then and there you can burn them. Anyway, the way you preserve all your hard-earned book pages is inside, yes, a plastic baggie—one with a self-seal capability, unless you're goofy enough to trust some damn sandwich bag to stand up against all the elements, which can include water from *you*. Don't be stupid. Carry a *couple* of damn good bags. Most likely the goofy dude you're running with will have forgotten his.

Not Winter though. He's a genius at everything else, so, by axiom, he does *not* forget a goddamned thing. Ever! And the logical corollary to that is that, since you are *not* a genius, you will forget *something* and have to beg your Lord and Master to give you an extra *something*, knowing he has it. Some ten books ago, I had to ask Winter for an extra baggie.

We're on The Bad Thing but, interestingly enough, these official all-precious Instructions don't tell us that. No, it tells us to find an old trail leading straight up to Indian Knob, but also that "if you can find this trail, you are very good." Well, screw that. All we're finding is sawbriars. We must not be very good.

Winter, however, has been to Indian Knob more than once in his sweet cantankerous old life, so I follow his whacking through the bushes. In the past though, we came from a different direction. In the past, before The Advancement of The Superpeople, we *all* would simply scoot along the highest ridgeline from the fire tower to the knob after having climbed the mountain hosting RatJaw *once*. Just once. Not goddamn twice like *now*.

And yet, miraculously, the length of each loop is the same: 20.0 miles. This is a true mystery around these parts, and woe be unto you who question it or even try to argue against it! You get nowhere. There is an old maxim (along the order of all that Murphy's Law nonsense) that purports to state "The Golden Rule." And that rule is: "He who has the gold makes the rules." It's the same thing here. "He who rules the race makes the course." And he can make it any which way he wishes. Even without logic. Which is the case here. My own *conservative estimate* is that all this Testicle Spectacle/Prison Visit/Bad Thing crap adds at least three more miles—vertical miles!—to the original so-called 20-mile loop. But it matters not to the maker of The Barkley Rule. So, *we keep climbin'*.

Directionally, it's fairly easy. That direction is UP. Most likely, Indian Knob is at the TOP. And after about a week, we arrive. I look around and only see more sawbriars. Winter looks around and *knows*, somehow, where that accursed Bad (Native American Knob) Thing is.

"It's over there," he says.

We get there, after only sparse and minor sawbriar piercings, and suddenly it's this gigantic rock. It's a capstone really, and it's big enough to live in, almost. Nature or some mad stone carver actually *hollowed it out*, sort of. The point is: you can walk *through* it. Yes, you can. So can I! So can Winter! And so we do.

"This is the Eye of the Needle, scRitch," he says. "Otherwise known as Needle's Eye."

"Sort of like Cotton-Eyed Joe?" I suggest. He ignores me.

"The book is in here. Ah, here!"

He's reached into what I would call another rattlesnake hole, except it's at *eye level*. I didn't know that rattlesnakes like to climb *up* to lie down. Seems to me they're better off on the ground. That's where all the field creatures live, and all the Barkers' feet and ankles.

We're *inside* this stone, there's this deep book *shelf*, Winter has just reached his arm in there and come out snakeless. But he has the book!

It's called *Nice Guys Finish Dead*, by some doubtless philosopher named Conroy. Apparently, he *wasn't* a nice guy. He survived, *eh?* Long enough to write his book.

We rip out our pages and I take some comfort in the fact that Winter's not a nice guy either.

"I guess," I say as I rip, "that either we'll get there alive, or else we won't finish at all."

"Don't give me any shit, scRitch, like you think *I'm* not a nice guy."

"Well, I hate to tell you this…"

"Shut up and put the book back and let's go."

"Right."

"You're so full of shit, scRitch, that *everything* that comes out of your body is brown. Look at the blood on your watch. That ain't red, asshole!"

BOOK 12 – Clockwise
Tales From Out There: *The Barkley Marathons, The World's Toughest Trail Race* (by Frozen Ed Furtaw) or later
Where Do We Go from Here: Chaos or Community?
(by Martin Luther King, Jr.)
(Your Twelfth Objective)

Taking my derision like a trooper, I follow my guru out of the rock and onto a ridge. It's, like, this high point and all down—I mean *all* down—in front of us is one steep motherfucking mountainside just *chock full* of sawbriars.

"scRitch," he says, "*that's* the Zipline."

"Right."

"You're likely to leak more brown blood."

"Right."

"Just follow me and try not to leak out your asshole."

"Right!"

Winter plunges downhill and in a minute I can no longer see him. The briars are that tall!

Holy shit! I think. *I might have to run!*

Certainly I need to move quicker. Winter's not a bad downhill runner. He'll scrape you (me!) at every opportunity. I know this, so I pick up my game. The only reason I'm still here and fairly on course is because Winter's old—probably ten years my senior—and he *can't* scrape me. Even on these severe hillsides with wait-a-minutes wrapping around your throat, his head still pops up enough for me to see him, then unwrap my latest briar and give chase. What saves me is that the head-high briars encircle his neck, too.

We work our way down through the misery and try not to stumble over anything and tumble to our deaths. We don't talk. Actually, the physical effort required to keep staying alive pretty much cancels the leisure for conversation. It's like this almost everywhere at The Barkley. But otherwise, of course, we do move *slowly* enough to talk. Except when we're pissed.

And I'm getting there. He keeps disappearing in the briars downhill ahead of me. He doesn't wait. Hell, I'm thinking he's *still* trying to scrape me! I start to drift back to our mutual history. And sure, it is *his*-story. The whole world, after all, revolves around Winter. Never mind the other three seasons.

This whole symbiotic relationship begs further review. The symbiosis, according to biology, refers to him counting on my bolstering of his ego, and to my total dependence on his course knowledge in order to survive. Parasites have the same pleasing feelings. Tapeworms, for example, have their egos fed constantly. Meanwhile, their hosts' guts generally enjoy losing weight. It's a win-win.

Too bad Winter does nothing for my stomach. And conversely, I'm sure, I do nothing for his, except maybe cause ulcers.

Continuing this "stomach" line of reasoning for the moment, the subject of alcohol *hasn't* come up yet, nor has addiction or even mental illness. But there's this sudden lightbulb popping on inside my head about the fine line between genius and idiocy, which suggests an even finer line between addiction and distance running, and that always suggests the numerous examples of former alcoholics morphing into great ultrarunners. Pretty much all of this is true, and there's causal relationships built in there someplace.

Now somewhere lost here both in thought and sawbriars, I like to think I'm beginning to get some handle on some of these things. The lightbulb thought just thunked, for example, is: *If genius were eccentricity, Winter'd be Edison.* The man is quirky as a damp wood campfire. He's a true rocket scientist. A math and physics whiz. A former NASA outer-galactic knower and understander of things. An honest-ta-Ja inventor, and I have personally seen some of his inventions developed for use in probing outer space. [Seen during my running of *his* 100-miler (another invitation-only race) to which I was invited by *him*.] But he won't squish a spider, and he purchases super-expensive computerized design-manufacturing equipment to make guitar picks. Oh, and he also makes classical guitars by hand. No need for fancy equipment to build guitars, just guitar picks.

Is *that* a fine line, or what? Same with the relentless *driving forces* of alcoholics versus the *driving forces* of ultrarunners. Certainly there must be a fine line there too, yes? It's been said that the drive is the same for both, just that the one behavior is so destructive while the other is so positive. (It is assumed the second is what happens *after* it "successfully" replaces the first.) Yeah, well, maybe—except for this present athletic endeavor. I cannot think of very much that's behaviorally positive about The Barkley; maybe it's just all mental. Which brings me back to Winter, who's *so* damn mental it's scary. He out-thinks me every moment, and out-argues me the rest of the time. I can't figure the guy out.

He's no *'hoolic*, but his drive's the same. He's not an addict—oh no, he is much too smart ever to sink into *that* condition—but he is hooked on kittycats. And, maybe, spiders? And he certainly suffers from no mental illness. No, his suffering comes from genius. Very few, if any, other humans on earth can understand him. Certainly not fully. Which is why, I suppose, I've always liked it when he says to me: "You understand!"

In my sweet short miserable happy life, I have come to know several (if not lots of) alcoholics, former alcoholics, excellent runners, addicts, idiots, paranoid schizophrenics, and "the best minds of my generation" (and thank you, Allen Ginsberg, for that opening line of *Howl*). [The fuller line from that poem, by the way, is: "I saw the best minds of my generation destroyed by madness, starving hysterical naked, dragging themselves through the negro streets at dawn looking for an angry fix, angelheaded hipsters burning for the ancient heavenly connection to the starry dynamo in the machinery of night...."]

Wow. Ginsberg couldn't have prefigured my arguments any better if he tried. (Heh.) I guess none of these past peeps I've known so well could be called stupid. But they have certainly managed to screw up their happiness, if not their lives in general. What happens inside the human mind that disables its owner to cause traipsing in the first place down some really sick paths? Drugs, booze, habits... sure; but there also must needs be a conscious mind that permits the first drug, the first drink, the first whatever, and to launch the brand-new habit. Or, are we *all* hooked in *some ways* on *something*?

Not all of us. Not Winter. IMHO, as they say, *all* of this aberrant behavior begins in the brain. You cannot be addicted, I believe, unless you first allow yourself to be. And *that* begins in the mental mind. [Even brainwashing to make peeps do things they *can't* control begins in the brain, no?]

And it's some *illness* of the mind that permits the self-destructive behavior in the first place, again in my humble opinion. Mental illness can manifest itself in all kinds of ways, like in all the behaviors just noted; but also in less obvious ways, like basic goodness versus badness, kindness versus nastiness, and generosity versus selfishness. Addiction is the sincerest form of selfishness there is.

Why? Because it's all about: *"Me! Me first. **I** MUST satisfy **my** cravings first* before I can do anything else—ever!—or even later today or in the next hour. And certainly before I can ever do anything for *you*."

Addicts *must* have their drug, their drink, their smoke, their roll of the dice, their roll in the hay, or their daily fucking umpteen-mile run before, hey, many of them can even function at all.

Anyway, finally and thankfully, *Mentally Ill R NOT US*. Not Winter. And (heh) not me.

So, I muse, now arriving *finally* at Zipline's bottom, why *am* I sticking with Winter? Well, besides the obvious (he knows the course), I'm also ransacking the ways of rhetoric to prove I am *not* an idiot.

He ends up on what I think is the wrong side of the creek.

"Aren't you on the wrong side?" I shout when I'm nearing the creek. The Instructions are very specific as to which side we're supposed to be on.

"Fuck no, you idiot! *That's* the wrong side!"

Really. I stop and pull out my Instructions. They specifically scream out in uppercase boldfaced letters: **Stay on the right. DO NOT TAKE THE JEEP ROAD ACROSS THE CREEK."**

"I still think you're on the wrong side!" I yell.

"Hell no. *You* are!"

Apparently the Zipline presents more of a hazard than just too damned many sawbriars. It warps your sense of direction, flips your gyroscope, and probably rearranges your whole chromosomal balance to boot. How the hell did I cross the creek?

"Left" and "right" are relative terms, right? I mean, correct? When he turns around and faces me, of course I'm on his left—if, that is, I'm on his right to begin with. Which I was, I think, until he turned around. But maybe we're not going in the direction I think we're going.

If I'm not mistaken, it was here or very close to this very place where two heroic race finishers actually, supposedly, disqualified themselves by being on the wrong side of the creek! *Can you just imagine?* Those gentlemen were the very next two finishers of this gigantic titanic footrace after The Brit did it in the second millennium. During the entire final century of that titanic millennium, that Brit was the *one and only* runner from any planet throughout the cosmos to actually finish the Barkley Marathons. Those that came after (and are still coming) are triumphant conquerors in the twenty-first century, the third millennium.

Hubba-hubba for these guys, huh?

It was Dr. Atomic and The Godfather who, in the very first year of the twenty-first century, became the Number Two and Number Three Finishers—official or not. They were heroes. I was here watching. Cheering, too!

And the whole thing was somewhat tainted because they actually *did* cross over to the wrong side of this frickin' creek. It was Iditarod himself who caught them. But they had no clue. It turned out that neither Dr. Atomic nor The Godfather had read the damned Instructions! Thereby establishing a very long tradition of practically nobody reading these damned Instructions!

Iditarod was running behind them down this Zipline, and he *had* read the instructions. He looked ahead and, probably, couldn't believe it! How could these two stalwarts of the athletic persuasion deliberately ignore the rules and cross over to the other side of this creek?

Well, believing his eyeballs or not, he nevertheless felt compelled to report the violation [which I'm told is "The Barkley Way"]. And Race Management was thrown immediately into angst and turmoil and waited and waited and waited forever before being forced to issue a "ruling," which was, of course, disqualification. You cannot write all these horrible intricate crazy fucking rules if you aren't going to enforce them. And Iditarod is an honorable and truthful man, very well known to one Lazarus Lake from past editions of this race wherein Iditarod himself was DQ'd. In that case runners were required to visit the fire tower water drop, even though it was slightly off course. Iditarod skipped it—he was racing *eh* and didn't apparently want to have to slow down to take water—and he was caught by... I don't know whom. So, you know, turnabout is fair play, yes? You can't DQ one hero at a previous race and then expect not to have to DQ other racers in following years, especially when their violations are of the same such silly rules.

So despite all three of these past heroes (Iditarod, Dr. Atomic, and The Godfather) being disqualified for whatever their goofy violations were, absolutely none of the other runners of this mega-silly footrace have given a shit since. Hey, in our eyes they did *the entire distance* entirely on their own two feet, by their own sheer power, and within all the management-imposed time constraints. They never took a ride, they never consciously took a shortcut, and they didn't *deliberately* thwart the integrity of the event by refusing to take water or run on the wrong side of a creek. Assuming that not-drinking imperils nobody but yourself (in a footrace) and that no "moving walkways" have been installed on opposite creeksides, all of us who've witnessed these things just throw up our hands and go, "What the hell?"

What *is* the point of drawing a line in the mud in the depths of the jungle, for example, and prohibiting hikers from crossing over and continuing their hike on the other side? If anything, crossing over to the opposite side—when *this* side is actually closer to the finish—in our minds just adds to the distance. Ha! So "violating" this rule just *adds* to (it does not lessen) your agony.

But of course, it's the "purist" inside Race Management. The whole idea of The Barkley is to run along the worst path possible. So if two paths in the jungle go along side-by-side, the "True Barker" must take the one you can't hardly see that's also full of water and mud and briars and thorns. Once again, the course is constructed more to encourage quitting than finishing. And yet, all the runners are on their own. There aren't any cameras (so far!) or course marshals "taking names." Perhaps this is The Great Conspiracy which has now evolved into nobody reading the Instructions! If nobody is aware of all the picayune nitpicks of "policy," then nobody can rat on another for not knowing them.

Ignorance of the law is, in fact, a damn good excuse! Unless there are sheriffs and deputies and marshals to enforce it. No course marshals? Then no sense in expecting all these cheesy nitpicks to be obeyed. Fuck it, man. We're all just *out here* trying to *get there* under our own goddamn power.

It's like that infamous performance contract of the rock 'n' rollers Van Halen. Reportedly, every venue contract contained a rider specifying all their required backstage drinks and snacks, including a big glass bowl of M&M's from which all the brown ones *must* be removed. They were all supposed to have been plucked out, or else there'd be grounds for cancelling the performance. It's not that Van Halen didn't like brown M&M's. It's so that immediately upon entering the room, they could tell if anyone had read the contract.

I'm thinking that perhaps this has practical application to The Barkley. These Instructions are given to runners the day before. Maybe there should be a rider in there stating something like: "If you show up tomorrow wearing a pair of green socks, you can have a two-hour head-start."

It's futile to argue with Winter what the correct side of the creek is. Whatever *his* side is, is the correct side. So I hurry to get behind him, while he *keeps marchin'*. Apparently, The Barkley Way is to avoid the convenient creekside road ("road"? you-gotta-be-kidding-me) that's, what, been built there since the last time *I* Ziplined? I'm standing *in* the damn creek and I don't see any goddamned road. But Winter's not on my side (of whatever we're supposed to be choosing sides with), so I follow Winter. He comes to a point where *two* creeks converge and—oh yes, following those strict Instructions—he crosses over to the *west* side, moseys down yonder, and then climbs up a short *steep* earthen embankment.

"There's that *son of a beech!*" Winter exclaims without humor.

There is this by-now-infamous "Beech Tree" with a hollowed-out bottom that stands on the embankment just above the confluence of those two creeks. It's amazing the way that this way twists and turns and brings you right back to where you started, but in a different place. Inside that hollow, of course, is *the book*. And the one we're supposed to use first is (of course!) *the* Barkley history written and published by Frozen Ed—*Tales From* Out There: *The Barkley Marathons, The World's Toughest Trail Race.*

No shit! I think. I also reflect upon Frozen's long telling me that *the* greatest honor an author of a book about The Barkley could ever hope to achieve would be to run the race and find his book, tear out his own page, and subsequently realize it's *all* being ripped to shreds. As I tear out my page, I have to agree. And I make a mental note, *eh?*

BOOK 13 – Clockwise
Six Seconds (by Rick Mofina) or later
61 Hours (by Lee Child)
(Your Thirteenth Objective)

The reason for this beech tree's infamy has to do with a several-time starter, who should be nicknamed Beech, and his companion at the time, and how neither one of them could ever find this goddamned tree! *They searched for hours!* Eventually they gave up and actually (somehow) wandered clear out of the park! They were both walking along the highway in front of the prison when, at something like two-in-the-morning, The Godfather (who was only a spectator that year and was then driving home) spotted them and gave them a lift back to camp. At race headquarters they regaled the multitudes with hyper-expressive tales of their own—from *Out There*.

Beech forever and ever thereafter, it seems, continues *still* to harp on that damned tree and how impossible it is to find. He, of course, didn't have Winter for a guide. And that is entirely because Beech is faster than Winter and, of course, me.

But at The Barkley, hey, speed kills. And that is one of the littlest-known axioms of one Max Axly, also known as Winter. *Speed kills.* In this particular footrace, you don't have to be fast; just persistent, dogged, knowledgeable, more powerful than a whipping sawbriar and able to fight your way out of a sack of wet paperbacks. Actually, you just need to be Superman.

As expected whenever you find some book at the bottom, you turn around and look UP. Yes, this infamous Beech Tree lies at the very bottom of Big Hell. The Instructions tell you this, and they also tell you that the way UP this thing is to keep climbing only the steepest inclines you encounter. Or, quoting the passage printed on the paper: "Keep taking the steepest possible way until you believe that death is imminent."

I've been thinking that death is imminent from the moment I left the Yellow Gate. Winter, I think, concurs. In a not-all-that-surprising move, he climbs about 50 feet, then lies down on his back, extends all his limbs outward, and is crucified. God didn't die some two thousand years ago; I'm witnessing him die *now*.

Eventually I reach his elevation, and pause a moment… but not to pray; to chastise my god.

"When I beat your ass to the Yellow Gate, sir," I say, "should I send a helicopter back for ya?"

"Fuck you, scRitch. If you weren't so fucking slow, I wouldn't have to rest so often for you to catch up."

"Right."

He gets to his feet and we *keep climbin'*.

"Up, scRitch, UP!" is what I *think* I'm hearing as I climb.

It can mean only one thing: my old friend Spyder is fast becoming "my *Big Hell-lucinaton* of choice." Back in the day when I still could halfway keep up with her (she's younger and much better looking) and we were both here at this selfsame race and struggling up this very same *Hell*, she would climb higher and quicker and holler back down to me. And she would holler that very phase.

"Up, scRitch, UP!"

I think I'm hearing it now. All up this mountainside, and this is a very *steep* mountainside. When all else was failing me at that time, as I recall, it was her voice that lifted me up. It's encouragement of the kindest kind. I'm sure, to her, it was merely friendship meant in the same sense that kids sharing some grand adventure will encourage one another, so that they *all* survive and get home in time for supper and not piss off any parents. There wasn't anything more than that in Spyder's plaintive encouragements. It's like the Barkley application blank itself: everybody is expected to stay alive because nobody wants to dig the hole to bury you. Maybe that is why (as I realize later) Spyder wanted me to keep moving.

At this particularly hallucinogenic moment, however, while being alone with Winter and struggling up these same steepest possible climbs, I wistfully concoct other reasons for her earnest encouragements: *She loves me! I just know it!*

"Up, scRitch, UP!"

This is just *one* of the conjurings in my mind. Here's another: *Oh my god, she's so passionate! She wants me to keep up with her so we can have a great flaming romance afterwards!*

"Up, scRitch! KEEP it UP!"

Spyder is, after all, a great friend whom I used to keep running into at various other ultramarathons around the country. Sometimes there'd even be hugs! But that was generally before the race would start, because afterwards she'd be gone (that is, by the time *I* got to the finish). Still, in my delirium, this must mean she loves me.

"Up, scRitch, UP!"

At another time, I became sure of it because she wasn't *in* the race; she had driven several hundred miles just to volunteer *during* that race. And I remember thinking, the person she most wanted to be there for was *me*. This was a long, extremely long, multiday race, and she brought me food. She would drive along and stop at various spots ahead and offer assistance, encouragement, and fresh supplies. And later, when I eventually quit (proof yet again of The Quit Imperative) she actually drove me to a motel. Had I been hallucinating like today, I would've sworn she meant to share the same room.

Didn't happen. *Couldn't* happen.

The next morning when I opened my door to see the cars parked outside, hers was gone! But I no longer needed a ride, because my own vehicle was parked just a short walk from there. Which was the whole reason for driving me there in the first place.

Still, that was possibly the last time I saw Spyder *until envisioning her right now*. Looking up forever towards the never-arriving summit of Big Hell, I can *swear she is here*! Just right above me, huffing and puffing and calling constantly downwards, "Up, scRitch, UP!" She vanishes, of course, every time I arrive at the spot where she just was.

As I'm dwelling upon that previous exasperated anti-*climb, Ax...* um wasn't there. Why? Because we were faster than him. So Max Axly Winter must've been a group or two behind. [Running corollary: If I used to be faster than someone I happen to be running with now, a long damn time has passed.] Anyway, Spyder was our cheerleader, the lovely embodiment of our *esprit de corps*. The others in our little group of one-loopers at the time included Redneck Wisdom and Mr. East. All three of them were seated comfortably on that mountaintop capstone by the time I got there—right at the exact moment when I just *knew* "death is imminent."

This time Winter is my cheerless leader. He's UP and ahead, of course, and I allow him to summit the mountain first, on account of him knowing where the book is and me having no clue. Last time I didn't find it either; Spyder handed it to me. This time Winter does, and I'm glad. I am *very* glad. For centuries this book had been duct-taped high up a small tree right at the apex of this last *steepest way up* Big Hell. I could not have found it then; I cannot possibly find it now. So that, dear reader, is why we have Winter! [Also by the way, that "small tree" by now must be huge and unclimbable, so Race Management instead wedges BOOK 13 "in a hollow under an overhanging rock." *Rock on, Laz!*]

82   Loop 1

"You have *Six Seconds*," he says, handing it to me.
"Is my death *that* imminent?" I ask, panting uncontrollably.
 "What are you talking about?"
"The Instructions! Didn't you read them?" Huff huff.
"Asshole," Winter mumbles. "Rip out your page and let's go."
"Ah," I say. "I see it's the book title. What a cosmic joke, huh?"

We both know why it is, too. And I'll think up those thoughts of explanation as soon as I catch my breath. [Then you'll know also.]

I tear out page 65, Winter leaves his seat on the "overhanging rock," I re-stash the books-baggie under it, and we begin our mosey back to camp. And of course there's a whole bunch of goddamned *instructions* about just exactly how to do that: **"We know that it is easier to loop around low, and hit Chimney Top Trail further down the mountain (avoiding the steep parts). That is not the Barkley Trail."** But also of course: *You-gotta-be-kidding-me.* Winter and I just go. Down. Around and down. We're finding this goddamn trail—wherever it is, wherever it goes—and getting our asses the hell down off this damned pissant mountain!

And yes, the Chimney Top Trail is candy-ass. One of two conveniently provided by the park for our convenience for ingress and egress. The other one, I'm now remembering to think of for *your* convenience, begins the race (up Bird Mountain) on the other side of the park. [If you're a clever reader, you'll think, *"But there's three!"* And you'd be right. It's the North Boundary Trail, but you'd be wrong. That trail is not used for ingress or egress. Laz's ways are rubbing off on me.]

You need to know *the why* of this 13th BOOK. One year ago there was a classic meltdown of a heartbreak non-finish. This superman, The Ginger Man, completed all five loops only to miss the final cutoff by *exactly six seconds!* Owe-My-Gag and U-Godda-B-Kiddin-Me. *Six* (that's 00:00:06) *seconds* over the limit. He did not finish! *He* is a DNF!

They (somebody) even made some sort of a YouTube movie about it. It was this big huge deal! It has since probably been viewed hundreds of thousands of times all over the world. I am now in the middle of the same damn race or else I'd cite you the link. [Look it up your own self, hey?]

Apparently, the dude somehow made the wrong turn before reentering the park or the campground—from the wrong direction!—and he busted his ass to get to, and touch, the damned Yellow Gate to beat the oft-publicized finish time of 60 hours flat. He made 60:00:06 and collapsed. It must've been awful. No, I didn't see it. I had to leave early that year to travel back home and report for work the next day as some kind of judge. Don't ask.

Six lousy seconds! And after sixty full hours of monstrous titanic misery, by which time everyone else's sinking ship had already sunk. [Everybody quits at The Barkley. Are you kidding me? This whole book is about quitting at The Barkley.]

Imagine the irony. Imagine the sadism. Over the course of a year, Race Management somehow manages to find a paperback book with the title of *Six Seconds*. Such a coup, huh? One goddamn brilliant *coup de grâce*. And he's back! The Ginger Man is back again, one year later, once again zooming along *somewhere* in or out of this crazy park. One thing's for sure: he is *way ahead* of me and Winter. And that means he's gotten to BOOK 13 *long before* we have. So now, just imagine the look on his face when grabs this book. "Priceless," yes? Well, that right there is the why of this race. So that Race Management can have a damn good laugh.

Or, something like that. Even if Race Management can't be there—here, there, everywhere, at once, always and forever—witnessing the point of the laughter itself, he hears about it, and that's quite enough. Something like bringing joy to an old man's heart is the whole point of all this silliness; seeing just how much people will do, or avoid, or try to accomplish in their perpetual quests for temporary glory. Oh, it's rich, isn't it?

"scRitch! Pay attention!" It's Winter barking, again. "The trail turns and comes this way!" he's hollering behind him, because he's ahead of me, probably thinks I can't see, and presumably wants to finish under the cutoff? *One* loop, that is; not five. Well, we'll see.

It's pretty much dark when I next look at my watch. We're allowed thirteen hours and twenty minutes to complete our loop. That's *one* loop. At nearly every other ultra I've entered, after thirteen hours and twenty minutes you should be in the motel showering. You will have most certainly completed *fifty miles* by that time; and only if the race is longer do you stay out there longer. Here, Winter and I haven't even *officially* made twenty. Although we have, but just not *officially*, nor even has it ever been measured properly. I'm guessing at this point we're into our *twenty-fifth* mile and it's getting darker than hell and even this candy-ass trail back to camp is a son of a bitch. It can trip you, mess you up, throw crap in your face, scare you, and—if, say, you're thinking too much—you can miss a turn and get lost. Utterly, horribly lost.

Maybe that's the reason for all these shout-outs from Winter. Maybe he doesn't want to scrape me after all? It's dark and horrible out here, and maybe even he—at this point in the festivities—realizes misery loves company. Actually, I'm guessing that he wants me close by in case *he* makes a wrong turn. Ah, what the hell. Winter just wants me around so he can belittle me.

Mostly Winter exudes the vibe that he doesn't give a hurled turd about me or my ideas, *especially* not my ideas. He thinks all I've got inside me is pure bullshit. Whereas what he has inside him is profound genius. I remind myself to re-think about all this later. Right now the main task is completing this goddamned loop in around thirteen hours or less. I look again at my watch. We have just over maybe forty minutes.

"Better pick it up, scRitch!" he hollers, again at me trailing slowly.

"OK!" I yell back. "I'm right behind!"

"Oh, you're *behind* all right. You're a horse's behind!"

"Thanks," I say, knowing he can't hear. "That's all for our commercial messages of genius. Now back to our regularly scheduled program of bondage-and-discipline and sado-masochism in the dead of winter."

Indeed there is more, *much* more, to all this silliness than one man's laughter. There's two men's laughter, one of them being Winter, although the latter rarely does. Laugh, I mean. But when they both have the fortunate chance to laugh at others' misfortunes, they can howl in ribaldry without missing a beat. I should know. I've set them both off into comic nirvana many, many more times than once.

The task at hand, though, is a far cry from funny. We have got to beat the clock! And now we have to fucking *stop*—to put our headlamps on! Actually it's just me who has to do this. Winter pulls a hefty flashlight out from somewhere and keeps moving. Bastard. No wonder he can stay ahead of me!

If my guess is halfway accurate (which I'll tell you right now, it isn't) and we're in about our 24th mile and each loop is roughly a marathon (which I'll tell you right now, it is) and we've got about two miles to go of rough-ass (though *candied*) trail zigzagging ever downward to the damned paved park entrance road and on to the campground *in less than three-quarters of an hour*.... Shit! Even that paved road takes half-a-mile to reach the campground!

I see Winter start jogging, pitifully, ahead, and so I start. It's laughable—although no one's laughing—because we can only take a few jogging steps before we have to walk again because of all the rocks and boulders and whatnot impeding our path. You don't lose much time, if any, by walking briskly *all* of the time instead of breaking into slow ungainly jogs for *some* of the time. I've known folks getting seriously injured out here just on the candy-ass trails. Hell, I know one who had to be air-lifted out! But that was in a different race. Today it's not happening (I promise myself) and we simply keep clomping on down this rocky path by alternating panicky jogs with "I don't give a shit" walks.

I look at my watch. Thirty-five minutes! I break out again into a panicky jog. Winter keeps managing to stay ahead. *He's got bigger feet*, I tell myself.

Thirty minutes!

This is full-on panic mode. I try picking it up, by picking them up and putting them down *quicker*.

I think we're not too far from *my Hilton* along in through here somewhere. That infamous "Hilton." Haven't got time for *that* rumination right now though. I make a mental note to think up my explanation for that "thing" later.

After a seeming eternity, we reach the old "dynamite shack." It's where the old original trail-builders stored their dynamite. Apparently, they had to blow up a few of these rocks that I'm now tripping over. This whole trail system was built around 1933. It was a make-work project of the old CCC (Civilian Conservation Corps) which was Franklin Roosevelt's idea for putting peeps back to work and ending The Great Depression. I guess it had some success. There's certainly a whole lotta rocks around here—on the ground instead of still-impacted inside mountainsides—but that's how you build trails through mountains. You blow 'em up!

You blow me up, too! I'm huffing and puffing and panicking! Winter and I only have about twenty cycles of 60-second ticks to make it to that goddamned gate! What the hell am I thinking about trail-building for?

We finally reach bottom, or just above bottom. We're above the visitors center and we can see the pavement. We also know we're supposed to stay on the trail all the way to the trailheads, but the hell with *that*. We both don't even have to say anything. We zoom right on down to the building and parking lot and *paved road* like a very small swarm of very slow bees. Gotta hurry!

Now we're out of the woods and onto the road. We can actually run here, and so we do. Not surprisingly, Winter, although older, is faster. I attribute that to his old college track running days. During my old college days, I hung out on bean bag furniture and got stoned. But I listened to a lot of great music! But none that I can remember. Winter, on the other hand, has never forgotten a riff or a factoid or a note or a sentence in his life. Why? Because he wasn't sitting; he was running track!

Like now!

Goddamn but the man can move!

Zoom-zoom-zoom and he's suddenly avoiding this other stupid half-assed trail, called the Flat Ass Walking Trail, or whatever, which was put there for tourists and then suddenly it shows up in our Official Instructions. Barkers are supposed to take that stupid little flat gravel path instead of keepin' on zooming along the paved road. Both are parallel and end up at the same place. What's to cheat? Well, some peeps might argue that taking that path is slower, but fuck 'em. We ain't got time for that.

We hurry up the slight incline, turn left, and rumble over the wooden bridge boards. Dead ahead is the campground and dead at the end of *that* is the Yellow Gate. Goddamn!

Again I watch-glance when I panic-push the "Indiglo" light as I boot-scoot scurry. *Oh-my-fucking-gawd-I-have-five-fucking-minutes!* Winter might have half-a-minute more because he's probably thirty seconds closer to that goddamned gate—which we can't damn see because *it's pitch damn dark!* But we know it's there!

Geezesus. It's now become an all-out sprint. Our lights jiggle nervously, just as we see others wiggle around beside and in front of us. They're the onlookers. The hangers-on, cloggers-up, getters-in-the-way-of. Omigod. I lower my head and just pound ground. I figure it's all pavement and I'll stop when I body-slam into the gate. Push-push-push. Life shouldn't be lived like this. We should have a few extra minutes!

We have *one*.

Laz is here and he's announcing my time. Winter has already grabbed the gate and is now holding on, breathing heavily. *Very* heavily.

"You made it with about one minute to spare, scRitch," says Laz. "Thirteen hours, nineteen minutes, and two seconds."

I slouch over the gate and am spent—very *very* spent—and, quite unexpectedly, grateful. Somehow, I shove book pages at him.

In the glare of his gate-post lantern, Laz is checking his watch, unwrinkling papers, nodding to Winter, and asking of *me*: "You two goin' for another loop? You have 54 seconds to decide."

BOOK 13 – Counterclockwise
Six Seconds (by Rick Mofina) or later
61 Hours (by Lee Child)
(Your Fourteenth Objective)

Within the next 54 seconds, *everything* that follows happens in my head.

The Official Instructions—after ransacking their contents for the umpteen thousandth time—confirm what I've long suspected. We don't just get 13:20 to finish a loop; we have 13:20 *to start the next one*. This means, yes, I will have to turn right around—right now!—and maybe hit my van (for supplies) and the bathhouse (for a pit stop) on my way back out of Dodge.

Why again the 13:20? Well, for the Fun Run, thirteen hours and twenty minutes, or thirteen and a third hours, represents one-third of the time allowed, which is 40 hours. The Fun Run consists of three loops. The printed verbiage on the last page of Laz's stapled sheaf of directives, as I look up later—or gawk down at *now*—specifically states: "You have until 13:20 to check out and commence Loop 2 in the opposite direction as you did Loop 1! If you plan to be a man and do the 100, you must be starting every loop within 12-hour increments."

Whereupon this killer is added: "Thus, while 40 hours is a legal Fun Run (3 loops) finish, you must be started on Loop 4 before 36 hours to prove your manhood with a 100-mile finish."

And the final paragraph of *The Official Barkley Marathons Instructions* reads as follows: "Loop 1 and 4 are to be run clockwise. Loop 2 and 3 are to be run counterclockwise. On Loop 5 the first runner out can go in whichever direction he prefers. Subsequent runners must alternate directions."

Well indeed, and WTF? Continuing on from here means leaving *immediately* and backtracking throughout *the entire course*. It means climbing back *up* Chimney Top Trail, finding the exact same book that Winter just found (and *he* found it, I didn't) and then plunging headlong *down* Big Hell. And then, of course, carrying on backwards from there—up Zipline, down to prison, back up RatJaw, and *yadda yadda yee whoopie whoopie shit*. Oh, and did I mention? It is now pitch damn roof tar *dark*.

Oh, and "be a man." I can't help *not* seeing "be a woman, too." I guess that the misogyny long thought to be associated with this race is still alive and kicking. It is apparently taken for granted that, if I'm a woman, I'm stopping—certainly before five full loops. Apparently, as it even says in the application paperwork, women are too weak. And so completing the syllogism, if I quit right now, I'll prove I'm too weak, and then and therefore the other half of the human race will have a new member.

How many times have I kidded around in my little circle of running friends that about the only way *I* could ever "qualify for Boston" is to have a sex-change operation! I have kidded this many times, no kidding! I have always felt that the rigid qualifying standards for the Boston Marathon are unfairly biased against big men. And they're also unfairly generous to all women. Women get nearly a half-hour more than men—in all age groups—to complete the 26.2 miles of a qualifying race. One great old seasoned veteran (himself an Olympic Marathon qualifier) told me: "scRitch, you couldn't qualify even if you did it on rollerblades."

So the Barkley Marathons is patently anti-woman, while the Boston Marathon is blatantly pro-woman, and I'm stuck in the middle. A man without a gender. I can't goddamn qualify for either one. And I'm sure as hell not very damn sure about turning right around *now* and going out for another loop!

If I don't, Laz'll ask immediately: "Why? Why aren't you continuing on? Are you quitting? *WHY ARE YOU QUITTING?*"

And if I do, I might make it out of the campground only to pass out cold in some parking area down the line. Probably that one we just minutes ago zoomed through—the parking lot at the visitors center. In the clockwise direction, I've watched as multiple loop attempters leave the safety and security of this Yellow damned Gate and mosey up the gnarly jeep road towards the first candy-ass trail a little ways and then collapse in the ditch. Sleep. It's all about sleep, or your ability to do without it. If you can stay awake and keep moving for three days—and *not* get lost—you have a shot at finishing this sucker, and immediately elevating your status from mortal man to idolized god. The throngs and media (that is, whatever media there is that gives a damn about stupid shit like this) will fall down and worship you. You'll be catapulted to herohood. Your sweaty, briar-punctured visage will appear on the twenty-dollar bill. There'll be commemorative postage stamps dedicated to the bloody bottoms of your feet.

Or, you could just go to sleep. Like I think Winter wants to do. I don't ask him. He's still propping himself up on the gate like death is imminent.

Hell, *I'm* still propping myself up on this gate like death is imminent. In fact, I think it *is* imminent.

There's a difference between *imminent* and *immanent*. Did I know this? [Who's writing this anyway?] Of course *I* know this. *Imminent* is, like, the very next thing to happen. *ItIsThisClose.* Like dying at The Barkley. It's what's next. It's like the sword hanging over my head; and in this position of me leaning it over the gate like a guillotine, it's all set to slice on down. *Immanent* is practically the same thing, as far as Barkley is concerned anyway. It means inherent. You know it's part of the experience. It comes with the territory. It's like, if you go to The Barkley, expect death. Because death is immanent there. Same thing. You croak under both terms. So there's your difference.

Well, OK, *quitting* is immanent; death less so. It's imminent all right, but if you can make it back to camp you're saved. You won't die. Probably. Although we are steadily compiling a growing list of runners who have made it back to camp, only to return to their homes and daily lives and die *there*. If I'm not wanting to be among them, *um...* well, that just might be a good argument for continuing. I mean, if I don't go home, death can't get me there. Which is exactly where death gets you most. Here at this Barkley you are relatively safe, huh? So far, nobody has died *here*. This is surely a dead-solid argument for turning right around and keepin' on goin'.

I'm wondering if Winter would buy the argument. In the Syllogism of Warped Barkley Reasoning, if Winter routinely likes to argue but considers all *my* arguments to be full of shit, and I proffer this argument to him about doing another loop to stay alive; well then, he'll likely tell me I'm full of shit, and quit. If I say nothing, I'll probably be better off.

Although we both may quit. But in the nanosecond I have left, that gut-check is being challenged.

Turning around immediately would thus allow another 13 hours and 20 minutes to complete a loop going backwards. And, oh yes, in the dark. The *pitch dark*. If I or we could just barely squeak in here under that time going frontwards (in the direction dictated by the Official Instructions in the daylight), how likely is it that the reverse direction is doable *on time in total darkness and without a clue?* Do I even think I or we could make it back up Chimney Top and once again find that bloody *Six Seconds*? Hell, I can't find it with the sun out. He found it! And if Winter ain't goin', how can I?

Every split-second in camp is a split-second that counts against you. The *Official Rules* (couched as Instructions) inform you clearly that first you must touch this infamous Yellow Gate, and only then can you go to your car or campsite to refuel, repair the damage, and have somebody you immediately hate convince you to "go back out there." However quickly your ministrations can be accomplished works in your favor, for only then can you return to the gate, be assigned another bib/page number, and head out for more imminent glory and immanent mortality. Meanwhile the clock keeps ticking. You have either 40 hours to complete three loops, or 60 to finish all five. Anything short of that distance or longer than that time means you're out of the race.

And right now I'm standing at this infamous gate, directly in front of said notorious Mr. Lake, with less than five more nanoseconds on my personal clock. If I don't move—*right damn now!*—I too will be out of the race.

The race that eats its young.

Well, how "young" am I?

Not very. I should appear rather unappetizing and quite indigestible to whatever "eater" we're talking about here. Thus, I shall *not* be eaten!

BOOK 12 – Counterclockwise
Tales From Out There: *The Barkley Marathons, The World's Toughest Trail Race* (by Frozen Ed Furtaw) or later
Where Do We Go from Here: Chaos or Community?
(by Martin Luther King, Jr.)
(Your Fifteenth Objective)

Oh yes, I shall! *You* may very well go back out there for *your* fifteenth objective—after first reaching your fourteenth, of course—but *I* won't. I'm quitting.

I'm looking Lazarus straight in the eye (as much as I can see eyes in the blinding glare of the lantern light) and I listen as the following words trickle out of my mouth:

"You *have to* be kidding me. I'm not sure what Winter is doing, but I am *not* goin' out there for another fucking loop!"

"Winter," Laz asks him, "are you?"

"Against all reason and sanity and totally contrary to 'the better angel of my nature'… no. Fuck no. *I am not.*"

"So what's y'all's excuse?" Laz demands. "*Why* are you quitting? Why are you not continuing? The whole secret for success here is just *not stopping!* So why are you stopping?"

"Laz," I say, "I could write a damn book about why. And some day I will. But for right now, the very best reason I can come up with is: *I am beat to hell!*"

"That's the poorest excuse I've heard," he says. "And it's the worst one you've ever used."

"OK, then let me make it better and clearer. FUCK THIS BARKLEY! I wouldn't go back out there again if you bribed me with *fifty* dead hollowed-out trees stuffed *full* of hundred-dollar bills!"

"scRitch." It's Winter talking. "You're full of bullshit. Again. You wouldn't go back out there now because you *can't*. You're a weenie. You are too weak and chickenshit. Not a real man. And you have no chance in hell of even hiking back out to the parking lot."

"Well," I retort. "Do *you?*"

"Hell no," says Winter. "I'm going back to my van. To sleep."

And he offloads from the gate, but of course he can't leave yet.

"Well, there you have it, Laz. Neither of us are *real men*."

"I'll write that down as your excuse," he says.

"You do that. Is there any chicken left?"

We should interrupt this "broadcast" by bringing you a fine commercial message. There is this exquisite feature of The Barkley that has nothing to do with running the race or with the race that eats its young, just with the race that eats its chicken. Indeed the whole damn thing has everything to do with a guy named Barkley. It was named for him.

But first: me and Winter must stand for *Taps*. The shout goes out, Danger answers the holler, and he shows up at headquarters with bugle in hand. We are now to be giving our undivided attention to that universal clarion call of the warrior dead. Danger blares the tuneful message out to Planet Earth that another stupid foolish Barkley runner has just *quit*. Oh, and he does this twice, once for each of us.

So now as I drag my sad and sorry ass over to the main campsite's campfire, I ruminate over Mr. Barkley, Barry by name. He is for real, he's a lifelong friend of Laz himself, and he donates all this chicken that we *young'uns* love to eat. I recall in the early days of internet and chatrooms, someone wishing to learn more about this godawful race emailed the following question to the cyber-group: "What's a Barkley?" And right away someone else answered: "A scruffy, unkempt, hard-assed Tennessee chicken farmer." [I've always thought that has a nice ring to it, yes?]

And yes, this is Barry to a *T*. Back in the day, the Barkley chicken farm raised thousands upon thousands of these plump poultry "fryers" (legs-and-thighs, or hind quarters) for, I was told, the Tyson Company. And we are talking some kinda majorly serious chicken scratchin' here! Laz once told me that in its heyday, Barkley's farm consisted of six chicken coops, with each coop housing *around 90,000 chickens!*

Those must be some henhouses! And they all must be hens, I suppose, with the occasional rooster to keep 'em all happy (and him too, *ya think?*). Just imagine all those (6 x 90,000 = 540,000) half-million happily clucking, to coin a phrase, *motherpluckers!*

Anyway, I'm told that Barry Barkley was friends with Laz and RawDog from the very beginning—from those scruffy early days when, apparently, the latter two would go off hiking and reconnoitering the early race editions in these weird woods of this deliriously evolving psychopathic park, and then show up later at Barry's farmhouse *to eat*. And if the very first Barkley race happened in 1986 [which it did; check Frozen Ed's book] then at least some of those half-million "fryer quarters" were there to help feed the half-starved crazies who ran that year, and the

Barkley farm has been donating well-received *frozen* chicken legs ever since.

You just can't beat a chicken leg that's been well cooked on an open wood fire raging inside a campsite fire ring with a permanent grill grate on top. I found this out early in my Barkley wanderings, after I'd just freshly DNF'd for some excuse or other and it was the middle of the night and all I had to eat that day were bagels and prepackaged junk in packages. RawDog tended the fire back then (still does, occasionally) and he had just finished grilling a well-cooked chicken quarter. He asked if I wanted a piece.

Man, you cannot physically even approximate the veritable culinary orgasm that *that hot piece* instilled and thrilled in my groin. Or stomach. Same thing. I became so ecstatic I could levitate. Burning my fingers on that hot flesh was just part and parcel of bringing those bodyparts up into my mouth. It might've even singed my lips a bit, but the chicken didn't mind. It was offering up its entire lusty self for my immediate physical gratification. I should've thanked the chick. It was possibly the single greatest pleasure I've felt in half a century. Outside of a bedroom, that is.

That hen was exquisite. Succulent. Moist. Tender. And *HOT*. From her lower leg to her upper thigh and back down again. No moaning, just sizzling. And all this could even be further enhanced digitally (yes) by dipping your fingers and lovingly slathering her incendiary flesh with hot zingy sauce! I tell you, eating her was better then than drooling over all the erotic pages from *all* these sleazy paperbacks I have been collecting lately. No writer could write better than I could eat that night. It was totally heavenly masturbatory, eating that sweet chick. I must have *mmm*'d and *oooh*'d and *ahhh*'d two hundred times during the course of just one oral consumption. I almost wanted to ask the hen for her phone number.

That, dear reader, is how good Barkley chicken is.

But somehow it has acquired a bad reputation. No, not from the Catholic Church, but from previous eaters. And why? Because our incredibly hassled and overworked race director was doing all the cooking—in addition to: checking everyone in, collecting all license plates, assigning all bib numbers, getting signatures on "hold harmless" legal waivers (to protect the park), displaying the unique official course map and magic markers to copy it with, as well as the Official Instructions and personalized "computer projections" (a joke if ever there was one). Oh, and also collecting cash from everyone that buys the T-shirt. As a result? Almost every piece of Barkley's frozen chicken that good old Laz had cooked was burnt to a crisp on the outside and still frozen solid in the middle. Over time this became the stuff of legend, and of jokes.

This further morphed into mirth over the years, courtesy of those first-time (virgin) Barkers who bought into all the *pre-marathon banquet hype*. Many have shown up (myself included) with this remarkable idea in their minds that somehow the Barkley Marathons was like, you know, every other marathon. The night before, they sit you down and feed you platters of spaghetti. Right? Well, back in the day, many marathons did just that. But today, methinks, if they offer it at all, you have to pay extra and possibly attend some supper-type establishment—other than the gigantic convention center where the "Expo Extravaganza" is being held that you *must* attend in order to get your bib number and your packet.

The problem is, everything you thought you knew about marathons *is wrong*. At the Barkley Marathons, there is no convention center and no spaghetti. There is no city! No taxicabs, no busses, no "Expo," no souvenirs, no salesmen, no sales on (especially marked-*up*) shoes, etc., or socks; in fact, you cannot purchase a goddamned thing at the pre-race Barkley, so you might as well leave your credit card in your tent. Oh wait. I've noted T-shirts for *cash*. Yes, there are always T-shirts for sale. And so far, at every Barkley every year these are wonderful specially-designed and screen-printed shirts that you can basically only get at the annual Barkley headquarters, which is usually campsite #12. So, leave the credit card but bring the wallet. And did you know this, too, that The Barkley is the only place left in The South that stills accepts Confederate currency? Hell, they still fly the Confederate Flag!

Foreign first-timers at this race have a hard time understanding all this significance. The war that all this hoopla celebrates happened well before their time. There hasn't, for example, been another 5-dollar-bill issued by The Treasury of The Confederate States of America, in Richmond, Virginia, for well over one hundred and fifty years! So you can understand the confusion of foreigners when they think the cash they've just converted at the airport is no good here.

But that's OK. There are always willing "moneychangers" around, like me, who will happily take any non-American's CSA 5-dollar-bill and give maybe ten more USA bucks in return (depending on the bill's condition). Otherwise, hey, Laz will happily take your green pictures of dead USA presidents in exchange for a T-shirt—twenty to thirty of them (depending on short-sleeve or long). And I'm referring to that many Washingtons. With a Jackson plus a Lincoln, you won't need to hand over nearly as many. I don't think this is impossible for our foreign racers and visitors to understand, but it could be confusing. In England and Canada, for example, Queen Elizabeth appears on *all* the currency. So, the dead president-per-denomination concept apparently doesn't apply.

Nevertheless, these T-shirts are *to die for*. I have one that says, "The Barkley Marathons: where your very best just isn't good enough." Another one proclaims: "Meaningless Suffering Without a Point." Here's more: "Bad Things Are Out There At The Barkley Marathons," "I Got My Body Pierced At The Barkley Marathons," and [on the back of the shirt with, I'm told, the castrated scrotum of a bull hanging from an appropriately photographed gate on the front] "I Left My Manhood At The Yellow Gate." Or how about this one more recently: [printed along with the image of a skeleton sitting in the woods still gripping the park's own trail map] "Barkley Marathons 100 mile trail run: help is not coming."

Ya gotta love this stuff.

Oh, and it wasn't anything called *The Civil War* that gave rise to all this hoopla pretty far back in the day, *eh?* No, we can assume there was nothing "civil" about it. According to Laz (who is himself a transplanted Oklahoman) it was in fact *The War of Northern Aggression*. There can hardly be any wonder, then, as to why The Barkley's Official Entry Form specifically states: "No Yankees; we don't want them buried here."

All of this, of course, is merely prelude to my somehow hauling of ass from the Yellow Gate up the tiny little incline to race headquarters and to the communal campfire ring with the iron grill permanently attached. I'm looking, of course, for the most succulent leg of some especially delicious hot damn chick.

And there is none. The grill may be hot, but it's empty.

BOOK 11 – Counterclockwise
Nice Guys Finish Dead (by Albert Conroy) or later
Get Tough! (by Major W. E. Fairbairn)
(Your Sixteenth Objective)

I practically have tears in my eyes. *Who's the asshole that ate the last piece of chicken?* I think, and continue thinking, *and didn't throw a fresh piece on the fire? Of all the goddamn nerve! No consideration for nobody!*

Is it this late at night? I check my watch, after once again wiping the face on my pants. *Nah. Hell, we Barkers go all night long. People are gonna come in here starving at midnight! And long after that!*

So, besides thinking, I do the next best thing. I shuffle over to the big cardboard box sitting on the picnic table filled with freezer bags full of frozen chicken quarters, and struggle with ripping open a new bag. Which probably explains why nobody was cooking any fresh pieces. They're all in here sealed in plastic. Nobody before I show up has the gumption, apparently, to figure out how to rip open a bag.

And there could be a good reason for that, too. Not only are these fucking industrial-strength bags hermetically sealed for all eternity, but here after just one full day of Barkleying all this chicken *is still frozen solid!* So not only do you have to somehow rip open the unrippable, but you then have to bloody your knuckles prying apart still-frozen chicken chunks, which are also hermetically cemented together for all eternity.

But I don't care. I'm fucking *starving*. My taste-lust is raging full of those fondest of all memories of RawDog's super-well-cooked chicken. Gotta have me a piece. *Gonna get me a piece. Right damn NOW!*

Without the good and useful use of a sterilized hammer and chisel, the cook is forced to use only his filthy trail-coated hands and fingers. Separating these cryogenically cemented legs and thighs from the ice block requires great patience, not to mention strength, not to mention hunger enough to want to go through all this rigmarole in the first place.

I somehow manage to tear open *with my teeth* a permanently sealed unbusted ice-block bag, pull out the block of iced poultry—I swear you could use this material to construct housing in the Arctic—and now I'm trying to pull legs apart using only my two bare hands. And when I see all the trail souvenirs left on the chicken block after I have, somehow, magically, pulled apart a piece, I'm happy nobody is witnessing all this. I have my dirty frozen piece, I re-box the bag, and I mosey over to the fire.

"Hey, scRitch! You cookin' chicken?"

It's The Wall. One of the nicest guys ever to show up here, and rather often.

"So what the hell are *you* doin' back already?" I ask. "You quit?"

"Yes sir! I know when I'm whipped."

"So how many loops you do?"

"Ha! *One*."

"Don't sweat it, dude. Me too."

"It wasn't a bad loop though," Wall says. "I did it in twelve-and-a-half hours."

"Beats the hell outa me!"

"So?"

"So what, dude?"

"Are you cookin'?"

"Sure. Mine's on the fire. Go chisel your own piece off the ice block, and I'll cook yours too."

The Wall, appreciatively, moseys back to the picnic table underneath the huge white tent that, incidentally, he himself provides for our use every year—says it's generally for family reunions; *big family*, I think—and he duplicates the painful process of piece-extraction that I've just endured. He happily brings the ice chunk over to me.

"Frozen solid," he says.

"Welcome to the sacred and profane reputation of Barkley chicken," I say.

"You gonna burn it on the outside while retaining its cool, refreshing inside?" he asks.

"Hell no. Dude, when I'm cookin' my own food, *it is fucking cooked!*"

He likes that. He then carefully places his frozen piece on the grill.

"Put it by the edge," I tell him. "That way it'll take longer and have half-a-chance at thawing first."

"You got it."

"Did you see any tongs over there?"

"Yeah," he says. "I'll get 'em for ya."

"Thanks."

We're standing around bullshittin', watchin' the chicken skins blacken, and suddenly something happens. A crowd forms. It's late at night, pitch dark, the weather is turning frigid, every other campground in

America is asleep, and here in the deep backwoods of rural Tennessee, around this blazing campfire, us total Barkley failures want to party.

"Don't Bogart that joint, my friend," I ruminate musically, *and please pass the moonshine.*

I stand here, tongs in hand, and suddenly realize that, if anyone could hear my thoughts, nobody would understand them. "Don't Bogart that joint" is a lyric from an ancient hippie song of the same name by this one-hit-wonder group called, of all things, The Fraternity Of Man. Speaking of misogynistic partying, huh?

The line refers to both Humphrey Bogart and joints, both of which *maybe* aren't known anymore. More specifically the ancient hippie music phrase refers to Mr. Bogart's seeming onscreen habit of *always* having a cigarette in his mouth, so "don't Bogart that joint" means do *not* keep that rolled marijuana cigarette in your mouth; pass it on. *"Pass it over to me."*

These days it seems most of my companions gathering around campfires are too young. Too young to remember Bogart, certainly, but maybe even black-and-white film and hippie music, too. I will bet, however, that cigarettes and marijuana haven't been forgotten, although I'm not sure about "rolling your own" in cigarette papers purchased at your local "head shop."

One of the reasons for Barkley's popularity, in my humble opinion, is in fact ancient hippies. In fact, I'll go so far as to suggest that ultrarunning itself is a logical outgrowth of ancient hippie culture. If it's true [as my thoughts explained previously] that ultrarunning is itself just the replacement of one addiction with another addiction (generally running to replace alcoholism), then I ought to be able to say that running for very long distances is possibly the result of bad-headed hippiedom suddenly wanting to get straight.

Even at the time us ancient hippies were all "laid back" and stoned on Mary Jane and sucking down big bottles of very bad wine (not to mention "the munchies" by which reefer smokers would suddenly *need* to binge on *all* the bad foods in the house—emphasis on *all*), well, even then we knew that what we were doing was bad for our health. [Lots of extremely popular young hippies in music, for example, were all dying! Try Janis Joplin, Jimi Hendrix, and Jim Morrison, among *many* others.] So then Frank Shorter comes along and wins the Olympic gold medal for marathoning [gold in 1972, silver in 1976] and is now credited for starting "the running boom" (or at least the jogging one). So, hey? All of a sudden a lot of us hippies *need* to get back in shape.

The other part of ancient college experience in these United States was Physical Education, or P.E. for short. P.E. was once a universal requirement! You couldn't graduate without taking some P.E. You could "elect" whatever physical activity you wanted, but in many or most colleges you absolutely had to pass about two full years of some kind of P.E. Generally this would be stuff like tennis or basketball or even golf, but sometimes there might be courses in wrestling or weightlifting or even track and field. If you expected to graduate college back in the day, you *had* to take and pass about four semesters' worth of damn P.E.

Unless, of course, you had good medical excuses. It could be—and often was—quite easy "to get out of P.E." Many hippies I knew were able to do it. And god—if there is one—bless 'em. But for the rest of us schmoes, we found ourselves, two or three days a week, tossing around big balls or hitting, or avoiding, various nets. Then after you graduate, you think, *what in the hell was all of that for?*

The far better question is: *Why in the hell did P.E. requirements disappear?* I don't think physical education is necessary to graduate any more, and if this is true, this is sad. Because even the most stoned-free hippie freak back in the day could somehow "get it" (understand) that physical shape is important. There were, for example, "chicks" and "studs"—each of which were ogled by the opposite sex. There were not, for example, "hippos" and "walruses." Even back in ancient daze, physical attractiveness meant some folks somewhere had to be in shape. And you didn't get in shape by laying back, smoking joints, sucking apple wine, and stuffing your face with Little Debbies and Cheetos.

Once you're out of school awhile and the fat starts bulging, somehow then you understand what your old schools were trying to teach you. By requiring some sort of physical education, they were actually humanitarian enough to *want* to try to educate your humanities ass *physically*. Yes, there are good (if not great) reasons for getting your ass to *MOVE*. And eventually it even dawned on we of the hippie persuasion. We actually realized that physical education is good for us! Imagine that. So then Mr. Shorter shows us how, and suddenly a whole lotta hippies start running again.

Just like Lazarus Lake. And RawDog and probably even Barry Barkley himself. And if the sixties were the laid-back years and the seventies became post-graduate fat years, then surely the eighties were our renaissance. Not so many footraces—outside of school—were invented in the seventies [even fewer in the sixties; the Boston Marathon, for example, was a joke for us serious hippies]. But! The 1980s brought a total transformation of, say, America's city streets. Suddenly there were people on 'em—not just cars—and then the non-psychedelic light ray somehow pierced the purple haze and illuminated the idea that maybe us hippies should join them. Unless, of course, we wanted to remain walruses and content ourselves with the hippos.

I maintain that serious foot-racing erupted in the eighties. And hey, guess what? That's when The Barkley was invented. The very first running event named after that scruffy unkempt hard-assed Tennessee chicken farmer took place right here, in these woods, back in 1986.

And you don't think Lazarus Lake is an ancient since-reformed-college-educated-P.E.-appreciating and at-one-time-damn-good-distance-running-young-spirited-former-hippie-freak? Just look at him!

Which, coincidentally, I'm doing right now.

Someone asks him—still holding up the westernmost pillar post of that goddamned Yellow Gate without falling asleep, apparently—if *he* wants a chicken piece. And he just glares.

He declines, of course, because in my mind—and maybe in his—there ain't nobody what can cook chicken like *he* can. So seeing him casting his cynical wanna-be-a-Rebel-wicked-ass-eyeball at *me* just naturally results in him not being hungry.

But it's OK, I tell myself. This is something brand-new: scRitch bein' campground cookie. I shouldn't be trusted. I haven't, *fer chrissakes*, done anything yet!

Until, that is, I stab two pretty-well-done chicken quarters with this long grilling fork found on the picnic table, see nothing red or pink inside, and flop one on a paper plate for Wall and the other one on mine.

"Holy crap, scRitch. This is great!"

"There's barbecue sauce over there on the table," I say. "Be sure to digitally prepare some all over your piece."

"Right-o!" he says. And we both get down to business.

Not bad, I think as I munch. *Maybe not up to RawDog's standards, but RawDog's asleep in his bedroll. So this is just gonna have to be the next best thing.*

That's when everybody *else* hangin' around the campfire wants to eat, too. So now I have to squeeze my own chowing-down in between *grillin' the hell outa more o' those motherpluckers* until damn near dawn.

BOOK 10 – Counterclockwise
Ultramarathon Man (by Dean Karnazes) or later
Weirdo Haven (by J. X. Williams)
(Your Seventeenth Objective)

Eventually I make it to my own damn bedroll. This year it's inside my van. Too freakin' cold to sleep outside in a tent this night. At The Barkley, this happens just about every night. It also becomes aromatically evident that I haven't showered yet.

By the way, for those still in the race or at home keeping score, y'all should by now be well on your way back around the course towards BOOK 10. That is, if you still want to finish a Fun Run. I'm thinking right now you're moving way too slow to finish the full race. You're going counterclockwise, you're tired, it's freezing, it's pitch dark, you've somehow managed two gigantic mountains, you should now be on The Bad Thing going down, and your next objective is the prison. That's where the book is, remember? Supposedly at the same damn spot where James Earl Ray went over the wall? Hey, it's your job to remember these things. I don't have to anymore. I quit.

Paraphrasing those immortal hippie words of Arlo Guthrie in his epic "Alice's Restaurant," which *long* song made him famous: *Well, we had another thanks-given-to-be-alive dinner, went to sleep in the campground, and didn't wake up until the next mornin' when we got a bugle call from Volunteer Danger down at the Yellow Gate's westernmost stanchion. 'Said, "Kid, it's time to roll yer lazy ass out the bedroll an' head on down for to hose yerself off inside a goll-dang frickin' damn shower!"*

And so this is what all of us by-now-happy-campers do when safely back in camp. It's how we roll. For the next obsquattamatillion hours, we're partyin'!

We laze around, pester Laz, eat stuff (constantly), hit the bathhouse (occasionally), and generally cheer like crazy for every single quitting runner who is hereafter getting "Tapped out" by the bugle. Yes, Danger (or his substitute whenever he, too, must sleep) blows the Official Barkley Bugle (this sad and extremely un-shiny ancient high school band instrument that Danger brings every year) and everybody must stand to attention, take his or her hat off, put his or her hand over his or her heart, bow the head and be grateful. Be damn grateful it ain't *you* being humiliated—I mean honored—like that. It's a ritual, this playing of *Taps* for all the losers. Don't want to have the mournful tune played for you? Finish five loops!

I crawl out and mosey down to the bathhouse to take care of "the three s's." I always have my nicely packed gym bag for these first-in-the-morning trips. I also remember my towel. One time—son of a bitch!—I actually drove all the way from home to the campground without having packed a goddamned towel. Thank goodness for the Dollar General in the nearby town. I was able to buy another one. Two in fact. They're cheap, only about a dollar apiece, and hence, I suppose, the name?

When I get back from the bathhouse, there's commotion afoot. Winter himself has apparently emerged from his van also, and is now excitedly discussing something with Henry Speir, who, I'm thinking, Danger just played the bugle for. Henry is telling Winter about the jacket found lying along the NBT trail somewhere.

"You're sure it's there?" Winter is pumping Henry for info.

"Yeah. I left it."

"What the fuck did you leave it for?"

"I didn't know who it belonged to!" Henry's hackles are beginning to raise.

"It belongs to ME!" hollers Winter.

"But I didn't know that!"

"But now you do!"

"Well, OK!"

"Why'd you leave it?"

"OK, Winter. I apologize. Really. Forgive me for not fucking knowing it belongs to *you*."

"You're an ass, Speir."

"Look, I saw it lying on the ground and picked it up and took it to the first water drop. I figured it's been there since Loop One. I'm on Loop Two. Someone coming behind me will see it and be able to reclaim it if it's theirs. Otherwise, I figured I would tell people in camp what I found and where it is, and whoever belongs to it can go get it himself."

"What if somebody *else* took it?" Winter is evolving into Exasperation Specimen One.

"Well then, I guess you'll have to deal with that. As it is, Winter, I'm done. I quit on Loop Two. Your jacket is where it is."

And Henry goes off toward the bathhouse, and Winter stands there and glares at *me*.

I go, "What?"

He goes, "I have to hike out there and get it. My wife gave it to me. She would be very angry with me if I don't hang onto that jacket."

"Maybe she'll buy you a new one," I carefully suggest. I can tell he's pissed and I don't want to rile him further.

"She's DEAD, scRitch!"

I just failed in my attempt to not rile him further.

"Oh," I sheepishly say. "I'm sorry."

"Fuck your fake sorrow. You wanna hike with me to get it, or what?"

Well now, here's a thing, isn't it? The man is my total nemesis—no doubt about it—he hates me for sure, I think, and here now he's actually asking for my company. This causes pause in my life. I have to consider this carefully. Examine it from all sides. Seek out its true meaning, its hidden message, its ulterior motives, its reason for existence. His rationale, too. I need to philosophize awhile before I can answer.

"Sure," I say.

So much for philosophizing.

"We'll leave in twenty minutes," Winter says. "Be ready. And don't forget to put your vest back on." Then he heads back to his van. I guess.

BOOK 9 – Counterclockwise
Run Faster You Bipedal Bitch, and Other Stories
(by Damon Knight) or later
The Lost Girl (by D.H. Lawrence)
(Your Eighteenth Objective)

I look at my watch. I have no idea what I'm looking at. I'm trying to imagine where on the course runners should be right now, but I'm clueless. Everyone is at least on Loop 2; but Danger has been blowing some wicked bugle, so this now means there's a whole lot less of everyone on Loop 2. Although it is morning, and gettin' on towards 24 hours into the race, so really there's people out there on Loop 3.

The thing about quitting at The Barkley is that, from "the quit moment" on and nearly forever afterwards, everything about the actual race reduces itself to mental mush. You're in a total fog. Well OK, I am. I don't have a single clue about where in the hell now in the race I'm *supposed* to be. Well OK, where *you* are supposed to be. I quit, remember?

But for purposes of keeping some semblance of order wrested out of the chaos, at this point in your reading, dear reader, you should be at BOOK 9, if that helps you any, and you're moving counterclockwise, but that won't help you at all. Anyway, judging from my own ripped-out page (Laz always offers to give your pages back to you after he's inspected and counted them), BOOK 9 is some trash pulp fiction sleaze entitled *Run Faster You Bipedal Bitch.* I have page 65.

As I'm getting ready for my hike with Winter, I am forced to delve back into my pack to see, for example, if there's any food and drink left. That's where I see my book pages, stashed in the plastic baggie along with my map and Official Instructions. [By the way, if you quit, Laz could care less about your collected pages. When I shoved them at him last night, he shoved them right back. He doesn't ever even *want* to see quitters' pages, which is why I still have them.] So now with my Instructions, it's a simple matter to deduce where the hell BOOK 9 is. Turns out, it's at the Fire Tower. Conventional wisdom (or wishful thinking?) has it that the Fire Tower is roughly half-way. So if y'all are gonna finish Loop 2 on time—within the allotted 26 hours and 40 minutes—you had best be at least halfway this morning. I look again at my watch. I still have no clue where in the hell we are with regard to elapsed race time. Maybe it's because I've already forgotten when the race actually started. I think, however, that it was yesterday.

[In retrospect, I later realize that I'm way off here. Y'all had in fact, by this time, better be damn near *done* with the loop to expect to make it in time. So feel free to ignore the spot locations I imagine the remaining runners to be at now and until the end of the race.]

The end of the race.

That's exactly what Winter and I start talking about on our hike, after the first mile or so. After, that is, we've both intellectually warmed up.

"How long you figure humans have left to live on this Earth?" I ask him.

"At the present rate of population growth coupled with diminishing resources," he says, "I give us about another thousand years."

"I'm thinking five hundred."

"Why do you think that?"

"Because," I say, "if humans have another thousand, they could very well figure out how to leave this poisoned planet and discover another habitable one to move to."

"But they won't be able to figure it out in five hundred?" he asks.

"At the present rate of global poisoning, coupled with the ignorance of politicians refusing to invest in space travel, no. I do not think humans can leave this planet and find another one in five hundred years."

"They're doomed anyway," he says. "The nearest supposedly habitable planet is too far away."

"You mean," I suggest, "that even if a mixed-group of space explorers left today—even if they knew where they were going—they wouldn't even *reach* the next planet in five hundred years?"

"You got it, scRitch. *Now* you understand."

"Space is that vast, huh?"

"You understand."

"But what about… let's say they're all asleep in the rocket ship? You know, cryogenically frozen like Walt Disney is? Like in that movie…"

"You think that'll work, scRitch?"

"I don't know. It seems reasonable to me. They go off on a 500-year space voyage, all frozen stiff, and then the computer wakes them up when they get there, no?"

"Do you know what's out there? What all flying, swirling, wildly out-of-control space shit? Asteroids? Debris? Radioactive rocks? scRitch that spaceship would be bombarded to smithereens within the first five years."

"But it would be piloted!"

"By whom? You said they're all asleep!"

"Well, by artificial intelligence!"

"Right. AI. You think computers will drive the spaceship."

"Sure! How else?"

"Computers will malfunction. With no humans in control, the mission is doomed. Besides the real control of these vehicles comes from Earth. And there are no people left on Earth!"

"There are now!"

"But you say yourself there won't be in 500 years!"

"But this spaceship is leaving now! This year! According to my argument."

"Get serious, scRitch. Your argument is stupid. There's no such thing even close to being ready to launch like you're arguing."

"No?"

"No."

"So what do we do? How does the human race survive?"

"It doesn't. Like I said, I give it one more millennium, tops. The resources we need, like food, water, even air—the atmosphere itself—will all become polluted, poisoned, or radioactive. And the only ones that'll make it that long will live and be able to sustain themselves on islands. Islands surrounded by dead ocean. And before the year 3000, they'll be dead, too."

"Well," I say, "we do know one thing for sure."

"And what's that?"

"Our sun is a star and in a few billion years it will swell into a red giant, like all the stars eventually do. And this red giant will swell in size to reach Earth's orbit and consume the whole damn planet. So, there's that."

"Right, in another five billion years or so."

"So humankind has absolutely zero chance of surviving on this planet for that long."

"You understand, scRitch. You understand."

We're walking on the jeep road out of camp, the one that the race actually starts on, but turns left off of within the first few hundred yards. That's the old white-blazed trail that leads to the top of Bird Mountain. It's a candy-ass, for sure, but a very long and strenuous climbing one. It's how you get "up there" to even get close to finding BOOK 1—which is actually a long ways away from here.

We're hiking out to where Henry Speir said he found and left that blue jacket, which Winter *loudly* claimed he must find now, or else face the imaginary wrath of his deceased second-or-third wife. I forget now which one he told me she was.

"Well, we'll never see it," I say. "We will both be long gone before five billion years."

"A drop in the bucket," he says. "In terms of cosmic space and time, scRitch, five billion years is like nothing."

"I hope we find your jacket."

"I do too. Rachel would never forgive me for losing it."

"Here we are talking about our entire existence being gone and forgotten in five billion years, and you're worried about a damn piece of clothing you forgot yesterday."

"DON'T YOU DARE SPEAK THAT WAY about that jacket!!!"

"OK! OK!"

"That jacket is precious. The sweetest woman I've ever known gave it to me. I owe her that much—not to lose it."

"OK," I say. "We're going to get it, aren't we? I agreed to hike with you, didn't I?"

"You had nothing better to do."

"Right," I say. "Except maybe cookin' chicken."

"For *yourself?*" He shoots me a look.

"Nah, for the whole damn camp!"

"Oh," he says.

"Or," I can't resist fuckin' with him a little, "maybe for the whole damn planet, *before the sun cooks it!*"

"You're just a total bullshit, scRitch."

I let that slide and we continue our trudge, which is actually a whole lot brisker than it was yesterday. Which I suppose proves the value—in recovery terms—of sleep.

"How do you suppose the race is going?" I eventually ask.

"The Barkley or the human?" he asks back.

"Well, both, I suppose. But for right now, the race that's going on around us."

"How do you think it's going?"

"Oh, you know. The usual."

"And that means what?" he asks.

"It means everybody quits!" I say. "Except for the one lone superman who might actually finish."

"And who do you suppose that superman will be?"

"Oh, I don't know. Who's in it this year?"

"I don't know either. We'll just have to wait and see."

"Well, one's thing is probably sure."

"What's that?" he asks.

"The son-of-a-bitch won't quit. And he'll keep us here until Monday night!"

"Where else do you have to go? What else do you have to do?"

"Oh, nowhere, I suppose, and nothin'."

"Then shut the hell up and keep walkin'."

BOOK 8 – Counterclockwise
The Whipping Room (by Florenz Branch) or later
Psycho Circus (by Andrew Shaw)
(Your Nineteenth Objective)

We're moving faster now, and so y'all had damn well better be at BOOK 8 or beyond. Hell, you probably should be at BOOK 7 or 6 before Winter and I resume our ruminations.

What I am (and actually have been, but never let on) pretty much excited about is being in the company of a *bona fide* certified genuine and for-real honest-to-cheeses rocket scientist. And having this wisdom all to myself and having the ability to interrogate it to death and bask in the belief that all of my *most-important-questions-in-the-universe* may finally be answered.

But nothing, of course, could be further from the truth.

This Winter himself is nothing if not chilly, cold, and frosty. And he delights in nothing so much as freezing you in your tracks and causing the very core of your being to stand and shiver.

"So," I resume, "What about UFOs and extraterrestrials visiting here?"

"Not very goddamn likely," he retorts.

"Why not?" I question, in my seeker-of-wisdom guise.

"Same reason. The distances are just too fucking great."

For him, this seemingly ends the discussion. But I haven't yet quit seeking wisdom.

"How about this," I conjecture. "What if these visitors in UFOs aren't even alive? What if they're all robots? You know, artificial intelligence?"

"They'd have to be programmed, wouldn't they?"

"Yes."

"And able to be controlled from a distance?"

"Sure."

"Well then, *that* distance is too goddamn far."

"How do we know?"

"We know!"

"How? Our own radio transmissions to our own farthest-out probes and machines seem to manage. Don't they? I mean, sure it takes time to reach there and back, but still…"

"Have our probes and machines gone out a billion light-years?"

"Well, no."

"Then there you have it. Look, scRitch, for those kinds of distances, your Earthly computer programmers would need to send out a signal when they're born, and the probe's answer would not get back to Earth until after their great-great-great-great-fucking-grandsons die!"

"Even traveling at the speed of light?"

"Even traveling at the fucking speed of light. Look up in the sky tonight, if it isn't fucking snowing or something, and have a look at those *stars*. Some of those stars are galaxies, and some of those that we're seeing now emitted their light a thousand years ago. Or more!"

"Wow."

"So *now* do you understand?"

"Well… but maybe there's life a little closer than that."

"Not very bloody damn likely."

"So all these UFO sightings are fake?"

"Either that, or some fantastical aeronautical experiments cooked up by the bastards at NASA."

"What about Roswell? You know, New Mexico? We're told they actually recovered alien beings—well, their dead bodies at least—from that alien crash site!"

"Have *you* seen 'em, scRitch?"

"Well, no. But there's photographs."

"Where? Where are these photographs?"

"I don't know. In newspapers, I think."

"Do you believe everything you read?"

"Well, no. Half of what Laz writes I can't believe."

"Then there you go. This Earth is buried under paperwork compiled by assholes that you'll never see."

"So are you saying Laz is an asshole?"

"No, I'm saying *you* are, for believing even half of all this bullshit!"

"How so?"

"You are *sitting* on all this Earthly bullshit writing, sitting involves the certain *placing* of your ass, and you can't see your own hole!"

"Huh?"

"Not without mirrors, you can't."

Sometimes these philosophical discussions with Winter arise to the sublime only to descend to the ridiculous rather quickly. I can't tell if he's making a joke here, or not. Almost no one can, as I've noticed in all my years here at Barkley. For Winter shows up annually without fail, but in all my observations of his interactive behavior with nearly all other Barkers, much of whatever he happens to be talking about no one else can understand. So it's easy to miss his jokes.

"Well, I'm not sitting on anything right now," I say. "I'm walking Quitters Road here with you."

"And so you are, scRitch. And so you are."

There are things here to be thought about, especially in the next few minutes, as we both hike the rocky, stony, gravelly jeep road that basically encircles the entire park. It starts at the campground, leads all the way to the Fire Tower, and where it goes from there I don't exactly know, except that you are able to come back from the tower and make a turn on a spur that leads out to Army's Gap. So maybe that's not a complete circling of the park, but it's close enough.

But that's not the point. The point is that every Barker worth his or her salt, or entrance fee, absolutely knows—or soon learns—that this jeep road is *the* way out of the jungle and back to salvation. This rocky and rutty unpaved conveyance right here under our feet. Oh, there are other candy-ass trails on the other side of the park that will also eventually lead you back to camp, but to end up practically at the campfire, you take *this* road.

And this road is presently our fastest track out to the first water drop, where Henry has promised Winter's precious jacket is. And he and I have already quit, so it's fitting we should be hiking Quitters Road, *eh?*

Quitters Road is one thing, annual race participation by one lone Winter is something else.

So one of the reasons for "why the Barkley?" is Winter. Yes, as I happen to have learned, it's been Winter himself who basically sponsors the thing. He puts up the money. Why might anyone think the ridiculous entry fee of *one whole dollar and sixty freakin' cents* is enough to cover costs? It's because Winter makes up the difference. He pays for, basically, all "the little things": park permit, race insurance, bib numbers, vehicle rental, headquarters campsite, maybe even the firewood. All of this is lumped into what's called the Barkley Fund. And most of that funding has been provided by this chilly Winter.

Is it a gesture of infinite kindness or a not-too-subtle bribe to get in every year? At this point we don't know. And we don't want to ask him.

And so we change the subject. But still we wonder: why does Winter get to be among the select chosen few year after year after year? To my knowledge, he enters few, if any, other races; his somewhat robust running résumé is all in the past; he barely runs or exercises at all anymore; and still he's *here*, and slow enough for me to keep up with.

Pretty hard to bite—or refuse—the hand that feeds you, huh? I change the subject.

"So why do *you* think this race is becoming so popular?" I ask him.

"Me?"

"Yes, you."

"It's The Barkley! It's the toughest fucking footrace on the planet! All runners worth their fucking salt want to challenge the toughest race there is, don't they? Why do *you* think, scRitch?"

"I think there's a couple of reasons."

"Shoot."

"Well, for sure one is to do like you suggest: challenge the toughest event there is…"

"I didn't say 'event.' I said 'race.'"

"Got it."

"And actually we should say *trail* race. Despite the fact that there is no trail."

"Right!" I agree. 'Cuzza the road ones. Like Poorwater."

"Which is shit, but you're right. Idiots invent 'extreme challenges' all the time."

"Like Spartan races and 'tough mudders.'"

"I don't think they're road races, scRitch."

"Sorry. I'm just suggesting other tough stuff."

"That shit is candy-ass by comparison."

"Right. I agree on that!"

"So what's your other reasons?"

"For why The Barkley has become 'the thing'?"

"Or whatever."

"Well, for one thing, ya gotta admit there's something very primeval about this thing. Very ancient. Most races have marked courses, and this one doesn't even have that. What you get here is, like, the closest that modern man can come to traveling back in time."

"What? Are you fucking crazy? This has nothing whatsoever to do with fucking time travel!"

"Oh yes, it does, my friend!" I say. "Just hear me out."

"You're another fucking idiot."

"What do you think Daniel Boone faced back when he went looking for pathways west?"

"Huh?"

"I'm serious. Back in his day, there were no trails, no aid stations, no cars to carry your supplies, no parking lots, no 'race officials.' No, there was only wilderness, just like here."

"Now you're comparing yourself to Daniel Boone?"

"No, Winter. I'm comparing route-finding at The Barkley with ancient route-finding in Kentucky, which, as you know, is just right up the road from here."

"So how is this traveling through time?"

"Well, we're here in the twenty-first century and he was here—or pretty close—in the eighteenth century, and he and I are both essentially doing the exact same thing: finding our way through the woods with no help at all from modern conveniences that either have or haven't been invented yet. This, too, is like raw discovery. It's the closest we get to being pioneers again. Just the basics is all we've got. So, twenty-first century down to the eighteenth. It's like, boom, three hundred years backwards in time!"

"You're nuts."

"No, seriously! This Barkley is the *only* event I know of that does this for you. That takes you back in time. Don't you think that has a kind of popular appeal? You know, getting back to nature and all?"

"I think you should've been born—or were you hatched, scRitch?—three hundred years ago, so that you wouldn't be bothering me now."

"I was born, not hatched, and I'm only making observations here. I'm trying to come to grips with the actual attraction of this godforsaken race."

"Just keep hikin'. It'll dawn on you. Eventually."

"The only difference," I say, "is wild Indians. In his day, Daniel Boone risked getting shot at by spears and arrows."

"Keep that orange vest on, scRitch. So you don't get shot at by wild hunters."

BOOK 7 – Counterclockwise
The Confusion of Languages (by Siobhan Fallon) or later
Maelstrom of Pee (by Roy Cohn)
(Your Twentieth Objective)

Winter is right, of course. Some years ago when all sorts of new "peace treaties" were being made with Icehouse Delirium State Park, one of the demands upon all Barkers is that they wear orange safety vests—or bright orange *something*—so that they won't in fact get shot by hunters.

Of course, the question immediately arises: What the hell are hunters doing *hunting* inside a *state park*? Aren't parks, by definition, hunting-free areas of public safety? I have no answer for this. Either the "safety conscious" park poohbahs really were genuinely interested in our safety from, say, *illegal* hunters, or else there really is a legal "hunting season" inside this park. But our race takes place in the spring. Most legal hunting seasons I know take place in the fall.

So I still have no answer. But in years past, almost everybody here in the race wore something that's bright orange. Today I'm one of the few who do. Apparently, the park's overbearing fear for our safety has waned in recent years. Maybe no one gives a damn if we get shot anymore.

Or maybe everybody just realizes—and thanks be to Cheeses for this—that nobody's bringing any guns into this state park. Whether anybody tries in the future to tote them in illegally—there is (or was) after all a deer stand over by the Buttslide—by entering the park via some other point of ingress is anybody's guess. Generally, I've noticed that somehow non-racing locals manage to "tote" their whole damn pickup truck inside the park via some other point of ingress, which I'd always imagined to be any of the jeep roads with locked gates across them which would otherwise allow egress onto the surrounding paved roads. Maybe these are clever locals and can pick the locks?

Clever for sure! And whenever I see a local in a pickup truck on some off-the-grid makeshift mud road somewhere—which is on The Barkley course precisely because it is off the grid—I always think *they know more than the park does about how to get a truck in here*. And so it goes. After having spoken at some length with some of these locals, I have to observe that there is no love lost between them and the park's grand poohbah.

They've had the same bitch that we've had all these years after the park became managed by new management. Back in the day (the *real old* day), I'm told this place was wide open. One lone ranger occupied a shed or a trailer at the entrance, and people could just come and go as they pleased. Apparently, that included hunters in any season. But that one lone ranger (I forget his name, although Race Management has told me) was also one of The Barkley's biggest fans. He (and by association, the entire State of Tennessee) had no trouble whatsoever with Barkley runners, not only scampering all over the park during the race but also showing up unannounced in any season to practice.

It used to be that park officials actually expected and gave a "pass" to Barkley runners showing up at all hours to run in all places. For the general public, the requirement even then was to be out of the park by nighttime unless they were registered campers or had a "backcountry camping permit." But for Barkers, all you had to do was leave a note on the dashboard of your parked car and no ranger would worry about you. Your note could say as little as "Barkley" and the powers that be would leave you alone.

In fact, the opposite came true. Whenever rangers were faced with the prospect that some general-public-idiot was lost "out there," they would routinely call upon other locals—known to be Barkley runners—to come over and help them find the lost people. The Barkers knew the park better than the rangers did. And generally, as I'm also told, whoever those Barkers were that voluntarily answered the rangers' call could and would locate those missing public idiots. The whole situation was a win-win for everybody.

"Voluntarily," *eh?* Well, isn't even the official nickname for the State of Tennessee, "The Volunteer State"? Yes, we believe it is.

But nowadays things are different. Everything about this race must suffer strict negotiations and constant concessions to appease the powers that be. The powers have changed, but more importantly they've tightened the reins. Barkers can no longer just show up willy-nilly, park their car, leave a note, and vanish. They can no longer explore the mountains and the jungle to try to figure the race out, to try to do as Daniel Boone did and *find* the way. Anything explored overnight must be covered by a backcountry camping permit. Anything explored by day must be confined to the park's public (candy-ass) trails. Indeed the only time Barkers are permitted to veer off these public trails is during the race itself.

And to run the race, every Barker must sign some sort of waiver. It's the typical "hold harmless" agreement, you know, so that the park can't be sued due to your getting hurt by deliberately going off-trail, which public trails have been provided by the good powers *for your damn safety*. Woe be unto those who, like stupid Barkley runners, dare to go beyond them. Woe, in fact, be to those who want to explore the damn public park! Only a damn tiny fraction of which is discoverable via public trails.

I am truly afraid that, as time goes on, fewer and fewer Barkers will even understand, or care, how and why all this park pressure using rules and regulations and negotiated peace treaties came about in the first place. In the very near future, if not already, no one will realize that this very Barkley footrace was once utterly *banned* from the park, by the park, and for keeping the park for parkers only—not Barkers.

Yes, our beloved Barkley footrace was at one time *banned*.

This banning was not only decreed by the park, but it was also meekly accepted for a while by one Lazarus Lake. In 2005 he sent out an email to all Barkers he had e-addresses for, indicating that whatever The Barkley had been up until then was now at the "end of an era." As of that moment, the whole Barkley experience was *history*.***

Well, that wasn't gonna fly. There were those of us who weren't buying this official decree by bullshit middle managerial demagogues who wanted to exert their imagined omnipotent *authority*. "Fuck *authority*," we

---

***It is worth quoting the full email:

Sent: Friday, January 07, 2005 3:50 PM
Subject: end of an era...

so the meeting did not go well this morning.
the state has forbidden the continuation of the barkley.

i am interested in how you, the soul of the barkley,
think i should respond:

.there is other state land in the same mountains, where i
could attempt to scout out a replacement course that we
would be allowed to run on.
.we could pursue any and all political means to pressure
them into reversing their decision.
.we could camp outside the park, do the run, and dare
them to arrest 40 people.

other suggestions?

anything goes. we no longer have anything the state could
hold over our heads and i think the decision is unjust.

laz (steadily growing more pissed off)

few reasoned. Middle management authority is always superseded by higher authority, and so to the higher authorities is precisely where we sent our cards and letters and earnest true-blue American appeals. Appeals to better consciousness, brighter wisdom, higher *power*. Our little group consisted of attorneys and human resources people and letter writers. And [Did I mention Barkley locals? Yes, I think I did.] we were blessed with one of our own Barkley locals having the good fortune of being relatively tight with his state representative, and even state senator, whom he convinced to help us. [As previously mentioned, his nickname is Tramper, and I shall never forget him.]

Badda-bing, badda-bang, badda-boom! Next thing ya know? It took "an act of congress" but yea, oh yea, The Barkley Marathons footrace was saved by an act of congress. Actually it was saved by a Joint Resolution of the Tennessee General Assembly at the Nashville Statehouse on February 13, 2006. (So, Happy Valentine's Day to The Barkley!) In other words, higher authority kicked middle authority's ass, and our footrace has happily continued ever since.

[Frozen Ed's book, by the way, reprints the entire text of that government document. My favorite paragraph: "WHEREAS, this General Assembly respectfully disagrees with the Department's decision, believing strongly that not only is the Barkley an appropriate use for (the park), the race is a precious jewel of Tennessee's outdoor recreation culture that is well worth preserving...."]

Thus and so, the hallmark of the true Barker is perseverance unto the finish, just as the hallmark of the race itself is perseverance right through the halls of congress, or the legislature. Even Laz couldn't believe we were able to do this. But now maybe even Laz himself is a believer. A believer, perhaps, in just how well a government of the people, by the people, and for the people really and truly *can* work.

But middle management, as expected, due to the people going over its head to undo its dastardly doings, is still pissed. Pissed as hell that it didn't get its way. And so that's why you have all these stupid painful negotiations each and every pissing year before the park will give The Barkley its park permit.

We used to have a section of the course called Little Hell. Well, the park poohbahs suddenly declared that part of the park off-limits. Why? Because of all the "rare" blooms of flowers that neither I nor anybody else sees, or has seen, or will ever see again because that part of the park is now off-limits! So then, I believe, ol' Lazarus made contact with whoever owns the property across the road, talked nicely to them (who probably couldn't believe that anyone actually wants or is actually asking for permission to trudge up and down their mountains of sawbriars), and they graciously consented. And thus and so, instead of Little Hell we now have the Testicle Spectacle, which is worse.

But the race is happier now, because at every opportunity to make it worse, the race is in fact made worse. Today as I hike Quitters Road with Winter, I am unhappily concluding that today's race course is almost unrecognizable from the old original race course.

And there are still other reasons for that, too. For example, our freshly pissed-off middle management grand park poohbah had gotten it in his head that one reason for the grand popularity of The Barkley was the thoroughly unkempt—not chicken farmer but—North Boundary Trail, which we think hadn't been maintained since its creation around 1933 by the Civilian Conservation Corps. That's over three-quarters of a century of weeds and overgrowth and felled tree trunks and horrible vines hanging off everywhere and trillions of horrible briars. So? So *His Nibs* the park guy rustled up a whole passel of (you guessed it) *volunteers* and they all went out over many summer weekends to make that trail safe for democracy. Dammit. They hacked and cut and dug and set stones and even put new blazes on the vertical tree trunks and presto: the whole North Boundary Trail was turned into, in the words of our fearless leader, "a super highway."

So, that good old NBT ain't what it used to be, but then neither is the rest of the race. What the park claimeth back in the form of another candy-ass trail, The Barkley further pusheth the envelope in the form of higher mountains, sheerer drop-offs, more confusing pathways, worse terrain, road and water crossings, creepy tunnel endurings, nasty-ass prison visits, and twenty trillion *more motherfucking sawbriars!*

A word to the wise now is (take it from me): Don't complain! If you have to sign something, sign it! If you can't go somewhere, don't go there! If you need a permit, get one! If you must pay a fee, pay it! If you need a campsite, pay for that too! If you must restrict your own further explorations of the park and its surroundings to raceday only, then do it without bitching. Otherwise? Otherwise I can promise you: future editions of this footrace will be *a helluva lot worse.*

And you don't want that. Trust me and Winter. It's plenty damn bad the way it is.

I'm thinking all this and suddenly, out of the crystal sky blue, Winter goes: "They don't want to have to bury you."

"Huh? What in the hell are you talking about?"

"I'm talkin' about getting shot."

"Getting shot? *What??*"

"By hunters, scRitch, you asshole. It's why they want us to wear orange! What the hell do you think I'm talkin' about?"

What I'm thinking is this line of thinking happened about a half hour ago. I'm thinkin': *Keep up, Winter! You're about five thought chapters behind!*

"Oh. I was thinkin' about something else," I finally say.

"You're just lost. Lost in the ozone... *again*."

We keep hikin'.

BOOK 6 – Counterclockwise
Southern Discomfort (by Rita Mae Brown) or later
Wait for Tomorrow (by Robert Wilder)
(Your Twenty-First Objective)

Winter must be another reason why The Barkley exists. In addition to being *the toughest trail race* on earth, attracting runners wanting to test themselves, and citing the Nashville "act of congress," we now have cold cash coming in from the cold (Winter *eh?*) and, of course, everything else that Winter brings with. Like people. Like camaraderie. (He always arrives here in the company of another Barker, Goody Two Feet, who's practically his neighbor.) So it's all like, for lack of a better term, family.

There is just something about returning year after year to a war zone. To some historic battlefield. Perhaps to honor the battlers, both living and dead. Perhaps to reenact the battle. Perhaps just to fraternize all over again with the visitors to the war zone who were never in the war. I think this explains those Civil War Reenactors. It's like a big party that goes on inside some big park and tries to prove, in vain of course, that the South *really should have won.*

There really should be more Barkley finishers by now, *wouldn't ya think?* And women finishers for sure! Why, really, *hasn't* a woman finished yet? Well, these are all some of the draws, the enticements and allures of the big race inside the big park. Peeps flock here every year to, what, try again? To re-try and finally-win the unwinnable war?

Or, hell, maybe it's all just an excuse for having one big long sweet back-to-nature party with all their closest friends—who have become like family—here in the backwoods of Tennessee. Cheering people come here yearly to cheer on, and keep on re-cheering, The Barkley Reenactors.

Maybe the Reenactors come mostly to cheer on themselves.

"Winter," I finally ask, "why *does* this race exist?"

"The same reason that you do," he says.

"OK," I say, "how's *that?*"

"You're an anomaly, scRitch, a real freak of nature. Just like The Barkley is. People seemingly flock to both of you to see the freak show."

"Thanks," I say. "So why do *you* come here?"

"I come for the mystery. Things happen here, scRitch, that don't ever happen anywhere else on the planet."

"Such as?"

"Such as the spirits of the place. I know I told you about coming out here myself years ago, and I explored around here for miles, and then I found myself in front of a strange mountain. I knew it stood between me and the campground, and I honestly did not know how to get over or around it. I told you this, right?"

"I think so. Is that the mountain that, well, you just somehow passed *through*?"

"That's right! I was drowsy and dopey and bent down to rest, and the next thing you know, I was on the other side! These spirits, scRitch, the Spirits of The Barkley? They conveyed me right *through* the mountain! I'm sure of it! Otherwise how in the hell did I get to the other side? And back in camp and safe for the night?"

"Maybe it was a ranger on an ATV and you had simply fallen asleep."

"Fuck you, scRitch! There was no ranger on a vehicle giving me a ride. I swear it!"

"OK, Winter. OK. It was the spirits."

"They took care of me. I don't know how else I could have possibly gotten through that mountain that night."

"The place is full of old coal mines," I offer. "Maybe your spirits just guided you through a tunnel."

"Spirits nevertheless. I don't remember any of it. I only remember being on one side of the mountain, and in another instant I was on the other side. How does *that* happen without something spiritual and mystical being about this place?"

"I give up. How?"

"It's a mystery! Don't be a wiseass. And remember that one year when you came upon me and Miss England right over there somewhere along the NBT, and we were lost and trying to figure our elevation and you came along with an altimeter watch. Remember that?"

"I guess so."

"And do you remember what happened when you looked at your watch? scRitch, do ya?"

"I'm not sure."

"The dial was *spinning*! Don't you remember? We were all staring right down on the face, and your dial did nothing but spin in circles!"

"It did?"

"Of course it did! It was like it was possessed! By the Barkley spirits! Don't you remember that? How could you possibly forget?"

Diving back into Thought Mode for a while here, now, I try to go back and revisit this scene supposedly so vividly remembered by no less a deity than Winter himself. But sad to say, I do not remember such a dial on any watch-face—certainly none that I owned—that did nothing but spin wildly out of control.

What I'm actually thinking is that Winter's wishful thinking is what's out of control. I recall having a Suunto watch—in fact I still have it—a distinguishing feature of which is how, instead of a second hand, little dots on the outer rim of the round face would sequentially advance (kind of like the lights on a theater marquee) steadily around the face clockwise like, you know, one second at a time. If you only looked at it briefly, I suppose it's possible that you *might* think the dial was spinning, but it would be an awful slow spin.

Maybe this is what Winter saw, or is now *convinced* that he saw. But beyond that, I have no idea. What's so marvelously troubling here is that Winter is so emphatically non-spiritual. I know, in fact, that he's an atheist. He's a dyed-in-the-wool mathematician, physicist, and rocket scientist for sure. I would have thought there's no room for a god or any spirits in a universe run by science. I could swear that, for Winter, there are no matters of faith—none at all. What there are, are unexplainable phenomena that, after giving science a few dozen or hundred years, *will* be explainable in the future.

"Spirits" conveying fast passage *through* mountains might be a case in point. I've told Winter that I am one, for example, who readily believes—not in spirit chauffeurs, but—in teleportation. Yes, evaporation, transfer, and reassemblage via particle beam acceleration at near the speed of light. To me, the old cliché "Beam me up, Scotty" is only one more inevitability awaiting scientific invention. We now have fax machines, right? And isn't having a fax machine on both ends of a telephone line a way of instantly teleporting tiny ink dots from Point A to Point B? Don't these dots *in effect* come off one piece of paper and reassemble themselves onto a different blank piece of paper up to thousands of miles away? And doesn't this happen fairly instantaneously?

So IMHO, what science is looking for are two "human" facsimile machines and something of a line or a beam or a wavelength instantly transferable in between. It's more than just a human fax machine, of course. With a fax, basically all you're transporting is an image. In the

Star Trek future of things, humans will be able to transport their own entirely physical beings.

And as I've suggested to Winter, the way this can be done is by literally and *within just a split-second* taking apart a human being atom by atom in order, row by row or column by column, from left to right and top to bottom and *instantly* shooting them *in exact order* across time and space at roughly the speed of light, and then reassembling them all, atom by atom, row by row, column by column, left to right, and top to bottom again fairly instantaneously—certainly within the time between one heartbeat and the next. If all of this can't happen in between heartbeats, the human who's supposedly teleported might die.

And there's your risk versus reward. And therein lies the initial "glitches" to this bold new system, *eh?* It's why you and I don't want to be the first humans ever to be teleported across time and space. "Hey, Scotty, until we work out the kinks, beam *somebody else* up!"

So I'm thinking, maybe what happened in Winter's case was: *aliens* visited our planet and beamed Winter straight through the mountain. *Ya think?*

Personally, I do not believe intergalactic distances are so great that non-living robots or humanoids or cyberbeings couldn't travel them. I think they've already been here. And I also think that probably the biggest reason why they don't, or haven't, stepped out of their spacecraft and shaken our hands is because whoever or whatever programmed them in the first place could not possibly have imagined creatures on any planet anywhere as weird as we are.

Yup. Me and Winter, for example, could easily scare the bejesus out of *any* alien artificial intelligence. Maybe because he and I ourselves are both artificially intelligent?

And yes, those Roswell, New Mexico, aliens could indeed be cyborgs.

Here is the Number One Question, as I have long argued, that really **must be asked** of the very first extraterrestrial alien that does indeed step out of his/her/its spaceship and offer to shake our hand: (ahem, are you ready for this?) *DID JESUS DIE FOR <u>YOUR</u> SINS, TOO?*

That's it! The bible, God, creation, revelation, Christ, sin, Holy Ghost, redemption, religion, Sunday school, our whole multi-millennia-old pseudo-metaphysical *reason for being here* will immediately be proved true or false depending on that visiting android's answer.

Boom! And there you have it, right there.

That'll explain just about everything, *won't it?*

Well?

Because *IF* any of these handed-down big beliefs accumulated today on Planet Earth were in fact TRUE, then God had to create Planet Uphxzmt also, and clue all *those* folks in on such divinely revelatory matters as: Genesis, Exodus, Deuteronomy, and yadda yadda yee, not to forget Matthew, Mark, Luke, and John tossed into the hodgepodge as well.

Hell, there ought to be a crucifix hanging on an interior wall of the Uphxzmtian spacecraft. And not to forget a Saint Christopher medal also for "safe travels." For, *um*, "traveling safely in Christ."

The Redeemer. The Founder of Christendom. The Numero Uno Muslim Prophet. The Fallen Jew. The Dying-on-the-Cross Dude that first made the world safe for sinning again. Just imagine—adjusting for the nearly impossible utterances differential—how *that* dramatic scene might play out:

> INCREDULOUS EARTHLING: So, did Christ die for your sins, too?
> STUPEFIED ALIEN: What these "sins" is you utter?
> INCREDULOUS EARTHLING: You know, bad shit! Like Barkley! Like, what was first committed by Adam and Eve in the Garden. So later God had to send his only begotten son down to our planet to… wait a minute.
> STUPEFIED ALIEN: You this guttural utterancing is nonsense.
> INCREDULOUS EARTHLING: Well, God's Son Jesus *had to* be crucified in ancient Roman times so that that Original Sin could be forgiven for all men—women and babies too, except they gotta be baptized—for all time and forever afterward. Cool guy, that Jeeze. Helluva sacrifice!
> STUPEFIED ALIEN: You Earthling must is talk about how everythings Earthlings believe in got started on Earth, correcty?
> INCREDULOUS EARTHLING: Correct! And in order for all our beliefs to be true, they *must* exist on your planet as well. *Don't they?*
> STUPEFIED ALIEN: You Earthlings is stupefyingly goofy. Here is the why all this is: In the beginning there let be a Committee. The Committee of the One True Party. They rule from on high sitting around a board room. Then they vote to make a universe, with a few dissenting votes. Nevertheless they made one. *This* one. And all their memos have been kept on file. We brought the latest file folder with us. It is inside our vehicle. If we were going to stay here, we'd thump it. But you need to know Uphxzmtian in order

to read it. And all The Committee ever demanded that we Uphxzmtians do is "go forth and multiply." Which be exactly what we is trying to do. But we need to take over your planet because ours is now so polluted and unlivable that we must move. I am a seeker-cyborg. I am on a scouting mission to find intelligent life.

INCREDULOUS EARTHLING: Good luck with that.

STUPEFIED ALIEN: Stop you interrupting. Once I telepathically Snapchat back to Mother Uphxzmt, billions of spaceships will begin their voyage. So you in big trouble. You best take yourself to your leader. Warn him/her/it that, in the end, building a wall between countries will not amount to a teensy bitsy byte of pixelated plasma—or one of your "bible" pages. Tell your leader that what his needs to happen is building a wall around your whole entire damned planet. Uphxzt-uphxzt!

[*And with that, the for-real Prophet of Doom and Other Delights climbs back inside his/her/its saucer and lifts and spins off to another galaxy far, far away.*]

[IT'S CURTAINS]

BOOK 5 – Counterclockwise
The Place That Didn't Exist (by Mark Watson) or later
The Places That Scare You: A Guide to Fearlessness in Difficult Times
(by Pema Chödrön)
(Your Twenty-Second Objective)

"There are spirits here, scRitch," Winter breaks our silent musing.

"From outer space?"

"What? What *are* you smoking? I'm talking about spirits right here!"

"Oh. Oh yeah. I guess my mind drifted a bit."

"Your damn mind is always drifting, scRitch. Stay on task!"

"OK."

"They're friendly spirits. They *help* you. If only you let them."

"Otherwise, this is a miserable place, yeah?"

"It's a wonderful place! This place is unique in all the world."

"I suppose so."

"It has its own climate. Its own biosphere. It's like it's totally self-contained and protected within its own wildness."

"It's like it has its own Zip Code."

"What? What are you talking about?"

"I was making a joke."

"Well, the hell with you and your jokes. They are all stupid."

"Yeah. Yeah."

"Wildness. You do know that over there somewhere that wooden sign has it totally wrong."

"It misquotes Thoreau."

"That's right, scRitch. The sign says 'Wilderness' but Thoreau said 'Wildness.'"

"In wildness is the preservation of the world."

"That's right."

"The sign was put there by the Boy Scouts, right?"

"That's what we're told."

"I guess," I suggest, "you can't send boys to do men's jobs."

"Hell, you can't even send men to do men's jobs."

"What's the job? Erecting wooden signs in the woods?"

"No. Reading. Reading is the job, and then quoting accurately what you've read."

"I guess that's difficult to do, huh?"

"Impossible! By and large people cannot *ever* read the damn handwriting that's right in front of their face. And they certainly cannot remember it accurately. Men or boys, women or girls, it makes no difference."

"Then everybody's stupid?"

"It's a pretty high percentage."

"Do you know where Thoreau said it?" I ask.

"That line about wildness?"

"Right."

"It must've been in his *Walden*."

"Actually no. I once looked up that quote and found he'd written it in some essay called 'Walking.'"

"'Walking'?"

"Yes. Not *Walden*. But good luck trying to find it."

"There's probably been a collection of his essays published somewhere, sometime. Or a textbook. Hell, every damn high school kid in America has had to study Thoreau for over two hundred years!"

"Actually, Winter, I think he died around the time of the Civil War. So, however many years ago *that* was."

"A hundred and a half."

"Right. And you know, of course, that nobody pronounces his name anymore the way he did, right?"

"OK, smart guy," meaning me, "how did he pronounce his name?"

"*THOR*-o," I say. "Accent on the first syllable rather than the second."

"Now how in the hell do you know *that*?"

"I have good friends who've actually gotten Ph.D.'s in literature. Even specializing in American literature."

"Well, bully for you, scRitch. A Ph.D. in literature and two dollars and a half can get you a bus ride."

"Right. And my friend the lit Ph.D. eventually got a job with General Electric."

"They need someone to proofread their propaganda."

"Right!"

"I got mine in something useful. Physics."

"Right! And so you got a job with NASA. Being a rocket scientist, and all."

"Reluctantly, scRitch. Nobody else was building rockets at the time."

"We really do need rocket scientists," I affirm. "Otherwise how is mankind supposed to get off this planet and move to another one?"

"Shit. Man-*kind*, as you say, ain't goin' anywhere."

"No?"

"No. Right now NASA doesn't even hardly exist. When was the last time we were on the moon?"

"Probably back in the seventies sometime."

"Right. And the whole bullshit organization has been trying to disappear ever since. We can't even shuttle our own astronauts back and forth to the space station. We're dependent on Russia to do that."

"I know," I agree. "It's practically criminal."

"It's practically insane! How would you like to be the last astronaut up there when the U.S. and Russia go to war?"

"Winter," I say, "if the U.S. and Russia go to war, one stranded astronaut will be the least of our worries. In fact, that astronaut will be about the safest person on earth—because he'll be off of it!"

"Well, I give him, or her, and *us* and Russia another thousand years. After that, all wars will be meaningless, because they won't exist. We won't exist. The entire planet won't exist! So however long you can survive in a space station, that's how long future generations can live."

"I give 'em five hundred."

"Didn't we have this conversation already?"

"But now we're talkin' about NASA."

"Fuck NASA. I stopped working for the bastards, and the organization has gone downhill ever since."

"I thought you were still a subcontractor for NASA?" I ask him.

"Part-time, scRitch! And reluctantly. I couldn't give a comet-sized pile of orbiting horseshit about goddamn NASA."

"Well, it is sad," I say. "Here the *one* area of earthly endeavor that's worth anything at all for the future of mankind—which is getting the hell *off* Planet Earth—is the one endeavor that politicians no longer seem to give an orbiting pile of shit about either."

"Fucking ignorant rich Republican bastards."

"Maybe there's hope in the private sector," I suggest.

"Fucking SpaceX you mean?"

"Yeah. Whatshisname, that Musk dude, maybe his company can take over for NASA and do the work that earthlings are now supposed to be doing."

"No money in it. Tell me how SpaceX is gonna make money by launching bullshit rockets. NASA survived this long because it didn't have to make any profit. It had our tax money!"

"Well, other companies pay 'em to carry their satellites up there, don't they?"

"Right. So, tell me, how is launching satellites like exploring space to find another planet for us to move our fat asses to?"

"Seems unlikely, I know."

"It's impossible, *I* know!"

"It's one of the very best things for government to be spending our taxes on, but government *isn't* doing it. Government only wants to build bigger weapons, higher walls, and fund more and more Earth-bound bullshit to keep us all enslaved *here* to the government!"

"Rich Republican bastards," Winter says. (It's something he always says.)

"By the way," I ask, "where are we goin'?"

"To the water drop," Winter says.

"The first one?"

"What do you think?"

"The first one. The second one's on the whole other side of the park."

"Sometimes, scRitch, your powers of reasoning and deduction must astound even you."

"Thanks, I'm sure. I just had a brain fart is all. I thought Henry said he found it on the trail."

"He did. But then he took it to the water drop. Better exposure. Better chance for assholes to steal it."

"Nobody steals anything here," I argue. "I'm sure he just took it to, you know, a more visible lost-and-found place."

"Just like they don't cheat here either, *huh*, scRitch?"

I stop arguing.

We continue *a little ways* in silence. Taking the path of least boulders, rocks, ruts, mud, and standing water. For a jeep road, this really isn't a very good road without a jeep.

Winter's strides are long. He walks rapidly. If he were a war machine, he'd be a tank. His size, his sarcasm, his omniscience, and his loudly trumpeted IQ I have come to know as his trademarks. He's a certified genius with size 14 treads.

"I just hope that jacket's there," he finally says. "If she could, Rachel would kill me if it isn't."

"I remember, I think," I say, "that the water drop is by the green gate. Isn't it?"

"Not too far from it. But the course hasn't gone that way for years. How in the hell do you know the green gate?"

"I remember it because the first time I ever came here, that's the first place I got lost."

"Is that right," Winter says without asking.

"Yeah, I was a total virgin and ended up following this guy I call Sandwich all along the North Boundary Trail. We got to the water drop and the green gate and he left me. The son of a bitch just quit!"

"Imagine that."

"Seriously!" I emphasize loudly. "He suddenly up and said he 'didn't have it' that day, and then turned around at the green gate and took this very road we're hiking on back to camp. He pointed to the vast wilderness on the other side of the gate and said, 'Go that way. You'll find the way.' And I'm, like, shit! *Now* what the hell do I do?"

"You turn around with Sandwich and follow him back to camp."

"Nah. I was still young and stupid at the time. I plunged right down that big field beyond the gate, not knowing where the hell I was or where I was going. That's when this guy Dorm suddenly showed up going the wrong direction. He was headed where I'd just come from, towards that damned gate and this road beyond it."

"Maybe it was the right direction after all."

"Sure, if ya wanna quit! But I didn't drive all the way down here to quit. I wanted to do the damn race! Well, at least one full loop of it. And after convincing Dorm that we needed to go the way *he'd* just come from, neither one of us completed that one loop."

"That's when you spent the night with him. Under some leaves?"

"No, under his space blanket. With our backs up against a fallen log."

"Thus the Hilton."

"Right. That goddamned Hilton."

"Wasn't there a cell phone involved?"

"Right. It was pitch dark, we were totally lost on that candy-ass Chimney Top Trail—trying to quit!—and so Dorm whips out his cell phone and dials up his wife, who's back in camp sittin' around the fire with Laz and the troops. He hollers into the phone, 'We're lost!' And all's I hear comin' out the earpiece of his phone is laughter. Wild uproarious laughter."

"Ha!" Winter at last emotes.

"I mean, it's loud! And just squawkin' out his earpiece. I could hear it five feet away."

"Ha!" That's good, scRitch.

"I mean, the more Dorm kept askin' for help as to where our location was and where to go to get back on trail, the louder the laughter through that ear-hole became. After about a half-hour of not being helped, but only laughed at, he decided to give up. And that's when we went lookin' for shelter. I mean, hey. It was freezing! We had freezing rain and sleet pelting our sad asses all night long. Later on, some dude told me we could've died, or something, from hyperglycemia."

"Hypothermia."

"That too."

"You and Dorm."

"Me an' Dorm in the night in the storm."

"Cozied up under a space blanket."

"Some marathon finisher hotdog wrapper."

"Freezing to death."

"Right. My worst thought in fact was, 'what *do* I do *if he dies?*'"

"Grab his cell phone. Call 911."

"Right. These were ancient days. I didn't know *how* to dial it. I couldn't have called for help if my life depended on it."

"Or his."

"Right. Or his."

"You were lucky."

"Right. I'll never live it down. Anyway, it was at that green gate where all *that* got started."

Suddenly, Winter stops and points.

"It's right over there," he says.

BOOK 4 – Counterclockwise
Left To Die (by Lisa Jackson) or later
Corpses Ain't Smart (by Rod Callahan)
(Your Twenty-Third Objective)

"Where?" I ask.

"The better question is *why*." And just like that, Winter's back to being the genius again.

"OK, why? *Why* is the green gate right over there?"

"Because it's not here!"

Winter doesn't laugh very often or even smile very much, but at this point of all this pointlessness, I think I detect the faintest gleam of a sardonic grin.

"Wiseass," I say.

"Besides, scRitch, we're not going there anyway. We're going to Coffin Springs. Because the best water on Planet Earth is at Coffin Springs. We'll refill our bottles with superior water, then head over to the water drop where the inferior stuff is. If my jacket's there, we can go home."

"So where's Coffin Springs from here?" I ask.

Again he points.

"There's the sign. See it?"

I can't at this precise moment read what's written there, but I do see what looks like a wooden sign on a post stuck into the right side of the jeep road.

"Yeah."

As we get closer, I can see the words "Coffin Springs" with an arrow pointing left onto what seems like a spur road or an offshoot.

We take that road and go left. After what seems like another long trudge, we suddenly come to some sort of other junction, where just over the edge and down the slope and into the woods is apparently the object of our non-thirsty desire.

Winter goes right over the edge. He's whacking bush through thickets and briars going down.

"It's down here, scRitch. See it?"

I confess I hardly see anything. But what's there, as I eventually discover, are these stone—or concrete—slabs surrounding a basin. A small sunken-trench-like thing that's been dug out of the hill and reinforced with these slabs. It's like a miniature koi pond built into your patio. Inside there's this pipe. It's sticking out from the hill, directly under one of the slabs, and there's water pouring out. It's like the spigot on the side of your house for a garden hose that never shuts off. The spigot just pours and pours.

Winter gets down on his knees and makes like to worship at the fountain. He cups his hands under the pipe and proceeds to splash, slobber, and drink. Then he fills his bottle.

"Get down here, scRitch, and taste this wonderful stuff. It is the nectar of the gods."

I stumble down to join him and go through the makeshift of ritual myself. I drink after filling my own bottles first (my hip pack has holsters for two of them) and then I have to admit, it's water.

I wouldn't rate it quite as highly as Winter does, but as far as *aqua vitae* is concerned, it is damn good water. So much so that I make a mental note of it, with a vow to return to this spot of refreshment during every future visit I make to this non-outpost of non-civilization positioned here at the ends of the Earth.

When the evil-ass aliens all come to invade, I think, *I am retreating to right* [spit] *here. This will be scRitch's Last Stand.*

We finish our ablutions and climb back up to the basically-dirt spur road and the junction and Winter now indicates the right direction. This, as opposed to the wrong direction. The Official Instructions, as thunked earlier, are full of crap like this. If you're told to go in "the right direction," that does not necessarily mean you should turn to the right. It might only be telling you to go in "the correct direction."

And from where we are to where we're going, it's only *a little ways* farther along the right road (of course!) until we come to the drop-off down the *right* side of it to where all the water jugs are. From above, it looks like an abandoned refugee camp. There's plastic milk-jug-type jugs sealed full of water, unsealed full of water, unsealed and even un-capped partially full of water, and of course all the empties. I make a mental note of thanks that I don't have to be involved with cleaning up all this mess.

There's also clothing. Discarded or abandoned or found items of apparel that nobody, apparently, is wearing. There's even abandoned equipment, like water bottles! And dead batteries and other stuff that ultrarunners wear out or wear (until they pitch it at dumps like this), like belts and vests and pocket-type things and who-knows-what. There's also a few piles of goddamn paper *wrappers*. Like as if, if you need to throw away your empty candy bar wrapper, it's never OK to do it on the course—but here where there's already a dump it must be OK. Anyway, whoever is stuck afterwards with having to pick up the water jugs is also stuck with cleaning up other people's trash.

But where's Winter's jacket that Hank Speir left here?

Winter is presently ransacking the place. He swings his swath a little wider, into the nearby bushes, and then: "There it is! There's Rachel's beautiful blue jacket!"

"Henry must've hidden it a little," I call out.

"What?" I've also learned over time that Winter is partially hard-of-hearing.

"Henry! Speir!" I say louder. "He, or someone, may have hidden your jacket so no one else would take it!"

Which, as I think of it, would be totally contradictory to the point of dropping it at a point where it would most likely be seen. Not very Speir-like.

"He's a good man, that Henry," Winter says as he comes back.

"Yeah," I agree.

"Not like some other assholes."

"Right."

"Some other asshole would have kept it with him. Then possibly lost it somewhere else where no one could *ever* find it."

"It happens," I say.

"Shit happens!"

"Right. So we can go back now?"

"I'm not sure what *you* would do, scRitch."

"What?"

"I mean, would you leave the jacket here, and hide it, and tell me later? Or would you be another asshole and take it with you?"

"Oh, I would leave it for sure. I almost never carry other people's crap. Too much extra weight."

"*You calling my Rachel's jacket crap?* You asshole!"

"No, Winter. Calm down. I meant in general. Other people's *stuff*."

"Well, watch it. This jacket is precious to me."

"I know. It's seven miles out here to get it, and gonna be seven more miles going back."

"That's to the tower, you idiot. To here it's closer to four miles."

"OK," I say, "and back."

"That's right. And back."

We proceed to "tidy up" the dump a little, to put like stuff into like piles and try to corral all the empties. It's a pointless task. The water drop is slated to be fully operational for three more loops of Barkley. And by the end of that time, this dump will no doubt *be* a dump.

But maybe not. Maybe no runner at all will be operational for *all* the remaining loops of Barkley.

BOOK 3 – Counterclockwise
How to Stay Alive in the Woods (by Bradford Angier) or later
I Should Have Stayed Home (by Horace McCoy)
(Your Twenty-Fourth Objective)

What is happening is, if you good runners and any of your ilk are in fact to be doing the full Monty out here, you had damn well all be done with Loop 2 by the time me and Winter get back to camp. This is Day 2, and you've had all night to boogie through just another 20 miles.

And ha-ha-ha to that. For one thing, it's hard enough just to find your way during the *day*. Nighttime is impossible. So that is why Winter and I put the night to its more useable use and *slept*. If you are battling the mud and the mountains and the briars *and the Instructions* in the dark, then god, if there is one, help ya. But by now the race has been in progress for well over 24 hours and it'll be another hour at least before we see camp again and hey: 26 hours and 40 minutes is your deadline.

Winter and I marvel at the fact that we're not seeing any runners here at the water drop. "Must all be fast ones this year," he guesses. "They must all be back to BOOK 2 and beyond by now."

"If they are to have any hope at all," I say.

"Do you remember where BOOK 2 is?" he asks. "Or how about this, do you remember its title?"

"I don't know. Bald Knob?" I guess.

"Close," he says. "What about the title?"

"I have no clue. Do *you* remember?"

"You have a page of it in your backpack, scRitch!"

"I emptied all that shit out from yesterday. Today is a new dawn."

"Well, I still have it," he says.

And so, right here at the first water drop on the course, just as we're about to leave, Winter stops everything and—using the excuse of safely securing his priceless blue jacket inside his own backpack—he pulls out his plastic baggie from yesterday. Inside, of course, are thirteen stupid ripped sheets of small printed papers.

I tell myself to endure. To bear up under the torment. Besides, I'm not going anywhere. And it's not like as if we're behind schedule or that we *must* make it back to camp before 26 hours-and-change is up. What the hell? We already quit!

Maybe, I think to myself, *I can still learn something from this man.*

"Here it is," he says with his baggie open. "*Ten Stupid Things Men Do to Mess Up Their Lives.* Wasn't that number 2?"

"Let me see it," I say.

He hands me the page and I see no author line at the top, but there is that title. Then I turn the page over.

"Wait a minute. 'Stupid Ambition' is at the top of the other side. So which one's the actual title? Do you remember the actual book?"

I hand the ripped-out page back to him, and he flips it over and back.

"No," he says finally, "but if you look down the page, it sort of suggests the overall title as including ten categories of stupidity. I'm guessing 'Stupid Ambition' is one of those categories, making this a chapter title."

He doesn't let me verify this, but I seriously couldn't care less. I just want to head back.

"OK," I say as he stuffs the paper back into his baggie. "Whatever you say. The only title I really remember is *Another Bullshit Night in Suck City.* How 'bout *that* title, huh?"

"That's BOOK 1!" as he obviously remembers.

"Right. I guess," I say. "Seems to me, though, that it ought to be placed somewhere where runners will get to it in the actual dark."

"But it is!"

"BOOK 1?" I'm not getting it. "BOOK 1 is the very first one we come to."

"What about Loop 2, scRitch? Don't you think all the frontrunners out here can finish their second loop in the dark?"

"I suppose, yeah."

"In fact, they'd better get back to number one in the dark—if they intend to make five loops! You're talkin' 40 miles in under 24 hours. Even *you* can do 40 miles in less than 24 hours!"

"Not on this course, I can't! And neither can most of the rest of us. Even you!"

"You understand. That's why we're here taking a hike after our race is over, and all those poor bastards are still in it."

"OK, well... anyway, I do like that title."

"And by the time everyone gets there in the dark, don't you think they'll all agree with it?" He asks as he's finally packed up and stands to go.

"Right. Kinda like 'Another Bullshit Loop in Barkley Suck.' Ya think?"

"Whatever you say, scRitch. And this must be one of those ten stupid things, don't *you* think? Let's go."

"Yeah, for sure." I agree, and we begin our long trek back to camp.

BOOK 2 – Counterclockwise
Ten Stupid Things Men Do to Mess Up Their Lives
(by Laura Schlessinger) or later
Good Luck, Sucker (by Richard Telfair)
(Your Twenty-Fifth Objective)

"I feel like an axman," I say after a while.

"What?" Winter's always amazed at what comes out of my mouth. "What in the hell are you talking about, scRitch?"

"In fact," I say, "I feel like we're *all* axmen."

"I always knew you were daft."

"No, Winter, hear me out."

"Right."

"There's this national or state park type place called Cumberland Gap. I remember it being in North Carolina, but it must be on the border with Kentucky."

"North Carolina doesn't border Kentucky. So now I know you're *still* nuts."

"Well, it's at some border of some state!"

"Virginia," Winter says.

"OK then, Virginia. Not Tennessee?"

"Tennessee is near there. But the so-called Cumberland Gap is between Virginia and Kentucky. Look at a map!"

"What am I, Rand McNally? I'm only carrying a map of *this park*!"

"Then you'll have to take my word for it."

"So what are *you*, Rand McNally, Senior?"

"I pay attention to things, scRitch."

"You've been there? To Cumberland Gap, I mean."

"Yes, I have."

"OK then, you saw the sign."

"What sign?"

"The historical roadside sign, or national park sign, or whatever. There's a visitors center there, and a sign."

"I don't know of any sign."

"Then you were *not* paying attention. There is a sign. I saw it! I read it!"

"What does it say?"

"It's all about Daniel Boone! It says that Daniel Boone—and I've remembered this phrase for twenty years—'and his band of 40 axmen,' yes *axmen*, first blazed the trail through that gap in the mountains which then allowed settlers to move into Kentucky. I believe what they were doing with all those axes was widening a path so wagons could get through."

"Very good. So again, what the hell does any of *that* have to do with any of *this*?"

"There are 40 Barkley runners! Every year 40 of us *uh* trailblazers start at the Yellow Gate and… well… *blaze!*"

"You're nuts."

"Well? It's what we do, *isn't it?* There is no trail. There are no markings. We're completely on our own out here! And we don't even get to carry an ax."

"You could carry one if you wanted to. It's just extra weight."

"Right," I agree. "But god help ya if you get caught actually chopping anything out here. Like, widening some 'game trail' for our fat asses to get through. Or jeeps. Like this very 'trail' we're on right now!"

"You remember The Godfather."

"The movie?"

"No, of Ultras. He's been here. He *fucking finished!* Him and his buddy, Dr. Atomic."

"Right," I say. "And technically they were disqualified."

"But not for swinging axes or blazing trails, as you say."

"Right. But that did happen, remember? The Godfather took a saw one day to the old North Boundary Trail and tried like hell—just like good ol' Dan'l Boone—to clear a damn path. Remember *that shit?*"

"Yes, scRitch, I remember. I pay attention to shit."

"So. Stuff that happens around here reminds you of Daniel Boone, too."

"No. Stuff that happens around here reminds me of just how sacred and mysterious this place really is. You fuck with it, you die."

"Or get DQ'd."

"That too."

"Anyway, I like to feel like an axman."

"Without an ax."

"Right. Without an ax."

"And no Indians are shooting at you."

"Right!"

"Oh, you're a damn *axman* all right, scRitch. I can think of a whole ton of bullshit coming from you that ought to *be* axed."

I let that slide. We continue walking, relatively briskly now because this whole vastly widened jeep road, or Quitters Road, is now actually grading downhill.

"So," I say finally. "Do you know where 'Kentucky bluegrass' comes from?"

"One of the axmen, *huh*, scRitch? After Mr. Boone and company widened the trail enough for the first Walmart wagon train to get through and set up the chain, his least favorite axman went into the nearest store and bought a bag of grass seed."

"Ha! Nice try. But no. That sign I mentioned also told of how, when good ol' Dan'l Boone first looked at Kentucky through that Cumberland Gap, the setting sun or whatever caused the grassy areas to appear blue. So he coined the phrase, and Kentuckians have thought their lawns are blue ever since."

"And that explains why you can't buy a decent lawnmower in Kentucky, only axes."

"Right! And especially not at Walmart!"

I chuckle a bit but, of course, Winter does not.

"You know," Winter suddenly blurts out of the clear blue, "that this race is a metaphor for a whole 'nother race, don't you?"

"Another ultra?"

"No, you ass, the human race!"

"*Hmmm*. Well, I suppose. I think we've talked about this."

"No supposing about it, scRitch. How about that line that someone else invented—not your damned Dan Boone but one of our own—Spooky Fotog. Remember him?"

"Sure. He took all those terrific old black-and-white pictures of the old prison and stuff around here."

"You remember. Maybe you're not completely daft."

"Right. So did Spooky Fotog invent that phrase I think you're thinking of?"

"*The race that eats its young*. That's right, scRitch. He probably should've trademarked the thing. Everybody seems to trademark everything else these days."

"*The race that eats its young*. That about says it all, huh?"

"I'll bet you don't even know that the Barkley Marathons itself now has a registered trademark."

"No shit?"

"No shit, scRitch. The very name of this race should now always be written with that little R-in-a-circle after it."

"A registered trademark!" I exclaim. "How about that!"

"But the phrase 'the race that eats its young' isn't trademarked," Winter says. "But it ought to be."

"It's part of a movie title though, I think. Doesn't that exact phrase appear along with the title of that wonderful documentary movie those good folks from Out West made about The Barkley a while ago?"

"Yes, I believe so," Winter agrees. "So maybe at least the phrase is copyrighted?"

"I don't know," I say. "But it sure should be."

"Anyway, The Barkley eats its young *for sure*."

"Yes. Yes, it does. That's why every year there's a 'sacrificial virgin,' eh? A 'human sacrifice.'"

"Always fresh blood," Winter says. "I had a thought a while ago about how the payoff for veterans is the constant influx of fresh blood from virgins."

In my mind, I connect the dots.

"So, it works like a Ponzi scheme!"

"I think so, scRitch. 'The race that eats its young' must be ultramarathoning's answer to the Ponzi scheme."

"That's good! You're a frickin' genius!"

"I have an IQ of 189. Believe it, scRitch. I found that out as an undergrad. Do you believe that?"

"Sure," I admit. "It might be one of the few things we're talking about that I *am* willing to take on faith."

"Well, good. Because it's true."

"Right. So every year our beloved 'race that eats its young' brings in the fresh flesh for all the old predators feast on."

"And scrape off."

"It's pretty brutal, huh?"

"That's right, scRitch. And I'd be scraping you, too, if only I could run again."

"Right." I think awhile, mostly about his initial observation. "So back to your metaphor, 'eating its young' *um* is what you're saying *the human race* does, too?"

"That's right, scRitch."

"How so? You mean, like cannibals?"

"Think about it. Didn't we already agree that life on Planet Earth will die? I mean, all life. All life upon the planet becomes extinct—you say in five hundred years and I give it a thousand. Well?"

"Well sure," I say. "But the human race isn't *eating* its young, is it?"

"It might as well be! We are certainly not doing our young any favors. Think about it, scRitch. Is the human race on Earth doing anything—anything at all—to preserve itself? To guarantee life will continue here until, like we've said, our sun swells to a red giant star and completely consumes our planet?"

"Well, we're certainly not doing much," I agree.

"Not much? Hell, we're doing NOTHING!"

"Recycling isn't helping?"

"Fuck recycling. It's a goddamn joke, scRitch! What are contemporary humans mostly doing today?"

"I don't know. Coming up with cannibal recipes?"

The joke falls flat before it even gets out of my mouth.

"Making more humans! More babies! More and more and more and more! That's what fucking humans are doing! They are effectively making more and more young so that later, well, what's left of the Earth—this totally poisoned and polluted planet that will not be able to harbor any life, *not any at all*—IT WILL KILL THEM! Or eat them alive, if you prefer."

"The planet isn't getting any bigger, is it?" I sheepishly say.

"No, not at all. And in fact it's getting—the habitable parts of it anyway—smaller! And more and more *uninhabitable!* The air gets worse. The water gets worse—look at what the hell the "town fathers" are doing to the water supply in Flint, Michigan, *fer chrissakes! A*nd the land gets worse and the oceans are getting more polluted every single goddamned day. scRitch, I'm telling you, we might as well be cannibals. At least then we could *enjoy* our youth—instead of letting them grow up in a horrible, ugly, poisoned world that can only kill them later."

"Ya know, Winter, Jonathan Swift suggested this a long time ago."

"What?"

"This! What you just said! He was writing during the great Irish famine, or whatever. He published this wonderful satire, called 'A Modest Proposal,' which absolutely declared that the best way for the Irish to survive the famine was to eat their babies."

"Oh, Swift. Right."

"It was devilishly clever," I say. "He was basically saying that the Irish were too stupid to do anything else *except* have more babies that they couldn't feed, and so they might as well *eat* their most abundantly manufactured gross national product, *eh?*"

"Swift was a genius," Winter agrees. "And a prophet. Look what's happening all over the Third World today."

"Nobody's eating, but everybody's fucking, *huh?*"

"The global population projections are off the charts."

"Out of this world."

"Precisely!" Winter says.

"So there ya go. The human race is effectively *eating* all of its young people—turning 'em into chopped liver maybe—which means *all* future generations."

"We're condemning the unborn," Winter agrees. "There's going to be nothing left for them. Certainly nothing *they* can eat."

"Ya know, my friend, this is why I'm childless."

"Me too."

"Ah! We agree!"

"Yup."

"I simply decided, way back in my wanton and reckless youth, that I just do not want any descendants of mine blaming *me* for their inevitably miserable existence. Great-great-great-great-great-grandpa scRitch cannot be accused of forefathering any agony."

"Nor, of course, do you receive any joy from your offspring."

"Right. It's the trade-off."

"Well then, you had better prepare yourself well for your own old age, because you won't have any kids to take care of you."

"Right."

"Of course, neither will I. I do have a good nephew, though."

"Some ancient philosopher or other claimed that it's a dirty trick to be born."

"Flaubert?" Winter guesses. "Gustave Flaubert. Or maybe you're thinking of Arthur Schopenhauer."

"Holy moly! You *know* this?"

"*I* pay attention to things, scRitch. *I've* also read *Madame Bovary.*"

"You *know* ancient philosophers?"

"I know something about philosophy, yes. And I also know that both those guys wrote about how it's better never to have been born."

"Wow!" I exclaim. "I first heard the idea while in high school, which helps to explain my not remembering."

"I think Flaubert's your guy, scRitch. And he wasn't actually a philosopher. He was a French novelist. But he was pretty passionate about *not* wanting to be a father."

"When did he live?"

"No doubt before you were in high school."

"Right."

"In fact, scRitch, there's a whole *school* of thought pertaining to that which you probably think is your own idea. It's called 'anti-natalism'—better it is to never be born."

"No, I can't claim that exact idea. I have a different one. It's about death. I call it my 1940 Theory."

"Oh, you're a goddamn philosopher all right, scRitch. What's this cockamamie theory of yours?"

"Well, it's about, you know, how all the people—in fact the entire human race, everybody!—has it in their heads that *there must be something else*. There just *has to be*. Otherwise, why live? There must be some *reward* for, you know, putting up with all this shit!"

"Like The Barkley."

"Exactly!" I say. "It's how religion grabs you and takes control over your life. So people who don't, you know, have a clue about what comes after, gravitate to the pseudo-bullshit high priests who don't, you know, have any clue either. Well, the high priests invent heaven, and how to get there, and hell, and how to avoid going there, and whammo: now suddenly there's meaning to life! Not to mention, they now have control over yours."

"Go on. What's the 1940 part?"

"So, where were you in 1940?"

"I was nowhere."

"You weren't born yet, were you? I honestly don't know."

"That's right, scRitch. I wasn't born until 1944."

"Good! I mean, that's good for my theory."

"*What the hell* is *your theory?*"

"Well, the date is arbitrary. It's always for some year prior to anybody's birth."

"*Go on.*"

"OK! So, my theory simply is that, just as you weren't anywhere in the years before you were born, you will be in the same exact condition years after your death. You will be nowhere! Why should after-life be any different from before-life?"

"You *may* have a point."

Loop 2

"No joy, no pain, no rapture, no sitting on clouds, no singing with angels, no harps, no heaven, no hell, no purgatory, not a goddamned thing. Just, you know, nothing! Poof! You *feel* just exactly the same as you *felt* in 1940. Which was nothing!"

"It may well be."

"Why in the world should it be a *given* that humans, once born, all of a sudden are guaranteed eternal life? In heaven or hell or elsewhere? Where does it say that?"

"In religion. Hell, almost all of them guarantee some kind of eternal life after death."

"Well, take away religion! That's the stuff invented by the high priests, who don't know diddle about after-death either! Look at all the whacky shit invented by the ancient Egyptians. Are all—or any—of those ancient pharaohs, queens, and princes *right now* enjoying eternal life? Or are they just dried up mummies wrapped in linen and in the same place *invisibly* as you and I were in 1940?"

We walk for a moment or two in silence. Only the bare branches of the roadside trees rub. I think I detect a smidge of a softening.

"I guess, for lack of a better philosophic companion," Winter finally says, "I'm with you, scRitch."

"Thanks. But, you know, the whole ginormous colossal cataclysmic thing is preposterous. That, you know, just because we're *people* we die, our bodies rot, and still we have an afterlife. Do dogs have an afterlife? How about cats?"

Then he whirls on me. *"Don't you say anything bad about cats!"*

"OK, OK," I say, meekly. "But the question remains, *uh* what happens to animals' remains? What happens to ours? For that matter, are *all* the *homo sapiens* from Earth's ancient history—*are all of* them *in heaven?* Are the Neanderthals? Where do you draw the dividing line between humans—who magically *have* eternal life—and the prehuman or subhuman apes—who magically *don't* have it? What about our friends the aliens from other planets? Are those dead slimy green warp-speeders in heaven also? And is it the same heaven, or different?"

"It'd be pretty crowded, huh?"

"It sure would! Anyway, Winter, I think because *homo sapiens* had evolved enough to think, and invent stuff, that people long ago invented places—invisible places—for where they want to pretend our fat asses all get parked for all eternity after those asses—like Yankees here at Barkley—fall down, die, and start to smell."

"Like down those still-open mineshafts over there by RatJaw."

"Right!"

"And Little Hell."

"Right! So anyway…"

"Anyway what, scRitch?"

"Anyway, I own *The 1940 Theory*, and in that same condition of nothingness is exactly where I expect *I'll* be. Eventually. But of course, I won't know it at the time."

"scRitch, I now bestow upon you ownership of a tenet of philosophy that nobody else on the planet will ever know about, argue with, or give you credit for."

"Thanks, Wintcr." I pause for a bask in the afterglow of accolade, then change the subject. "So, how far from camp are we now?"

"Too far," he says. "It might as well be 1940."

BOOK 1 – Counterclockwise
Another Bullshit Night in Suck City (by Nick Flynn) or later
Defiled by Chickens (by G. Alexander Trebek)
(Your Twenty-Sixth Objective)

Suddenly at this point along Quitters Road, as we are heading back to camp, we see the vague outline of some other *homo sapiens* running—that's right—and at full speed, uphill, and straight toward us. Talk about daft!

And when it draws closer, we hear *it* singing at the top of its lungs.

Surely it's an *it*. No human still alive out here could possibly be running that hard. Besides here, on this road, they're off-course and cannot possibly still be in the race either. And all of us quitters are *not* running. Like as if we ever did.

"Honest ta Ja, Winter," I say, "if *that's* not a hallucination, then I don't know what is. I see a sprinting dude running uphill singing his lungs out! Do you?"

"It's Cayman," Winter says.

"Cayman! You mean…"

"Yep. The very same."

We watch him approach. I knew he was in the race, but I never really saw him during the race which, of course, ended for Winter and me yesterday. He must've been ahead of us? Which is easy to imagine because in his day, Cayman was *fast*. He used to win ultras, not just run them. He's set records. He's run against—and beat—many of the best runners there ever were.

I remember one of his peculiar race preparation habits. For lubricating his feet against blisters—for which today's sports retail marketplace is just chock full of products to sell you—good ol' Cayman used motor oil. That's right, motor oil. In case, I suppose, his hyper-powered engine might burn too hot.

But these days he's old, like us. And he never did try this Barkley previous to this. It's not exactly what they call a "flat and fast" course. I'm actually starting to think, maybe he was *behind* us?

"Well, if it's not the Cayman!" Winter announces when we're all within earshot, and Cayman finishes his song. Winter and I have no idea what song it is. When he stops next to us, I swear I can hear air brakes being applied.

"I'm on a mission," Cayman says, breathing really hard. "Don't bother me."

"OK," says Winter, slamming to a stop himself, although without the need for air compression. "We won't. Carry on."

"I'm practicing windsprints," explains the Cayman.

"Uphill on Quitters Road at The Barkley," I say, sarcastically.

"What better place?" Cayman asks, quite surprised, probably, that anyone could possibly think that anything might be amiss about this.

"But you were in the race?" Winter asks.

"Sure!"

"How far'd you get?"

"I think we quit around Coffin Springs."

"We?" I ask. "Who else was you with?"

"I don't know. A bunch of new folks. OK, maybe two, three," Cayman says.

"Were you all moving fast?" I can't resist asking.

"Oh, hell no. That was the longest six miles of my life!"

"I think it's closer to eight miles," Winter says, "to there and back."

And so we never did, or could, figure out if his group beat us to Coffin Springs, or if Winter and I beat them. Neither we nor Cayman had kept track—or "splits" as they say—of our times for that distance.

"It was horrible," says Cayman. "That's why I'm out here today, to try and redeem myself."

"This place is not exactly like a 400-meter track," I say.

"Nope," says Cayman. "Hey, I gotta go!"

"Have fun!" Winter tells him.

"Should I get the USATF officials out here," I tease, "in case you set any speed records *sprinting uphill along Quitters Road?*"

"Sure!" he calls out behind him as he continues, and then slowly, but slowly, disappears over the nearest hill crest behind us.

"That Cayman," says Winter. "What a character."

"Listen," I say. "He's singing again."

"He's daft."

"So what's that song he's belting out?"

"*Waltzing Matilda*, I think," says Winter.

"That's a pretty old song," I say.

"That's a pretty old runner."

"Right!" I conclude.

We walk along in silence for *a little ways*, Winter and The Amazing Rachel Technicolor Dream Jacket, which is safe inside his pack, and he's carrying his dream bottle which is full of his amazing dream water. I continue with my double-holster-water-bottled waistpack cinched in place with "wildness" and "preserving the world"—or destroying it—on my mind.

"Did you know that *Thor*eau's family business was making pencils?" I eventually blurt out.

"What?"

"Pencil makers! The Henry David Thoreau family business was pencil-making. Well, it was his father's business. H.D. himself, I think, thought of himself as the Lazarus Lake of his day."

"You're daft," Winter says. "I don't know about making pencils, but THOR-eau had no clue about anything having to do with *Laz* in his day."

After a beat, I say, "Do you suppose they were Number 2 pencils, and all the high school kids in Cambridge used them to take their SAT exams?"

"You're nuts."

"Or, how about 'advertising specialties' for your company to give out? The *Thor*eaus could've made ten thousand pencils with 'Winter's Rocketship Enterprises' stamped on the side."

"They wouldn't have needed to make that many. My only goddamn customer all these years has been NASA."

"So what about this 'Big Bang Theory'?" I ask, taking this opportunity to switch my inquiry into probing astrophysical science.

"What about it?" Winter shoots back.

"Well, for starters," I say, "is it true?"

"You mean, did the universe all get started with one big explosion?"

"Right. Is that how it happened?"

"I don't know exactly, scRitch. It seems to be the prevailing current conjecture—I hesitate to call it a theory. But maybe it all did happen the way they now assume."

"Well," I say, "I think the whole idea is short-sighted."

"*What?*"

"Short-sighted! I mean, this is what the god-fearing religious power-mongers have as a final say over the planet, right? I mean, as far back as the universe is ever found to exist, all the Sunday-collection-plate collectors can ultimately say: 'Well, it was God that created all the matter that *banged*,' eh?"

"So, if not a god, then what?" Winter asks.

"Nobody!" I say. "No one, no thing, no deity, no nothing."

"So, it just suddenly appeared? Out of thin space?"

"No," I continue, "it's what I mean by short-sighted. I mean, how do we know the whole humongous cosmic thing isn't cyclical?"

"Cyclical?"

"That's right, cyclical. Forever and for ever and for all eternity and all there ever was throughout history and for all future time to come, well, in my humble opinion, the entire universe could indeed be expanding, just like they say, but maybe it's expanding around some equally humongous curvature, so that eventually the entire universe compresses again upon itself, and then, BANG! It explodes again."

"You're arguing that there is no beginning and, I suppose, no end."

"*Exactamundo!*" I exclaim. "The whole thing is cyclical. Always was, always will be. And THAT's your eternity right there!"

"You might actually be onto something there, scRitch. *Might*," he emphasizes.

"Let me tell you about *my* theory, OK?"

"I suppose if you gotta tell me," he says, "you're gonna tell me."

"What else we got? It is the very purpose of The Barkley to get people to think. I, at least believe that, and so here we are at The Barkley…"

"Thinking."

"That's right, Winter my friend. That is absolutely correct."

"Go on. With your *theory*, that is."

"I developed this in grad school. I call it *The Brute Universe Theory*. The first tenet of The Brute Universe Theory is that we humans are all limited in our thinking precisely because we're human. Humans have a beginning and end. Birth-death, ya know? So it is impossible for us to think otherwise. We think beginning-and-end, and so the entire universe *must* have a beginning *and* an ending."

I pause for a second to let this sink in (in *me*), then continue…

"Hence the Big Bang. Except the Big Bang doesn't theorize the end of things. 'The End of Days,' as they say. The time when the whole damn universe ends. Stops. *Quits*."

"Right. Quits," agrees Winter.

"Nobody is theorizing—I mean scientifically—about how the entire cosmos *kaputs!*"

"Sure."

"*They* all say God will do it. But I say," I say, "that *can't* happen because everything that's endless—you know, no beginning and no end—

which is historically attributed to 'God' is, in actuality, the basic property of the universe. The *uh* Brute Universe. *It* is what has always been and always will be. Not any god."

"Why do you call it brute?" Winter asks.

"Because that is exactly what it all is. It *does not give* one projectile shit about you, about me, not even about itself. *It* is all, all of it, umpteen obsquattamatillion mega-lightyears across, up, down, inside, and outside—ALL OF IT—brutally inanimate. *It* does *not* care! Mainly because *it* can't."

"This so-called Brute Universe of yours doesn't care."

"That's right, Winter. And it exists totally outside the realm of human beings, so therefore we humans cannot possibly comprehend it. Certainly not all of it. We can only think in terms of beginning-and-end, whereas the entire universe doesn't *think* at all. It just *is*. Always was. Always will be. Replete with totally cyclical explosions, expansions, contractions, and explosions again. Endless. Yadda yadda. Forever and ever."

"So what else is there about this brutish reality?" Winter asks.

"Well, the next tenet of The Brute Universe is that, if we humans are to coexist in harmony—not only with it but with each other—then we *all* had damn well better coexist! Peacefully! Because, my friend, *we* are all we've got! There is nothing else! When we have our little ends, we're back in 1940, *eh?* We are suddenly nothing. Again! It will be like you and I and we and them and all of us *homo sapiens* never existed at all."

"Maybe, scRitch, you *do* understand."

"The afterlife is politics. Power. The pseudo-religio powermongers have held sway over the human condition for eons. It's how they control other humans. It's how they make them *pay* every Sunday. It's all what keeps *them* in business! And they don't know any more about anything than you or I do. In fact, less. Certainly less than *you* do!"

"Well thanks, I think. And this is all well and good, scRitch, but there are a few gaping holes in your theory. For example, how do you explain the paranormal?"

"Ghosts?"

"That's right. How about clairvoyance? How do psychics solve murder mysteries? How do whackjobs like Nostradamus predict the future?"

"Right, my friend. And this is where my theory ends and your science takes over. All these things you mention, all this so-called paranormal activity, all of it! Well, it's just that we haven't figured it out yet. There are brain waves, yes? Centuries ago nobody had even heard of *waves* period! And now all that invisible shit powers radio, TV, cell phones, telekinesis, mental telepathy—everything that we cannot see! But it's there, right? And so eventually your science will indeed figure out all the weirdo-psycho-ghost-story bullshit. It's all explainable, Winter. Eventually *homo sapiens*—if he lives that long—will figure out everything. Why? Because *homo sapiens* has invented everything in the first place. Including their god! Including their imaginary afterlife!"

"Except the universe," Winter corrects.

"Right," I agree. "The universe was here first. All's we've done is exploit it."

"One more thing, scRitch. One more possibly gaping hole in your precious little theory."

"Yes?"

"Life."

"Life?"

"That's right," Winter says. "Life."

"You mean how did it get here?"

"That's right, scRitch. And while you're at it, how does life get *anywhere*? Anywhere at all in your Brute Universe-that-doesn't-give-a-fresh-launched-shit-about-life, the very thing that put us here! On *this* planet. In *this* park. On *this* road, right now!"

"It's another tenet of my theory. You, we, everybody keeps thinking that, you know, some *god* had to create all this life because—Geezesus—it *had* to start somewhere, right? Life *has to have* a beginning because, obviously, it has an end. Isn't that the so-called prevailing opinion?"

"Is it?"

"Well I think it is. The prevailing wisdom, that is. Everything, once again, comes down to *boom*. To what? To some ONE thing that gives start to it all. Which came first, the chicken or the egg? Well, I believe it was the science. The biology. The pissant first zygote! BUT!!!"

"But what, scRitch?"

"Here again the popular myth believes that it all—all of this, this life, life on this Earth—had to start *with just one thing*. And my theory says to hell with that. Life spontaneously generates *all the time!* And on every planet throughout the cosmos that's pretty much like ours."

"What?"

"You heard me. The atoms and molecules and fucking—yes, *fucking* must get tossed into the mix somewhere, *eh?* Well, all of it, yes, *all of it*, simply continues! There was no *once*. No Adam and Hoozits and the Garden of Whatchamacallit. The minute little teensy thingies that start life *happen all the time!* This beginning-and-then-evolving process is constant and continuous!"

"You can prove this, I assume?"

"Science can prove this, and we both know it! Once science figures it out, yes! I believe we *can* create life in a test tube!"

"I'm not sure about that."

"It's happening already, Winter! Haven't they successfully cloned, like, sheep? Haven't they even gone so far as to create replacement human bodyparts in a petri dish? A laboratory? On the side of someone's face? Man, this is Frankenstein-come-true after all!"

"Maybe. But all of that *starts* somewhere, with some *one thing*."

"Right! So far! But hey, you know about that dude—what's his name?—Higgs. Hasn't he actually given us the 'Higgs boson'? It's what some call 'the god particle'?"

"You don't know shit about the Higgs boson, scRitch."

"Maybe I don't, but maybe I don't have to. But I personally believe it *uh* lies at the core of all life. And because it does, and because—you know this, right?—they seemingly keep on finding new life, like in the Amazon Rain Forest and places—you've heard of all this? Today scientists are finding more and more and more previously unknown life, like insects. Like tiny smarmy things. Like weird shit and new fish at the bottom of the sea."

"That argues for taxonomy, scRitch, not spontaneous life. There may just be a backlog in identifying all of what is already on this Earth."

"I don't believe so, my friend. My theory says that the very idea of once—just once, one time for the beginning of everything and anything—is false. It's false because it's a convenient human cop-out. Humans cannot fathom continuous spontaneous creation, because humans have to have a beginning and ending. *One* beginning, *eh?* God *had to* create the first—what?—replicating atom! It's a god that kick-started this whole gigantic humungous life-and-evolution thing in the first place. Right? *One* god. *One* beginning to everything!"

"And you're saying, because of the Higgs boson, new life pops up all the time. Is that what you're saying, scRitch?"

"Yessir. That's pretty much what I am saying."

"Do you know the math involved? Have you any fucking idea what Peter Higgs, the mathematician went through to come up with that theory of *his?*"

"No," I confess, "but neither do I think I have to. It's the philosophy of spontaneous life that intrigues me, Winter. I leave the science and math to you guys."

"Well, you need to go back to school, scRitch. I have felt for the longest damn time that you have no idea what in the *hell* you're talking about."

I pause my talk, and try to think better. *Crunch crunch crunch.* Our running shoes are crunching along this rugged, gravely, totally uneven gnarly jeep road. Quitters Road. Very faintly, other footsteps now suddenly seem to be pretty far behind us.

"It's like a cotton candy machine," I finally say.

"Like a *WHAT?*"

"Well, this is how it was explained to me. The Higgs boson, I mean. Apparently, there are—all over the place—these tiny subatomic 'force fields' which are kind of like that vibrating shivering oscillating and invisible sugar-bed that cotton candy machines create. The 'field' is just, you know, *there*. So then the exactly correct atom or particle or proton or quark or whatever-the-hell—which already exists—comes along and either rolls or blows across the field—or boson *eh?*—and boom! Presto! An exactly correct little microscopic teensy thingy emerges that wiggles! Divides! Splits off! Has energy! Grows bigger, and is perfectly capable of evolving into higher and ever higher lifeforms after this boom-boom boson micro-bit begins!"

"You have got to be kidding."

"Kind of like subatomic cotton candy!"

"Scritch, you're nuttier than all the nut farms in Georgia."

Suddenly, what I was thinking were footsteps are now right behind us. It's Cayman. On his return sprint. He screeches to a stop and is completely taken aback. He cranes his neck around my left shoulder and practically hollers in my face.

"You *are* totally nuts!! You think life got started on this earth *in a cotton candy machine!!??*"

"I tried to tell him he's daft," says Winter.

"Daft? *His V-8 is three cylinders short!*"

In addition to his other racing talents, Cayman's involved with racecar driving.

"I don't suppose you gentlemen want to hear my further explanations," I say to both of them.

"*NO!*" they both sing out in unison.

"OK then," I say. "I know when I'm not appreciated. Or welcome."

Then Winter goes, "Hey, Cayman. Why do *you* think this Barkley is so popular?"

"Certainly not because of any cotton candy!"

"OK," I say. "We were just, you know, exploring the secrets of the universe. I guess we got a little off-track from the footrace."

"I don't have any idea about this race," says the Cayman, "or how—or even if—it's popular. This is my first time here!"

"So why did you come?" I ask.

"It sure wasn't to explore the universe with weird freaks like you!"

Winter chimes in. "Never mind that shit, Cayman. Just why *did* you show up?"

"Because I was invited! Isn't that, really, the reason why any of us are here?"

We all hit the imaginary *pause button* for a second while we walk. And think.

So, I'm now supposing that—after all *this*, and after all *that*—the only real reason as to why any of us are here is because, hey, Laz invited us. We received his goofy "condolences." That's the sarcastic method, via email, that Race Management uses to let you know you're in the race. Nothing else. You submit your—whatever—intentions, essay, beggings and pleadings via email at precisely *the* correct instant point along the known universe's space-time continuum, you hit "Send," and then you wait.

If Race Management (Laz) selects you from among the *thousands* of emails submitted [one day, I swear, the entire internet server known as Hotmail *will* crash because of this instantaneous deluge]; well, he sends you "condolences" expressing his *sympathy* at having to inform you that you are now *in for untold agony and suffering*. It's cute, I suppose, and totally effective. Most new entrants—virgins and/or human sacrifices all—immediately become afraid ("be afraid, be very afraid") and express their angst all over the Internet, which totally defeats the purpose of trying to keep things secret. But also, if you receive no condolences, you might find yourself publicly posted on the "weight list"—which is, naturally, a "wait" list with "weights"; that is, the greater the heft to your history, the higher your height on this next-in-line list. Or in plain language, the more he wants you, the better your chances of getting in.

I think about all this for a second, but then immediately decide I have no time to think about it. The Cayman is about to speak.

"For the love of Mike, this Lazarus sent me *condolences!* What the hell is *that?*"

Winter responds. "It's his way, his way of jabbing you yet again, before he has the chance to do it *here* in person."

"Heck, Cayman," I say, "all this time I didn't think you even *wanted* to enter this race. It isn't your style. There's no speed here. No road. No track. Maintaining *race pace* in these pathless mountains full of thorns is like a joke."

"I *didn't* want to come!" he exclaims. "Out of the clear blue sky one day, somehow, some way, Laz's whacky condolence shows up in my Inbox!"

Whoa. So much for submitting your intentions and essays and beggings and pleadings. It really does come down to who exactly His Nibs wants in his footrace.

After a brief pause for self-registering this shocking new news, I find it in me to suddenly blurt out:

"Well, Cayman, did you pour motor oil on your feet yesterday?"

And now comes the equally shocking response, "Of course I did! Today, too! And I still have what's left of a quart of 20W-50 in my car."

I'm sorry I asked.

BOOK 13 – Counterclockwise
Six Seconds (by Rick Mofina) or
61 Hours (by Lee Child)
(Your Twenty-Seventh Objective)

A little ways farther down Quitters Road, we're that much closer to reentering camp. I can practically taste the chicken.

"Isn't that the first turn off this road onto the White Trail going up Bird Mountain?" I ask Winter.

"That's it!" he replies.

All of us walk past and gawk at the sign on our right where the two separate trailheads are: one is the correct left turn (as you start the race) onto this, your very first candy-ass trail, and the other is the shortcut—which cuts short the right angle formed by the trailhead at the sign and the jeep road—which is quite a few feet closer to camp and gives mute testimony to hikers and Barkers both wanting to cut switchbacks. Indeed, as we've all learned, the White Trail itself consists of 14 switchbacks going from this trailhead up the mountain to where the course takes yet another left turn, over to the Pillars of Doom.

It's a pretty big sign, but it is easily missed coming from camp in the actual course direction. In fact, I have missed this sign—and the damned left turn, either by shortcut or right angle—every single time I've tried hiking up Bird by myself. Most folks don't know that about me, so of course I don't tell them.

Very quickly after this, we cross the wooden bridge over some creek—which might even be identified by another sign, which I've also always *not* noticed—that probably gets encountered somewhere else along the course, but I don't know where. My work on the course is done. The three of us hikers (OK, one's a sprinter) have now most assuredly and completely and resoundingly and thoroughly and totally *quit*.

Our next task is chicken eating. We're hungry.

Just across the bridge, following a wide easy left turn, we can see the camp. I start sniffing to see if I can smell it—and the open-flame chicken being grilled to perfection—but no. It's daytime, there's nobody cooking (for my hoity-toity convenience), and the smoke rising from the fire does *not* smell like chicken.

"I don't think they've been waiting for us," I say.

"They don't give a damn about us," says Winter. "We're not in the race."

"Maybe," Cayman jests, "I could sing for my supper?"

The first thing we want to do is, of course, see who else has quit versus who's still in the race. So we essentially bypass the campfire and the surrounding hangers-on and head straight to the small stone pillar, the business half of the two old "posts" that hold up the Yellow Gate on either side of it. I suppose it's the western post. Anyway, it's the one that Laz uses for his "office." It holds his lantern for nighttime, that goofy big red "easy" pushbutton, the bugle, and *The* Book—a loose-leaf binder that contains the record of everyone still in, and also out, of the race, together with their loop finishing times and all the excuses of all the quitters. Even though being "timed out" is very real, Laz doesn't actually think of it as an excuse. If you were moving so slow as to be timed out, there must be some excuse in there somewhere for *why* you *chose* to move that slow.

So we first check in with the boss, who, of course, is basically annoyed by our presence. He's distant and aloof and can't be bothered with us because we're quitters. But he lets us look inside *The* Book, where we are immediately surprised by how few runners are still in the race. It looks like there may be less than a dozen, among whom three are "out there" already on Loop 3, and the rest have yet to get in from Loop 2. As it looks now, the frontrunners themselves must be "choosing" to move too slow. Laz figures it might not be possible for anyone to finish within the 60 hours.

The numbers of quitters today are legion. We note Henry Speir (who, after all, was done when he told Winter where his jacket was) and Mom, Beech, Beans, Poorwater Basin, Miss England, Running Boom, Mungo Jerry, The Wall, The Arm, The Stomach, The Admiral, and the Dime Man have all quit, among many others about whom I know neither their true identities nor their nicknames.

Among those still out there are The Ginger Man, Dr. Metallica, Jam-Jam, a couple of "furriners," The Swede, Bama Boy, The Librarian, Mathmagic Man, Frozen Ed, and Buttslide. Still representing "the distaff side" are Leather, Yeeva and The Swimmer.

Even Laz reckons that, for this year at least, there might not be anyone heading out on Loop 4. There's good likelihood that everyone will time out at 40 hours. To go out on your fourth lap, you need to beat 36 hours for three. So maybe a Fun Run is all we'll see.

Winter decides to take his newfound priceless jacket back to his campsite (and no doubt lock it tightly inside his van), Cayman (who has apparently had enough speedwork for the day) heads for the showers, and I (who still and always am dazed and confused) decide to cook chicken. Visiting briefly with Laz has done nothing to diminish my starvation.

From "the office" to the campfire is about 30 steps. But these damned moss-and-slime-covered boulders in between are slippery—and there is a slight uphill—so you need to be a little careful and try to walk only on the leaves and dirt. Jumping around on these slippery rocks are for younger peeps, and their even younger families, many of whom have all been showing up *en toto* in recent years. Running Bare and her brood are a primal example.

I like Running Bare. Despite her seeming "baby factory" reputation, she is svelte and swift and built like she belongs on the covers of most running mags. She is also, I'm guessing, the physical envy of most other running women.

Over the years she's spun some fantastical stories, the most memorable of which is her *tradition* of running every New Year's Eve in the woods around her Southern house completely unclothed *and* unshod.

Nothin' could be finah than to be in Carolina, I muse, *in the woods after midnight in the morrrrrrning*. It must be awesome. Forest rangers have apparently witnessed this. I'm jealous.

Running Bare is also the author of the following line, now permanently affixed to the memories of the other women who were there when she spoke it and who later *hysterically* quoted it back to me: "My thighs don't even remotely touch!"

Aye, I muse, *there's the rub*. And I'm still jealous.

The women of sense (which are just about all of them) don't participate in this reckless rock-hopping behavior. I find three of my favorites now sitting around the campfire on regular chairs—canvas chairs, the kind you fold up and stick inside a long cloth bag with a cloth handle. They are Kate, Hail, and Cassandra.

"Hey, scRitch," one of them says, "are you going to cook us something?"

"You mean," I reply, "you all haven't cooked it already?"

"That's not our job," says Kate. "We're the cheering section. We're here to encourage *you* to do it."

"Well, all righty then. Is that the box full of frozen chicken?" I ask.

"Right over there, scRitch," says Cassandra. "Have at it!"

She's pointing to the "big picnic table" inside the big white headquarters tent. This is a *big* table only because it's *two* tables, one of which belongs to this campsite (#12) and the other of which is stolen from next door (campsite #11). My per-usual site here lately has been #11. So I have no table. It's no picnic, this, as I also per-usually tell the peeps.

All of which means, of course, that I do my eating at campsite #12, and now it seems (if I want any) that here is where I'll do my chicken cooking, too. The *thing* of it is, all we get (and have ever gotten) from the Barkley chicken farm are "quarters," which is basically the dark meat of the chicken. It doesn't ever matter. I have yet to hear anyone complain that it's not white meat. Maybe there's some weird subliminal message in that for the Civil Rights Movement, but probably not. It's pretty hard to philosophize when everyone's starving.

But the contents of the big brown packing box are *frozen solid*. It is, by the way, one of the "why's" of this aspect of The Barkley: Barkley chicken. Because there is no refrigeration (generally speaking) inside a campground, the best way to preserve food over the course of three days or so is to keep it frozen—or try to. Laz tries to. He keeps the unopened chicken boxes stuffed inside his rental van, underneath about a half-a-ton of *stuff*. Foam rubber, mattress pads, blankets, tarps, and other kinds of stuff make for makeshift insulation. It works pretty well, too. Plus the fact that Icehouse Delirium State Park is figuratively in a whole different time zone, Zip Code, weather pattern, and metaphysical universe—all of *that* contributes to your (generally speaking) chilly discomfort and keeps shipping boxes of chicken pretty well frozen. Even outside the van and on top of the picnic table. No matter. It's Icehouse, after all, *eh?* The nickname for our beloved state park here basically explains the why of the chicken being always frozen.

And that's also why the traditional "Barkley Chicken" is burnt to a crisp on the outside and still partially frozen on the inside. But such "tradition" over the years is mostly due to really incompetent chicken cookers, like Laz.

The other convenience that campsites generally lack is a microwave. Because if I had one right about now, I could rip open this chicken bag, thaw a piece, and grill a near-perfect hind quarter in *way* less time that it takes to talk about it.

"Anyone happen to have a hammer and chisel?" I ask at the box, which is open and revealing several stiff plastic bags with maybe a dozen quarters in each bag, and my grimy hands are wrestling wildly with several pieces stuck—solid—to all the other stiff frozen pieces inside the bag. It's like ice sculpting without the chainsaw.

"Use your fingers, scRitch!" Hail calls out. "Isn't this chicken *digitally* prepared?"

Which is the other joke about Barkley Chicken. It *is* digitally prepared, not by microprocessor or microwave, but by the griller's damn hands. And how this came about was due to barbecue sauce which, of course, has always been digitally applied to the blackened chicken skin by the cook's filthy fingers. You simply pour out a little sauce pool onto your "digits" and then smear the stuff all over the outside of the still-frozen inside. Then you serve it on a paper plate. *Mmmmmmm, huh?*

But I'm telling you now, with no matter what tools you either have or haven't got, it takes all the skill of a diamond cutter to pry these frozen gemstones loose. And soon, it seems, I am to be acquiring this skill.

BOOK 12 – Counterclockwise
Tales From Out There: *The Barkley Marathons, The World's Toughest Trail Race* (by Frozen Ed Furtaw) or
Where Do We Go from Here: Chaos or Community?
(by Martin Luther King, Jr.)
(Your Twenty-Eighth Objective)

As I carefully place the froze-solid chick piece, chipped off the froze-solid ice block, on top of the grill grate which is, by ironwork design, forever imprisoned above whatever fire is built below—and repeat this process another half-dozen times—I take a pause in my thoughts in order to step back (from these huge flames now wanting to singe *my own* hind quarters) and review.

We (all of us here) are milling around, barely moving, at a footrace where runners are practically killing themselves to get back to where we already are, generally due to having never left. These are the lucky ones, the fortunate ones, the ones who never had to suffer the loss in the first place that enabled "condolences" to show up where those others reside and *not* be fortunate. The less lucky ones suffered the loss, received the condolences, and have now proceeded as fast as possible to get *out* of the thing that caused their need for sympathy to begin with. The even lesser in luck have come full circle back to here to stock up for more "out there," and then leave here again in their continuing quest for ever higher and more exalted levels of suffering. And the very least fortunate of all haven't come back, period, and are in fact *still* "out there." In the Zen of Barkley, surely the loftiest level of oneness with the universe must lie in the suspended state of being forever lost.

I may not have achieved the ultimate Zen of one mind mining the universe, but I have been forever lost many times.

Thus, I automatically know how every *body* that *isn't* here is feeling. It's a kind of a kōan, I think: *To know what it's like to be horribly lost at The Barkley, it helps to be milling around the campfire enjoying yourself.*

Over the years I've managed to concoct a few scRitch's laws. The first, already noted, says something like: *Before you can know what's not enough, you first have to know nothing.* But now there needs to be a corollary: *After you know everything, sign up for The Barkley.*

Another scRitch's law is: *The only things that actually happen in life can never be imagined in advance.* And for its corollary: *If you* really *want something to happen, don't think about it.*

Other crap already thunked up so far includes stuff that really ought to be Barkley laws, such as whatever becomes emblazoned on its T-shirts; *meaningless suffering without a point* and *where your very best just isn't good enough* are two decent examples. And I wish I could claim authorship of both those maxims, but I can't. Maybe Winter came up with that first one.

My reverie is interrupted by the first notes of the mournful bugle tune of *Taps*. Obviously, Danger is also in camp, because he's about the only bugler here who can actually do justice to the sadness of the song. Also obviously, we have another quitter, or timer-outer.

Why Danger is the bugler of choice is because he was a Boy Scout and learned to bugle for his troop. He is also RawDog and Kate's son, and RawDog has always supported this wonderful evidence of the Laz's love on earth, even to the point of *sacrificing his only begotten son to it?* Nah, that's only a joke (however sacrilegious, *eh*). As far as I know, Danger comes here willingly. He also has a brother; so, you know, he can't *really* be compared to Cheeses, the Risen Crust, because of Cheeses's being an only child, or pizza.

But from earliest Barkley times onward, Danger has been drafted to show up and blow *Taps* for the suddenly enlightened, which means the quitters. I personally have quit long enough now to have witnessed the lad's musical prowess grow from when he was, in fact, a lad. Why he became "Danger" is due to his growing up and becoming a daredevil. Oh, and he's also run the hell out of this course—many times—which is always dangerous, especially to those trying to follow and keep up.

He too is *a chip off the old block* and has in fact invented a "thing" or two his own self. Danger's Climbing Wall is an impossible—and dangerous—case in point. When Winter and I first encountered the nearly vertical roadside cliff that one must climb to get up to the highway that one must cross to arrive at the bottom of some new mountain that one must also climb, well, we soon learned just how nearly vertical—and dangerous—this "wall" is. Hell, it *is* vertical! You have to grab trees and shrubs and even sawbriars just to place one foot higher than the other. And as soon as you do, and let go to grab an even higher thing to hold on to, you either slip backwards two feet or the new thing you're grabbing comes out of the earth in your hand—and again you slip backwards two feet.

Since then (and is it any wonder?) most Barkers have figured out a way *around* this thing. But thanks are due to Danger all the same.

There are words to *Taps*. I go over them in my mind [but only after having anachronistically returned home and looked them up]:

Day is done, gone the sun,
From the lake, from the hills, from the sky;
All is well, safely rest, God is nigh.

[As I also anachronistically discover later, there are supposedly five stanzas of lyrics to *Taps*, but of course, ain't nobody gonna stand for five repeats of the same tune for each and every single quitter! Besides, as Wikipedia rightly points out: "*Taps* is a bugle call—a signal, not a song. As such, there is no associated lyric. Many bugle calls had words associated with them as a mnemonic device but these are not lyrics. A Horace Lorenzo Trim wrote a set of words intended to accompany the music." So the words I am scrolling—but not at this time in my head—are, according to Wiki, those of this wordsmith H. L. Trim.]

Words or no words, I pause in my chicken-grilling to stand, face the bugle, plant my tongs-less mitt over my chest, and listen. I also strain my eyes to see who in the hell has just quit, but I can't make the lost soul out.

The mournful clarion ends, I resume my double-fisted feasting prep, and then the bugling starts all over again. Shucks, this means there's now *two* less runners in the race.

This time I don't bother straining my eyes. After the song is done, I assume if they're hungry they'll mosey over to me.

And they do. Eventually. The two who've just quit are an unknown "furriner" (a Frenchman) and our very own Mathmagic Man. They were out on Loop 3, but quickly decided against it. The latter is why our beloved Fyte Doc is here. They're sharing site #11 with Grateful, Lovey, The Swimmer, and me. She accompanies Mathmagic to the fire.

"The weather turned *too* good," Mathmagic answers with a grin after I ask, first, if he would like a chicken piece, and second, why he quit. "I didn't know how to cope!"

But he magnanimously declines the chicken because, he says, he's vegetarian. That's when his lovely crew person begins to explain how he's already eaten.

Fyte Doc (yes, she is medicine woman and intellectual fighter both) reminds her man that she had specifically grilled on a portable camp stove his wonted grilled cheese sandwiches last night between loops.

"Grilled cheese and knife," she says.

"Knife?" he asks.

"Yes. I didn't have a spatula, so I had to use a plastic knife to turn the sandwiches."

"So?"

"So the knife broke and half of it was embedded in the cheese. And you ate it."

"Ha!" he laughs.

"And you didn't even notice."

"Must've given me the artificial strength I needed to get back out there," Mathmagic surmises.

"Of course," I pipe up, "that *could* be considering vegetarianism to be a cut above, ya think?"

They chuckle. But really, the Math Man is pretty tired and beat and, also really, The Barkley is notoriously cruel to vegetarians. They don't want my hard-chiseled chicken pieces. So they both retreat to the site next door where, I can only assume, Mathmagic's Fyte Doc will whip him up some camp stove breakfast. Maybe cheese and scrambled eggs—garnished, of course, with embedded plastic. Maybe a broken fork this time.

But the Frenchman—*ahh, zee Frainch*, ya gotta love 'em—indicates that he—yes? no?—*wooed laik zee shickeene*. So, somehow in broken French, I indicate to him that he's next in line for a piece. But it'll take a while. All the chips off *that* block are still frozen.

So he goes off to the showers and I again pick up my tongs. They're not *my* tongs; they belong to Race Management, I think. There's also this other tool. It looks like a flimsy spear with two points. I'm guessing it's a long fork-like thing used to stab the chicken—after it's thawed of course—to "test" the inner "doneness." Right now it's doing me no good, so I leave it on the tree stump that serves as a kitchen countertop.

Good ol' Beans, who tells me he actually finished a loop—obviously ahead of Winter and me—wanders over from his car, which is parked as close as physically possible to the ominous Yellow Gate. His car, he tells me, is all the campsite he needs. It's got a heater and a back seat he can stretch out and sleep on. And he's able to park in the closest non-campsite space available to where Laz blows the conch. Beans is always worried he won't hear it.

Beans is also not a huge man (he can fully stretch out in his own back seat) but he is a remarkably generous and a religious man. He donates at least two gigantic cans of baked beans to the cause every year he's here, which is nearly every year. He's like me in that we've both been known to show up even if we haven't received any condolences.

He also keeps a hatchet in his car and uses it—often—to chop firewood into kindling. So he walks up and asks:

"You think the fire's hot enough, scRitch?"

"Compared to hell," I say, "probably not. But we don't want it *too* hot right now, or else we'll convert all the chickens to godless cinderism even faster than usual."

"Right," he says, missing the lame joke. Then of course he goes back to his car to fetch his hatchet to cut more kindling.

Thus and so, in deference to Beans and his scriptures:

And it was lunchtime and afternoon, the second day.

BOOK 11 – Counterclockwise
Nice Guys Finish Dead (by Albert Conroy) or
Get Tough! (by Major W. E. Fairbairn)
(Your Twenty-Ninth Objective)

For an agonizing, nearly impossible, footrace full of *meaningless suffering without a point*, we're doing pretty well. Those of us here in camp, I mean. As I'm standing by this wood fire roaring inside the site's fire ring, supposedly grilling frozen blocks of legs and thighs with borrowed tools of fork and tongs, the small gathering we started with is swelling into a crowd.

And they all *want a piece*.

Suddenly, I'm a short-order cook. And I start taking—like a complete dummy—all the short orders.

"Can I have a piece?" asks somebody.

"Are you taking orders?" asks somebody else.

"Sure!" I answer like a dipshit. "You get the next piece, then you, then you're on deck after that." All I ever wanted to do here was cook *my own* damn lunch. But now, suddenly, there's a very real possibility that I won't get any, unless I can maintain my last place in line—and nobody wants to usurp it.

Thus and so, a brand-new chicken chef is born unto The Barkley.

In deference to Beans, who's still chopping: *And Laz begat RawDog, and RawDog begat scRitch*. And the dozen Tribes of Israel are waiting to be fed.

"Can't y'all just wait awhile on the manna?" I ask of the gathering assembly, mainly in yet another vainglorious attempt to crack a joke that nobody *gets*.

"What?" asks Kate. She's left her camp chair and is now walking over.

"Never mind," I say. "I was just making a little 'funny.'"

"I know what you were doing," she says. She is a very bright lady. "You're thinking like you're the anointed one, some Hebrew that's been called upon to cook chicken for everybody following Moses in the desert, aren't you?"

"You're right, Kate. I was fantasizing."

"Just cook the chicken, scRitch. Everybody's hungry!"

"Well," I say, "where's your worser half? I always thought that *he's* the guy that feeds the hungry."

"He's napping in the tent."

"Oh," I say. "Oh well then."

"He also said that, if all these people want chicken, they are perfectly welcome to cook it themselves."

"Well, all righty then. That explains it!"

"So just cook, scRitch. *I* welcome you, if that helps any." She goes back to her chair.

Turning pieces, moving them as much as possible to the edge of the grate so as to forestall the cinders, and watching all the campers now grabbing and holding empty paper plates... is how I'm about to spend the rest of my Barkley. Maybe even the rest of my life. Maybe even until, you know, *The Rapture* and *The End of Days*.

Or maybe this *is* heaven?

Nah. More likely: the *other* place.

Suddenly, again, the bugle blows.

In deference to *Taps*, we stand in silence, bow our heads, and place our paper plates, hatchets, and tongs over our hearts. Then we all crane our necks to see who's newly arrived in camp and *ain't goin' back out there again*. Maybe not ever.

It's Buttslide. I'm guessing he's quitting after finishing two loops.

Buttslide is incredible. He never misses. I can't recall a single 100-miler he's DNF'd. Oh, maybe one: an extreme mountain range event in Colorado. But Buttslide kept at it until he did finish that monster, and by now methinks more than once! He's got pacing down to a science. In all the finishes that I personally know about, he's managed to cross the finish line with only about 10 minutes "left on the clock." No matter what the distance or how much time is allowed, if Buttslide's in the race he'll be finishing with less than 15 minutes to spare. And I mean *always*. That's why he's incredible.

Except, of course, at *this* race. He (like damn near all of us) has *never* finished! But he's done way better than damn near all of us also. I know for a fact he's finished two complete loops—and under the cutoff. Just like today!

After "visiting" awhile at the Yellow Gate, he walks—slowly—over to the rest of us gathered around the campfire. He sees what I'm doing, and so what the hell? *The more the merrier*, I'm thinking.

"You want a piece?" I ask him.

"OK. OK," he answers, almost as if satisfying his raging hunger is just an afterthought. "I'll take a piece."

"You'll have to wait for it," I tell him. "You're about fourth or fifth in line."

"OK. OK. I can wait." And without saying anything, he leaves. I'm assuming his leaving headquarters here is merely corresponding to his journey to the bathhouse to clean up. I could be wrong though. Buttslide has been known to be unpredictable—except when finishing any other ultra besides Barkley. For his per-usual finish elsewhere, you can set your watch by it.

Beans carries over his fresh-cut kindling and makes a higher pile near our raging inferno, now doing its damnedest to convert every chicken bodypart on the grill to a congregation of cinderism.

I gawketh at his woody burden and sayeth unto him, "You have done well, my son. When hell freezes over, we'll be able to light up a new one."

"Sure, scRitch," he says. "This is just in case."

BOOK 10 – Counterclockwise
Ultramarathon Man (by Dean Karnazes) or
Weirdo Haven (by J. X. Williams)
(Your Thirtieth Objective)

One of the new and totally unexpected duties of a freshly hired Barkley short-order chicken cook, as I am quickly discovering, is using The Chickenman's magical powers to know at every moment right where everybody else still on the course *now is.*

[Oh and there was, by the way, an ancient (pretty much goofy) super anti-hero character called "Chickenman" that was broadcast over radio, of all things—WCFL-AM—when I was a kid, which just goes to show we should never lose track of our inner child, especially now when we're pretending to be working during adult recess.]

[*"Bwawk-bwawk bwawk-bwawwwwwwk! He's everywhere! He's everywhere!"* That was that golden-oldie radio shtick's tagline.]

All kinds of people constantly mosey over and ask if I've seen their loved one, or ones.

"Do you know where Jam-Jam is?"

"How about Dr. Metallica?"

"Is [fill in the blank] _____ still doing OK?"

"Where do you suppose he is?" they *all* ask, eventually.

I look at my watch and make a big ceremony of answering.

"Right about now, at this particular moment, he is definitely near the bottom of RatJaw—where, you know, he can't easily be seen—with his pants down around his ankles and the Official Instructions torn up in both hands, taking a dump."

"Oh," the loved ones say. "I never thought about there being no facilities out there."

"Right," I inform. "The other option, of course, is to just 'hold it' for the whole loop until they get back here to the bathhouse."

They look at me like I'm crazy.

"Tell you what," I always say. "Go over there to that ancient bearded wizard-looking guy holding up that stone pillar beside the Yellow Gate, and ask *him*."

182 Loop 3

Laz almost never appreciates too many people hanging around him at the finish "line" begging for information that he just doesn't have; but, if you ask him nice and bring him another can of some cheap Dr Pepper-imitation *cold* beverage, he'll open his black loose-leaf binder and tell you what loop your lover's on. And if you bring that knowledge back to my campfire, I'll know too. You can skip the beverage for bribing me. I keep Gatorade in my backpack.

In just this fashion, I now know *some* of the unhappy totals. And it's, like, everybody's home and nobody's still out there—except the hardiest few. And most of those have completed two loops and are now on number three. The Ginger Man is in the lead, we think, followed by Dr. Metallica (no relation to Pepper), Jam-Jam, Bama Boy, The Swede, one or two dudes that I don't know, and our three lovely ladies: Leather, Yeeva, and The Swimmer.

Over the next several hours and just prior to many more bugle tunes, runners trickle in from both Loop 2 *and* from Loop 1, and in usually only a few more minutes, *all* of them are timed out. And at this stage of the race, convincing those—who still have time—to stop is not hard. They all can easily see what fun the rest of us are having telling jokes and stories, complaining about lovers, and throwing ever more and more chicken bodyparts onto the hellfire.

Frozen Ed comes in, along with The Librarian, and they both bring with them tales of bitter woe. They have only officially finished one loop. They "had to quit" during Loop 2, they tell us, due to the extremes of weather that come from nature, added nastiness on the course that comes from Laz, and those horrible weaknesses that come from age. Hell, I could've told them that. And they're older than me.

They take themselves to the showers to try and warm up. I figure it'll be awhile before they come around for chicken.

Next back to camp is our friend Bama Boy. I have seemingly known this man forever. What I have known is how he *wins* all the races I see him at. But here, at *this* race? He's a constant DNFer like the rest of us. *Equal prestige*, I think. It doesn't matter if you slug it out for one loop—or two or three or even four—if you don't *complete* all five, you're a Did-Not-Finisher.

If you want to know who those precious few true finishers actually are, you need to read Frozen Ed's book or log onto websites. If you have to ask The Chickenman, you might never in the world know the truth.

But if you've read this far, you know that already.

I let Bama Boy cut in line for chicken. Anybody who comes here with his credentials (he also happens to be a Ph.D. rocket scientist) deserves a little preferential treatment. My excuse for doing this—should anybody ask, or object—is "oh, I'm giving him *my* piece." Which is true. But at this stage of these weird rabble-roused proceedings, I'm actually giving *everyone* my piece. It doesn't look like I'm going to get to eat until, yea probably, hell freezes over.

By now it seems that practically everybody *else* is chowing down on my first or second rack of cinder chicken. I tell them all that, contrary to popular belief, Barkley chicken is no longer "digitally prepared." This *especially* includes the high-tech precise digital processing of each individual's preference for barbecue sauce.

"Here's your piece," I tell everyone receiving a cinder from my tongs onto their paper plate. "There's barbecue sauce over there on the picnic table. If you want digital processing, you can use your own damn fingers to smear the shit."

Most customers are *way* too hungry to care. And they either grab a sauce bottle and pour, or they don't. But I have to admit, the murmuring silence caused by no talking and just chewing is music to my ears. Maybe there *is* something to short-order cooking! *Maybe,* I think, *I should quit writing and start cooking for a living. Maybe Colonel Sanders will hire me.*

BOOK 9 – Counterclockwise
Run Faster You Bipedal Bitch, and Other Stories
(by Damon Knight) or
The Lost Girl (by D.H. Lawrence)
(Your Thirty-First Objective)

This feeding of the multitudes with no loaves and no fishes, just chicken, necessarily must pause for the next several minutes due to, guess what: more bugle calls. This time there are *three-in-a-row* soundings of *Taps*. Danger is over there at the gate blowin' his lips off.

It's "The Return of The Three Feared Sisters: Leather, Yeeva, and The Swimmer." Apparently, they have all decided to quit together. Apparently, too, I'm about the only dweeb in camp who did *not* know they were—all three—out on Loop 3, and fairly hot on the tail of The Ginger Man, Jam-Jam, and The Swede. Other dudes still out there that I don't know—and are *still* out there—must've all fallen into line behind these three sweet sterling specimens of female strength and stamina.

But it means, of course, that there won't be a woman finisher this year. Not even a woman Fun Runner! (In years gone by, there have been quite a few.) And these three strapping lasses here *should have* become Fun Runners—all of them—because they are certainly more than capable. All three of these gals have won ultras, some even outright—beating all the men! They are awesome. Everyone in camp agrees. And after the final *Taps*, the whole place erupts into a round of cheers and applause the like of which I've rarely ever heard before.

It makes me sad. I so want a woman to conquer this race that I can taste it. I—who have been "chicked" (as they say) during thousands of races (watching helplessly as they zoom past me)—know full well that the myth that men are stronger is bullshit. Maybe *the* strongest man *can* out-lift *the* strongest woman, maybe, but (and this is another reason why I love this sport) *the* fastest man is many times utterly defeated by *the* fastest woman. In races that go beyond the marathon distance (those paltry 26-miles-and-2-tenths) women can indeed compete on the same playing field. There is *no* difference, as far as I can see and believe and have known. Women can in-fact flat-out out-*kick men's haughty-ass asses*.

Loop 3

So they *should* be able to do it here, too. And I pantingly, slack-jawed and with tongue-out, await the day.

Sometimes I fantasize about being a lapdog to some great woman champion. I keep imaginatively trying to argue my worth to her. I *so* want men to be needed in this life that I can slurp it. I tell everyone who'll listen that, these days with sperm banks and artificial insemination and whatnot, women are far more capable of doing without men than men can do without women. If this Earth were full of *man*kind only, I can assure you for sure they *wouldn't* be very kind. If there weren't women to supply the kindness—to, as it were, quell the raging beast lurking within every man's breast—then the first male hominid ever to stride out from the primordial ooze would have stopped civilization in its tracks. There can be no "planet of the apes." The first thing that ape-men do is destroy the planet.

If women ruled the world, I also tell anyone who'll listen, there would be no war. No horrible weapons. No vast masses of armies perched across from each other on opposite hilltops ready to swoop down and kill. There might only be catfights. Women throughout history would hissingly shame one another over lunch. Maybe there'd be back-stabbing, but even the strongest woman cannot stab every other woman in the back all at once. It takes a man to do that. It's why men invented the atomic bomb.

Look at this. Here comes three of the top women in all of ultradom, obviously together, obviously *choosing* to join together and cooperate—and quit together—no doubt for the "safety in numbers" idea, but also for the furtherance of civilization and improvement of the human race. You don't see three men doing this. Well, you do—but not often! No, women's natural tendencies are toward togetherness, cooperation, support of one another, conversation, *society*. Men's natural inclinations are to maim and kill. Certainly to compete. To be king of the hill, top dog, the one *lone* hero, *the* best damn bull in the pasture, the one that gets all the cows. And I mean *all* of them.

Here at The Barkley, who was it that invented the idea of "the scrape"? It couldn't possibly have been a woman. It was a man. Most likely several men. Each one trying to best the other. All of them wanting to be king of the hill, or at least top dog at The Barkley. One of the topmost ever called himself Cave *Dog*. A quick check of his website (when he had one) revealed that all of his friends and associates were also accorded "dog" nicknames. Peeps like *Supply Dog, Water Dog, Food Dog, Car Dog, Truck Dog*, and his girlfriend *Sugar Dog*. Cave Dog came here *once*. Studied the layout and hiked the woods for about three weeks in advance, and then unbelievably finished the race! He even set the course record at the time. Then he went back home to Oregon and hasn't really been heard from since.

Boom. In and out. One and done. Conquer and move on. A real Barkley man's man if ever there was one. And to this day, Race Management can't even spell the man's name right. It's been misspelled on the "official" race application each and every year since Cave Dog really did come and conquer. I have personally "waged war" against Race Management to have his damned boilerplate amended to spell Cave's damn surname *correctly*, and each and every year it shows up in His Nibs's chosen few Inboxes misspelled as always.

Once I even e-mailed Cave Dog myself, notifying him of the consistent error, and even *he* didn't appear to give a damn. He certainly didn't vocalize an orthographic protest, or else the damn misspelling *would* be fixed. So there ya go: even the topmost dog doesn't choose to join up or cooperate with any of his other male canines, underlings, or inferiors.

The number one male inclination to *be* number one even transcends accurate communication. So, it is absolutely totally unlikely that Laz and Cave Dog will ever sit down to have lunch and catfight over how to spell either one's name. And *Laz*, by the way, is more accurately spelled *laz*. [He absolutely totally *refuses* to use capital goddamn letters!]

But not even *laz* gives a shit either about spelling. In his own little doghouse of ultramarathoning male canine competitiveness, *he knows he is Top Dog*.

And he's a dog lover! Lazarus Lake has even authored quite a few books about dogs. But that's a whole 'nother topic for a whole 'nother day. Another book perhaps, written by *him*. It goes way beyond the material specifically selected by me to be included in mine. But it could be germane here to note that the Top Author and Race Manager himself has selected just *one* of several of his dogs to be the top. His name is big. No capital letters please. No, apparently this is yet another singular choice for establishing uniqueness. Trying to get laz to use uppercase is as lost a cause as the Confederacy was. Indeed, the entire civil war itself, according to him—and no capital letters please—was as previously cited, "the war of northern aggression." Once again, this is only yet one more tenet of the male philosophy of *dominance*.

I think all this while continuing my labors at the hearth, still waiting for The Magnificent Three—capital letters preferred and usually necessary please—to finally get tired of *talking and talking and talking* at the Yellow Gate and come eat.

Loop 3

Finally, still together, they mosey over. Leather, Yeeva, and The Swimmer rock-hop the mossy boulders and make their way from the gate to the fire with nary a hint of self-aggrandized greatness. I offer them *gratemess* instead.

"Well, it took you all long enough," I say. "Aren't you hungry?"

"We didn't know you'd be cooking," says The Swimmer, flashing her pearly whites. "Otherwise for sure we would've quit sooner."

"Ha! Right!" I scoff. "You all damn near bagged a Fun Run. So why *did* you quit?"

"We just got done explaining all that to Laz," she says. "Do we have to repeat it again?"

"Just to get a piece of chicken?" echoes Leather.

"Nah," I say. "Of course not. You all don't owe me any explanation. Holy moly! You did *more* than two full loops! I'm insanely jealous."

"Don't be," says Yeeva. "We were not making cutoff."

"You have all day!" I counter. "You have forty hours to complete Loop 3!"

"Yah, but we only were Chimney Top. Impossible to make twelve more books."

"It didn't help that I fell and almost broke my back," says Leather.

"And I was hallucinating," says The Swimmer.

"In middle of day!" Yeeva adds. "And I was vomit and could not swallow even water."

"So y'all bagged it?" I ask.

"Yes," Swimmer says. "What's the point?"

"It's meaningless suffering without one," I remind them.

"Yep." They all nod in agreement.

"So, again, are you hungry? I have three well-cooked pieces, if I do say so myself, right here for you."

Swimmer answers for the three of them.

"We can't, scRitch. We're vegan and she's nauseous."

Which covers the three of them. Yeeva is the puking one. But of course, I did not know the other two weren't carnivores. Which also of course strikes me as odd. In the jungle, prides of lionesses, for example, kill and snarf down every other creature that moves. But here in these woods, the toughest felines in both the human and in the foot race—of whom we are all very proud—refuse the meat, however raw or cooked.

Enter Beans, who's been hanging around chomping at the bit to chop more wood.

"Hey, I've got some nice baked beans simmering in the can!" he offers enthusiastically.

"Is there pork or bacon in there?" Our fat-free meatless Swimmer asks.

"Oh. Maybe. I think there is," Beans admits, and I concur.

"That's OK," she says. "We've got our own food. Thanks anyway. It's been nice talking with y'all!"

The three of them, in all their magnificence and being totally unaffected by choosing to quit, walk off together towards the bathhouse for their showers and, of course, for *the* most amazing transformation known to man-sometimes-kind: each one's morphing into the *she-cleans-up-pretty-good* tough female athlete. *Oh my god*, I pipedream. *If only there was music, I'd ask them to dance.*

BOOK 8 – Counterclockwise
The Whipping Room (by Florenz Branch) or
Psycho Circus (by Andrew Shaw)
(Your Thirty-Second Objective)

So now what? I'm standing here with a rack full of chicken that nobody's eating? Pretty much *well* done chicken if you ask me. So, I fulfill the next expectation of *noblesse oblige*: I ring the dinner bell.
"HEY! ANYBODY WANT ANY CHICKEN???" I holler.
Instantly there are fifteen paper plates in my face.
"Sure, I'd like some!"
"I'll take a piece!"
"I thought, no? That *I* be next?" It's my Frenchman. I stab a piece for him.
"Blimey. One for queen and country. Good show!" An Englishman.
"Roity, mite. Pluck me a cluck off the barbie." An Aussie.
"I'd be happy to take a leg off your hands, *or hips*."
"Good one!" I say to the dude who says this. And I tong-and/or-fork over all the pieces. *Just that quick* my grill grate is empty.
I have now succeeded beyond my wildest imaginings. The entire immediate vicinity is chowing down, munching silently and licking sauce off its digits, and I *still* haven't had lunch.
Only one thing to do of course: go back to the bags in the box and chisel more chunks off the sculpture. Then pop another cluck on the barbie.
As I'm doing this, Lovey hurries over from next door.
"My Swimmer!" she exclaims. "Has she come in?"
"Yes, she has," I say. "And now she's in the showers. Didn't you see her?"
"I was asleep in the tent! Oh My God! *She'll murder me!!*" And with that she turns on her heels and hurries off to the bathhouse.
I doubt that, I muse. *Any babe lucky enough to have a crew here can't be a bitch. I'm thinking, crews can only assist in camp here, and it is one helluva long time in between meetings with your runner. Falling asleep ought to be expected.*

Loop 3

It's what *I* did, all last night in fact. And Winter and Beans and everybody else milling around the fire today, too. We may still be starving, but we are well rested. It's one of the perks of quitting. You get to sleep and eat.

Except when you're a brand-new freshly hired short-order cook. How in the hell did I get this job anyway?

Having now successfully—but barely—split off more iced chicken from the uncarved block in the bag, I carefully lay out another rack on the grill. Best I can seem to do is put eight quarters on there, without any falling into the fire or sliding off into the ash pit. This is culinary science *not* made easy. I'm learning it's damned tough to keep everything rotating around the BLAZE OF HELLFIRE enough to both defrost the iced chicken chunks without turning the outsides to charcoal, and to try to warm the insides toward the pink end of the spectrum. Before you can have *cook*, you first have to have *thaw*.

And with a full rack and no space to move things, this is a lot to ask of your novice just-hired short-order chief chicken chef.

But none of this is as tough as still being *out there*. Only men still remain *somewhere*, and they must be having the time of their lives. Women are all here, having the time of *their* lives. They've proven themselves to be fully equal to both the beginning and ending of this strenuous task; and to their credit, they've also succeeded in cutting out the middle *man*. You start in hope and expectation; you end in DNF and failure. It's the same for every body. Everybody's the same. So you might as well just go for a little exercise, then come back and party. That's what *I'm* fixin' to do—*par-tay!*

I try to think of what books are out there that whoever's left needs to keep finding—and in the reverse order from how Winter and I found them—but I cannot. I can't at the moment think of a single book title—not one!—and yet a page from each is right over *there* inside my backpack. To me, here, now that it's over, the whole concocted Library of Folly is about as memorable as graffiti on subway walls (sandwich shops included), or the misspelled carvings of lovers inscribed on meaningless trees.

I'm thinking now about The Ginger Man. What a heartbreak a year ago. I just can't even *imagine* completing **five full loops** and still ending up a non-finisher by all of six (6!) *lousy teensy tiny miniscule miserably ridiculous microscopic* **SECONDS**. If *that's* not "meaningless suffering without a point," then I don't know what is.

And Ginger's out there right now! So, I'd like to give him some advice. To wit, and toot sweet: *Bail, Dude. Come back and party! It looks like for this trip, you're even gonna be timed-out for the Fun Run.*

Let's all grab hands and circle round, I think. *We'll sing Campfire Girl songs and toast marshmallows. We can party all night and pack up and leave in the morning. Surely* some *of us have less party-hardy companions to go home to. And the reason they're not here is because they have more sense, which is why we married them in the first place.*

The least likely hardy partier is the one main inventor of all *this*. Or so it might seem to the uninitiated. But no one on the planet enjoys a good laugh more than Race Management himself concerning this monstrosity, this *uh* "experiment in terra." What this race ought to inspire are horror movies. Instead what you get is ribald comedy, and the greatest jokester in all of Tennessee is now making his way over here to our party.

"Is there any chicken, scRitch?" he asks.

"Iced, de-iced, raw, warm, or incinerated?" I ask him.

"Cooked!" He looks at me like I've only recently arrived from Mars. "Is there any ready *to eat?*"

"No," I say. "It'll be awhile. You could, I suppose, eat some digitally prepared snacks in the meantime."

"At least I know where my drinks are," he says while continuing to mosey toward headquarters.

For indeed, The Wall's family's great white tent serves the ceremony very well as both race headquarters and leftover food depository. It's like a shelter for the homeless, without the soup kitchen. Laz knows his rot-gut imitation Dr Peppers are inside a big green cooler stashed in his corner of the tent. Of course, I happen to know that there aren't quite as many now as before—because I too have known all along where he hides them. Sometimes cooks get thirsty, no?

At this stage in the race, whatever snacks are still on the table most homeless peeps wouldn't eat. No, but after *evening and morning, the second day* of Barkley, there is no shortage of disheveled rag-taggy and questionably alive humanlike zombies who will eat *anything*. Including the race director. Yes, I'm quite sure everyone here would even eat *him*.

He'd be tougher to cook, though, than his chicken. Too damn ornery.

I continue quietly minding my business at The Barkley Non-Bar and Grill. *"This ain't no party, this ain't no disco,"* I think, singing along with the Talking Heads inside my head, *"this ain't no foolin' around."*

"Is it too early to start our disco?" I ask of anyone hanging around close enough to listen.

Loop 3

"Nope. Start dancing, scRitch!" It's The Babe. She who famously entertained—everyone lucky enough to be awake—the troops in the past by spreading rose petals for finishers in front of the Yellow Gate in the middle of the night while dressed... *just barely*.

"Not me, Babe," I say. "I think *you* should strip down to your rose petal outfit and get us going."

"Ha! Not this year, scRitch. It's too cold!"

Nevertheless, now as the sunlight is starting to fade, the party does begin to get started. She pulls up a cloth camping chair (nobody remembers who donates these things) near the ladies who are already seated, and then others begin to circle round. Each time I look up from the grill, there's somebody new joining the crowd.

In addition to my three fave ladies who urged me into this chicken-griller role—Cassandra, Kate, and Hail—other sittees and standees here on "the patio" by the fire include Bubbles, The Arm, The Babe of course, Fyte Doc, Leather, Poorwater Basin, and here coming back from the bathhouse are Lovey and her Swimmer. The menfolk now gaining strength include Beans, Beech, Danger, RawDog, Traildog, Henry Speir, Mungo Jerry, The Librarian, The Wall, Dime Man, Frozen Ed, Buttslide, Mathmagic Man, Bama Boy, Cayman, and quite a few *furriners*. Coming up the paved drive I also note Winter coming back from wherever the hell he was, and Grateful's walking with him. Laz is already here, but inside his headquarters where he's currently being assailed for T-shirts and autographs. His books are largely available throughout the galaxy (thank you, Amazon) and right now the French *furriner* babes are hero worshipping.

It's getting so that legendary icons of sadism can't catch a break to sit down by the fireside and regale the troops with war stories. Which is, by the way, one of the things the iconic founding father of Barkley Universe does best.

Others that I expect to show up soon to party their chicken skins off include all the furriner dudes whose female crew members are over there chatting up The Icon because they (the babes' runners) have all quit—but, of course, they're not back to camp yet. That could take hours.

I should know. For years The Icon good-naturedly ascribed to me the record "for taking the longest time to quit." During my ill-fated very first time here—when supposedly my Hilton was founded—it took over nine hours to make it back to camp after Dorm and I had timed out after the thirteen hours and twenty minutes it took to get irretrievably lost in the first place. [Our total time for a partial Loop 1 was 22:21, according to Frozen Ed.]

I'm now happy to report, however, that another legend of a man, The Grammarian, has since surpassed Dorm's and my "record." I believe he was out there for 36 hours. Oh, and prior to all of our "dubious achievements," the previous record-holder was Old Gristle, who actually completed the full course in 21 hours (severely overtime, of course) because she kept moving instead of sleeping against a fallen log underneath a space blanket. This proves that you can lose a lot of time by sleeping, even though Dorm and I couldn't. His teeth kept chattering like a teletype all night, which pretty much succeeded in keeping us both pretty much awake.

BOOK 7 – Counterclockwise
The Confusion of Languages (by Siobhan Fallon) or
Maelstrom of Pee (by Roy Cohn)
(Your Thirty-Third Objective)

The reason humans are "social animals" is because of fire. Specifically campfires. And this philosophy isn't new. The first caveman (it could well have been a cavewoman, you know) to discover the thrill of rubbing sticks together rapidly, and watching what happens, did this so he or she could learn how to talk about it later. If you look around the animal kingdom, almost no other species deliberately burns wood and gathers round to *yak*. Not even yaks do that.

Most other animals aren't generally afraid of the cold and dark. Most are prepared for it. They have fur which keeps them warm, and fear of being eaten which keeps them moving (much like today's Barkers). I happen right now to be attending a grill grate full of species that lost that motion and succumbed to their fear. The human species, however, is happy about this. And we're all standing or sitting around yakking.

So that proves we're at the top of the food chain, doesn't it? We have no fear, for instance, of another—higher—species evolving and routinely eating *us*. Unless they might come from another planet. But as it is, we are all being drawn to the fire, and the food, in an ever-increasing gathering of garrulity. Time is seemingly standing still, except for those miserable human beings still out there without the benefit of many companions, perhaps, or of fire. If those miserable shivering strivers were to happen upon the warm glow of a campfire, don't you think they would stop?

This is *not* to say that we humans don't have a fear of being eaten. Witness grizzly bear attacks in national parks and the fear that grips us when tigers—or even big snakes—escape from zoos; but that fear only comes upon us when we're *not* hanging around a campfire. Besides, we all know we can outrun the snake.

So, hanging around a campfire gives us all a warm and fuzzy feeling, if not sometimes a hot feeling caused by sparks. And the keeper of the fire is duly, if unceremoniously, "appointed" to keep the crowd warm and the food cooked. If left to the crowd's own devices, someone eventually *will* volunteer to step forward and add a log, kick the embers, or turn the chicken. Perhaps it'll be the hungriest *crave*-dweller. Hunger produces great adrenaline. The primordial fear of being eaten can easily be overpowered by the profound urge to eat.

All of this is to say (if anyone's wondering otherwise) that, by god, *scRitch is fucking starving* and *that's* the reason for the fire, the yaks, the yuks, and the cooking. And the disinterested reader should note that "The God of Hellfire" has suddenly succeeded in cooking a decent piece that nobody else has spoken for.

Life is good. We have no fear of grizzlies. We are warm and entertained by the fire, and the cook has finally begun chowing down on his damned decent digitally-prepared sauce-smeared chicken leg. Even the conversation is non-argumentative. But not for long! Here comes Grateful and Winter.

Grateful is otherwise a great guy. We have a "history," he and I, that dates back a few millennia. Coming from what might seem to modern runners, and readers, as the Pleistocene Epoch, Grateful could be the jungle congo drummer and I could be the dinosaur. Didn't, say, Alley Oop use drums to communicate? Well, Grateful uses Twitter. And I, of course, am still the dinosaur.

Although it's possible that Winter is even more of one. He's older, recall, and pretty cold-blooded. He wasn't born in 1940 either. And neither *for sure* was Grateful. Grateful is a comparatively young man—although, surprisingly enough, he's a fan of dinosaur music. To be precise: the Grateful Dead, which is why I've nicknamed him after such fossilized musicians. He's a good trooper, and I personally am guilty of having helped further his worship of ancient, seemingly appreciative long-dead rock 'n rollers. I don't believe that half the camp here has ever even heard of the Grateful Dead. I, however, was alive at the time but preferred that other dinosaur group, the Rolling Stones. Three-fifths of those near-fossilized original Stones are *still* touring! The joke is that lead Mouthosaurus Jagger keeps getting married and repopulating the planet, so he has to keep working to pay them all after the divorce. And speaking of dinosaurs, I also believe that Winter's a great fan of Mozart.

What interrupts my lunch/dinner now isn't Grateful and Winter, however; it's the call arising somewhere in the distance, "Runners! Runners coming!" And that sends Laz, who leaves his soda on the picnic table—along with all the previous half-full cans he previously left when similarly summoned—and hurries over to his stand (some might call it his podium) at the Yellow Gate. Again, it's that rock post on the right of the gate as the runners *should* be facing it now; but these runners are facing the wrong way.

I see two coming. They're supposed to be on counterclockwise loops (either #2 or #3) which would mean at the finish of their loop they'd run right past the campfire and want to touch the gate with Laz's "podium" on their right. It's where Laz keeps the official results book (already noted) along with his lantern, bugle, and that stupid "easy" push-button. Yes, at some time years ago someone gave Laz the gift of that prop from an old TV commercial which button the customers would press and the gizmo would speak: "That was easy!" Right. So ever since, Laz encourages all end-of-loopers to press the button and entertain everybody with what comes out of it, and them.

"That was easy!"

I hear that twice. The two runners reporting in now, apparently, want to announce this silliness. *Their* silliness, of course, is reechoed to the camping masses when Danger bugles *Taps* twice. So, amidst all this pomp and pageantry, two more runners have just quit. It's what runners around here do best.

They are also the apparently remaining Frenchmen, whose wives or girlfriends, or both, have most recently been chatting up The Icon for, presumably, special favors of which nobody else knows what. So the joke of the "easy" button is that, when pressed by the French, its silliness is announced in English.

But that in itself is nothing. Most all the French visitors here speak English, if haltingly and so heavily accented that, well, I marvel at how they can possibly function here in Tennessee. Talk about accents! I have long amused myself by imagining conversations between, say, local business people and these visiting furriners from France.

"Whutcha'll lookin' fer, buddy?"

"Zeese ees zee whay far ze Ice Park, jes?"

"Whutcha sayin'?"

"Ze freez-zing park?"

"Oh, we ain't gots nuffin' laik gat chere. But dawn giss road harr thar's a Diahry Quine. Mebbe y'all's wantin' gat?"

It's the Tower of Babel reenacted afresh for the French by the Volunteer State. It's also fun to imagine Tennesseans visiting Paris for the first time.

But that, right there, in some circles brings up sore points. It just so seems in recent years that quite a few *more* Barkley acceptances are given to French applicants as opposed to other furriners applying from other places around the planet. This is a complaint I hear from various and sundry Barker-wannabes who live in the seemingly *non-favored* countries. Social media provides the platform. Complaints are universal. Thankfully, most of the intergalactic commentary about The Barkley is favorable, but not all of it.

Some of the complaints about favoring the French arise from Race Management's use of the same social media to broadcast happy pictures of Race Manager enjoying Paris and the rest of France.

The overwhelming impression is that Race Manager doesn't use personally earned or saved money to take these trips. No, most protestors of perceived unfairness in the Barkley applications process believe that such French vacation money is coming from somewhere (or someone) else. France perhaps?

But of course the reason for all the perceived unfairness dates back to the beginning of the race itself. From day one Race Management has chosen whatever select few runners *he wants to choose*. As thunked earlier, Barkley was one of those "invitation only" races. In other words, the way it used to work was: there was no "applications process." You would first have to receive an invitation to apply before you could actually apply. It worked a lot like the notoriously expensive Poorwater race. Interestingly enough, however, Poorwater used to allow (and maybe it still does) runners to pay a fee upfront in an effort to *become* invited. Back when I tried it, that non-refundable fee was $250. Even then I thought this was tantamount to bribery. And I think maybe by now there've been lawsuits, which is why I don't have a clue anymore as to *how* runners run *Poor*water without going broke themselves.

I actually didn't know then, either. I never ran it. I don't believe I completed the applications process anyway. I certainly never sent in the remaining thousand or so dollars of entry fee after I received my "invitation."

The Barkley's problem in the beginning (if anyone today can believe this) was that *nobody wanted to run the damn race!* Yes, Laz had considerable trouble filling the field for many or even most of the Barkleys in the 20th century. And the reason for its immense popularity in the 21st is precisely because of this social media and the proliferation all over Earth of email, websites, blogs (short for "web logs") the Internet, and the World Wide Web.

When it all got started—and by the way, the politician Al Gore did *not* "invent" it—there was indeed a difference (there still is actually) and distinctions were maintained between the Internet and the World Wide

Web. The "Web" was in fact invented by a British dude (now knighted) named Sir Timothy Berners-Lee, an engineer and computer whiz who's still alive and is, also in fact, younger than me. (*Oh, to have been born a whiz kid!*) Meanwhile the Internet evolved, from the 1960s onward, here in the good ol' USA as part of (according to me) what President Eisenhower first termed "the military-industrial complex."

In my view, it all goes back to warfare. Eisenhower himself, you know, might even be credited with "winning" World War II. The so-called *civilized* world sure promoted the hell out of him afterwards, and that spelled a pretty easy shoo-in to the White House, just like it did nearly a century before for Ulysses S. Grant who supposedly won the Civil War. They both may have been great army generals, but their achievements as Presidents were dubious. "Ike," for example, served two terms and mostly coined phrases, designed Interstate highways, and played golf. He also—it might be argued—helped design the Cold War. So, as with anything else involving our military, the Pentagon (which was built during WWII) tries forever to make annihilating Earth easier and easier; and setting up some way of linking computers to computers to missile silos and to telephones to boot is probably why and how the Internet began.

At any rate, email generally became a thing of this *Internet*—an expression of connectivity perhaps—and websites were a product of the World Wide Web, which itself is what we today might call an "app" (for application) of the Internet. E-mail could be identified at a glance through its use of the "at" symbol (@) and World Wide Websites were distinctive through their use of "online" addresses beginning with three *w*'s, although, strictly speaking, the full address (even today) is generally prefixed by *http://* or *https://*.

Wikipedia—also a website—explains all this history rather well, I think. And it informs what those prefixes mean: *HyperText Transfer Protocol* and *HyperText Transfer Protocol Secure*. Sir Timothy invented "transfer protocols" but he attributes "hypertext" to originating in the 1950s (probably with Eisenhower, possibly on the golf course) and he also built and published (on August 6, 1991) the world's first website: *http://info.cern.ch/hypertext/WWW/TheProject.html.*
Those last four letters, by the way, stand for HyperText Markup Language. As a former English teacher, I'm now wondering if "markup language" had to be written in red ink.

By now, however, common usage has all but eliminated the name "World Wide Web." Today most everything that's online is referred to as the Internet, and by the way *all* of this has come about because of computers and telephone modems. Modems work kind of like fax machines. (Remember fax machines?) They "digitize" everything into "bytes and bits" and shoot all of it—byte for byte and bit for bit—over the damn telephone line (or these days "cordless" over transmitted wave frequencies). At the other end of whatever "line," another modem works to put it all back together again inside some new computer. Exactly how many zillions of these teensy tiny bits and bytes that can be torn apart, shot across space, and reassembled again help constitute your "baud rate." Current machines can do, what, a couple of gigabytes per second? It's because of modems that I personally believe [I'm thinking I thought all this before, *eh?* Ya think?] that "particle beam teleportation" *of human beings* (like they do in *Star Trek*) is very possible. Hell, inevitable! Except that, unlike Sir Timothy, I *don't* want to be first.

Also this *inter-netted* computerized connectivity, of which we speak, these days probably connects more little personal computers than it does those gigantic mainframes, which were in use for many years *before* those geniuses that we all know and love first got to work inside their garages inventing operating systems that could work for the little guy. And "amen" to that! It's how I got here.

So, really, there isn't even an Internet! If you think about it, all that this "net" thing is, is telephone lines and microwave transmission towers all hooked up just like "Ma Bell" built the tangled wiry monster in the first place. It is literally just computers all over Earth talking to one another. And of course with satellites and other outer-space hurled projectiles, "talking to one another" is no longer confined to our own planet. One day, I swear, some NASA computer will receive an email from a galaxy far, far away. And it'll be SPAM.

Nevertheless, this wiry twisty Medusa's head of a communications nightmare is indeed available to each and every semi-intelligent being that inhabits our Earth. And when this Internet started taking over our Earth, that's when The Barkley got freaky.

For one thing, this Internet made old-fashioned paper, envelopes, and stamps obsolete. [And the Internet remains one of the United States Postal Service's biggest problems today. Think of all the first-class letters that *aren't* being mailed! So to counter "IT," the USPS keeps raising the price of stamps. Have you purchased any lately? Do you realize that around a hundred years ago, you could mail a letter for *three* lousy cents? Do they even *make* pennies anymore? But I digress.] So Barkley Race Management has whole-heartedly embraced this new technology, basically without having a clue as to how it works, or how to make it work for the race. And for another thing, what do you do when you run out of people you either know or have heard of *to invite?*

How, for example, does one pay his *application fee* through the Internet? Oh, you can do it all right—Amazon-dot-com, not to mention PayPal, thrives on it—but it can't happen if Race Management doesn't have a clue *how to* collect such fees. Other races have figured it out, of course. But other races' management isn't Lazarus Lake. What we have here, is a dinosaur failure to communicate. Or, more to this point, a dinosaur business still trying to collect dinosaur money.

[Can there be any surprise, then, that it still honors Confederate currency?]

So, what's this come down to? It varies, depending on whether you live *here* or over *there*—*uh* overseas. Furriners have a whole different application process than domestics. The former sends in early, and the latter sends in later. And just what do they early send in? Be damned if I know. Rumor has it that some "essay" is to be transmitted. If that is true, then why on earth would such essayists be required to fill out some kind of form later—which is never available earlier—and the last "question" on the form is to write an essay! What? Applicants *begin* the process by submitting an essay! So what is *this* essay? Applicants must write *another one*? Recopy the *same one* they've already sent in? (Isn't it, like, *in already?*) So, are they required to be redundant? Submit the same shit twice? WTF???

[This goofy situ has since been corrected methinks, but it took a while. In the early Internet days, we did basically submit an essay twice. But these days Race Management is accepting your essay first, then later on subjecting you to answer some ridiculous questions on some test that now serves to replace the essay section on the entry form.]

The whole thing has gotten completely out of hand. Centuries ago, with paper and postage, it made sense because: A) Laz knew who he wanted and whom to invite (not necessarily one and the same). He had already researched everybody enough to know they wouldn't embarrass him by "dying" on his course and needing to be rescued (or buried). B) Runners *must always* be able to self-extract, and both he and they knew this. C) If you were invited, the application blank would *be* in the envelope along with the invitation (actually that was one and the same). And so, D) if you wanted to apply, you would fill in the blanks, write your essay, and mail it all back (along with the $1.60 fee; which even longer ago was $1.55—I know; I paid it) to arrive as close to the "deadline" as the Post Office would allow. In fact, the joke was that your order of entrance would be determined by how close your envelope was to the top of the stack, as retrieved by Laz from his mailbox.

Well, that's how it *used to* work. Adapting all those Barkleysaurus habits to the new ways of the Internet has proved troublesome. At least to my way of thinking. None of it any longer makes no sense (just like this sentence).

Why?

Because The Barkley is no longer an "invitation only" race. Although it is, of course, because only those who are inevitably selected get in. Which also possibly makes no sense. But it's the process that's inevitable, not the selectees. In other words, you basically have no shot unless The Icon (our idolized god)—going through his own crazy unfathomably inevitable process—chooses you. What's changed is how the "pool of possibles" is compiled. What hasn't changed is: you can beg all you want, but if His Nibs doesn't want your ass in, *you ain't gettin' in.*

As I've noted, it used to be that the *pool of possibles* was well-known enough to be able to select in advance those to whom the invitations should go. But that was back in the Stone Age of Ultrarunning when there were only about a thousand such idiots, period, who did this *ultra*-running. These days there are easily tens of thousands, maybe hundreds of. So Race Management cannot and does not know enough about who's out there to begin the process with. Plus ultramarathoning is now a popular *global* thing, and it would be impossible to know, for example, who the "stars" are in Outer Mongolia. But now there's this worldwide Internet-thing whereby, for example, the great runners of Outer Mongolia know who *you* are *and* all about your infamous footrace.

So they all wish to apply, and the Internet allows them to do just that. Thus, at the rumored "appointed hour," thousands of emails come pouring into the Lazarus Inbox (itself maintained by the rapidly aging digital dinosaur called *hotmail-dot-com*) which are and is, quite frankly, unable to be contained or restrained by this ancient selection process. And all the lofty promisings of previous years (like, for example, if you quit and vacate your "slot" *now*, next year you'll be reinstated at no worse position in the queue than you are today) is bullshit. It is completely impossible to guarantee crap like that when there are thousands upon thousands of applicants *every single year!*

I have often thought that one way out of this quagmire of having promised more than is possible to deliver is to, well, just *stop* accepting *any* new applicants at all! Then for the next dozen years or so, simply fill the starting slots with only the runners who've been promised all this place-holding baloney in the past. Coupled in the future with all the per-usual dropouts and good (and bad) excuses for abandoning one's place in line now in exchange for receiving a slot later, well, this shift in policy really should "clear the slate" fairly quickly.

Every other ultramarathoning event on the planet that has *way too many* applicants every year is now conducting lotteries. It's probably the only "fair way" to do this. And The Barkley *needs* to do this.

What other way? And—omigod *don't say it's so*—what happens after The Icon up and dies? Even Lazarus won't live forever. And there are certain limits on his uncanny ability to be resurrected. Jesus himself is dead, no? "Ascended into heaven" is it? So *now* who's going to lay his earthy hand on Lazarus to wake his ass up and bring him back to life? Even if he's got another 50 years, who's going to give him *another 50 after that?*

Thus and so, if The Icon is unable to convey and continue his super-secret selection-process methodology (I used to think he sticks names on his wall and throws darts)... *well?* What then? Well then, I guess, The Barkley just up and dies also. When The Wizard climbs into his balloon and flies back to Kansas, who's gonna run Oz? Dorothy? "Women are too weak." There's probably misogyny even there.

Well, this camp cook can't take the race over. *The damned camp cook is older than Laz is!*

I sit on my camp tree stump near the fire, thinking up all this doubtless inflammatory stuff whilst tearing apart my chicken leg.

Damn, this is good chicken! I think as I munch. *Maybe the damned race* will *smarten up after all and join the 21st century. Use a lottery. Have* one *set date for applications from everywhere! Make the date earlier for all if more time continues to be needed by furriners to arrange their travel. And have only* one *"weight list." Consider a better Internet provider. And get with PayPal® for heaven's sake, and then charge everybody the nonrefundable $1.60* application fee *when they actually apply! Oh-my-god the race will be solvent by this time next year. Thousands upon thousands of dollar-sixties annually! Are you kidding? Do the math!*

And then, of course, Race Management can pay for its, or his, own damn holidays and vacations all over the planet, and hence be beholden to no one else on the planet. But The Icon *could* eventually, I suppose—after another 50 years—be beholden to the invaders from outer space.

Ack. Here comes Winter. Wanting, I suppose, to interrupt my (by now) supper.

BOOK 6 – Counterclockwise
Southern Discomfort (by Rita Mae Brown) or by now
Wait for Tomorrow (by Robert Wilder)
(Your Thirty-Fourth Objective)

"Why don't you quit all this, scRitch?" he asks.

"What?" Inwardly I'm suddenly petrified. *Can this guy read my mind?* "Quit all *what?*" I ask right back.

"All this cooking! What did you think I meant?"

"Oh, *uh* nothing."

"I mean," he continues, "what chef in the king's castle quit and made *you* cook?"

"Nobody. I was just hungry, I guess. So I 'put another shrimp on the barbie,'" I mock, "and the rest is history."

"Is it good?"

"Scrumptious!" I say, licking my fingers.

"Don't offer to cook *me* any."

"You said *quit!*"

"That's right, scRitch. Besides, I just had a nice visit with Yeeva and Doctor Bourbon over there at the Virginia campsite. They made me a nice grilled cheese sandwich."

"Did you check it for embedded plastic knife parts?"

"No. Should I have?"

"Never mind. It was a lame joke."

"Do we have any Fun Runners yet?"

"Not yet. There's only a few possibilities out there still."

"Who?"

"Well, I think Dr. Bourbon's son Dr. Metallica is one. Also Jam-Jam, The Swede, and Ginger Man, I think. And that's about it."

"So it looks like this is going to be another year when the course wins."

"Well, for the full five loops, I think. Nobody left here in time for a real Finish. But probably those guys can make a Fun Run."

"Maybe not."

No sooner does he say this when the shout goes out that three more runners are coming—also from the wrong direction.

Winter hurries over to the podium where Laz yet stands with the "easy" button. I get up and pitch my trash. Then I close up the still half-full (and still frozen!) Barkley chicken box, leave alone whatever chicken pieces still happen to be on the fire, and stand to pay my last respects to the three grateful not-yet-deads who themselves are standing for *Taps*. Three times.

That's when I decide to quit.

Might as well, huh?

Everybody else has!

Except The Ginger Man. But he's got something to prove. And besides, a Fun Run finish is *still* a DNF! He too will be *Tapped* out. **All are punished.**

Might as well head back next door and just…

…what…

…revisit the in-camp franchise of my own damn hotel?

On my way over to site #11, I suddenly remember a couple of book titles—*Southern Discomfort* (yes, this definitely is) and *Wait for Tomorrow*.

Right. I guess I'll get some sleep, then pack up and hit the road first thing in the morning.

*These Whole Pages Intentionally Left Blank
(you failed to collect them)*

Back Words

The Race That Pukes Its Old (and refuses to bury its dead)

Similar to the fore words, these back words also take their inspiration from words that have gone before; and just as I would have you first read Frozen Ed, I'd now like you to give a complete listen to Arlo Guthrie's classic recording of his rather long song *Alice's Restaurant* [from 1967, and you can easily find it on YouTube].

In it Arlo strums guitar and sings (actually he's just talking) for almost eight whole minutes when he says: "And we was fined $50 and had to pick up the garbage in the snow, but that's not what I came to tell you about."

Right. And you've just read 34 whole chapters (of failure), but that's not what I wanted to tell you about either.

Arlo came to protest against the United States Selective Service System (otherwise known as the draft), and I'm here to bitch about the future. Earlier in this stack of not-yet-ripped-out pages, I was giving Planet Earth another 500 years before it no longer harbors any life whatsoever (certainly not human). I'd like to change that. That is, I would like *you* to. I'm probably not going to be here to do it myself.

The thing that I would most like to change is the planetary death, not necessarily my prediction. Sort of like biblical old Lazarus himself, I'd like Earth to come back to life as well—and *keep coming back*. In fact it really shouldn't die in the first place.

But let's go from the sublime to the ridiculous for a moment, shall we? [And BTW, as the peeps all abbreviate today, I've had more than one English professor with an ironclad rule of rhetoric which is: "DON'T introduce a whole new topic in your summary at the end of your term paper." But I am nothing if not a rule-breaker. *Reckless and wanton rhetoric*—that's me! *PLOYS R US*. Besides, this isn't my term paper.] My point is, I just spent a whole book building up to a conclusion that doesn't have anything to do with the book.

Or does it?

But first, the "facts": This story about the Barkley Marathons® never happened. A lot of this stuff did happen, however, just not during the same event nor all at once. There were several years when no runner at all finished—just like here—but most years there would at least be some runners who finished the Fun Run (three loops) just as The Ginger Man was the only one to do it in this book. [Yes, he made those three full and complete laps around the park, and did *not* miss the final cutoff this time by a mere six seconds. He was still a non-finisher though.]

Another "fact" was that everyone could leave camp a day early, and we did. I had to speed home to meet a job obligation. Others probably hung around to try and steal my chicken recipe. (OK, that's not a "fact.") But Winter and I had long, long conversations during our races—just not this one, nor all-at-once during others. I've painted him as a real non-scruffy out-of-state highly educated hard-ass, but he's much more than that. He's a *bona fide* inventor, and NASA hired him to invent stuff. Some of his stuff was attached to the old Space Shuttle missions. And on top of that, he gave me a job. (But not the one I was speeding home to after this event let us out early.)

Imagine that. And after all our bickering, too!

More "facts": I've never done this race with a Race Management-issued wristwatch on. Neither has Winter. So you can't blame him for hallucinating over a spinning dial if it was my watch all the time. We also never did the race when Loop 2 was counterclockwise. In fact *we* never ever—not even once!—finished *one* full loop together. All of our attempts were partials. You know, half-assed.

I also never submitted the filled-in form appended to the back of this book. Its use here is for… I don't know what for. Maybe just as an example. Oh, I remember. I filled it out to show somebody else how to fill it out. You may in fact deduce a little tongue-in-cheek there?

So, during our unreal running of our imaginary loop, it ought to occur to somebody that we should have encountered other runners coming against us on their second loop (counterclockwise) while we were still on our first (clockwise). That didn't happen. Hey, it's imaginary!

Winter and I never went both forwards and backwards (alternating directions) during the same race either. We never got that far. So where I came up with these weird introductory and summary sections for this book I'll never know. But, oh yeah, the title of this end piece is also only a play on words. Just like the prefix. No, preface. The pre-fix is how race entrants are *infected, detected, inspected, injected, neglected, reflected, and see-lected.* (Thank you, Arlo Guthrie.)

The Why of The Barkley 213

So far (knock on paper reams) nobody has died out there, so the policy of non-burial has never fully been tested. Park authorities (and other authorities, like the Air Force) *have* scrambled their best fighters, hunters, and gatherers, however. You know, hunting for lost Barkers to gather them in and fight off their attackers—like sawbriars. But (again doing the paper knock) so far everyone has been quite successful at self-extraction.

Which brings us right up to the future, folks. As soon as some Barker does *not* get his or her own butt out of trouble and does indeed need the National Guard to trample down these lovely wicked woods in full-scale search-and-rescue mode, *that* will spell the end of this footrace. Don't let it happen! Wear good shoes and leggings. Carry a compass. Study your geography. Worship Ra the sun god.

These lovely dark and wicked woods are beautiful, serene, contemplative providers for your very worst footing and your very best thoughts. Winter has held it sacred, and Winter's as godless as they come. The smartest man I've ever met, he. Able to work math magic across three axes, and catapult theoretical physics at warp speed throughout this or any other galaxy. He's delineated and differentiated between String Theory and Quantum Physics, whereas I can barely recognize string cheese at the grocery store. And thanks, BTW, be to Cheeses, the Risen Crust. [I like that, sorry. I come from the City That Made Pizza Famous. Well, deep dish pizza. Hell, I used to bartend at the most famous deep dish pizza joint of all! But, no, I didn't have to speed away from The Barkley to go work a bartending shift. Although I'm guessing some will read this and wish that I *had* vanished, and saved everyone from this after-the-fact armchair footrace quarterbacking with all the disturbing chickenshit philosophizing thrown in.]

By the way, Winter used to complain that his own writing was too full of parentheses, brackets, and braces—just like mine—which is why he hired me to edit the manuscripts of his invention project reports to NASA.

More future: Hey, these bad old ugly Tennessee woods are precious. Just like Earth is. Please protect these places!

It was recently noted in, of all places, a printed magazine (one dedicated to no less a cause than saving the environment) that another great writer, Kurt Vonnegut, Jr., (author of the appropriately titled *Welcome to the Monkey House*, a paperback short story collection that, I'm sure, has made it onto the Barkley course) had a major complaint against the U.S. government. He asked why there is no President's Cabinet post for a Department of the Future. Indeed! *Why?*

Back Words

DO NOT, I caution, allow Earth to become Mars in just one more half-millennium! DO please find another planet for humankind to move to before our sun swells to a red giant and burns y'all worse than Barkley chicken.

[BTW, one last bracketed parenthetical before I break camp and hit the road: I used to espouse the theory that life on Earth *came* from Mars. (Yo. Here's the parentheses within the brackets.) Right. The Martians had completely ruined their great planet with pollution, greenhouse gasses, carbon emissions, trashed oceans, strip-mining, and poisoning all their insects while killing all their crops and ruining all their soil and being too stupid to recognize the *real* causes of cancer; and so they launched a rocket ship full of teensy little one-celled amoebas with their last dying breath before their atmosphere got sucked into outer space; and thus did their rocket crash-land on the third rock from the sun. (Of course, in their ineptitude, they missed. They were aiming for the second.) But fret not about amoebas in the future crash-landing from Saturn; I've since changed my mind about that.]

So, what else for the future of Earth? It's actually pretty simple. It's why I've written this book! *Why?*

Why, to entice Race Management to set it out somewhere along the course, of course, and have Barkers in the future rip it to shreds.

This Whole Page Goes in Front of Append Dick's (whatchamacallit)

Real Men Never Grow Up
(They Just Get Bigger)

Official Entry Form: 2016 Barkley 100 Mile

[scRitch's Note for Book Publication: Just *some* of the following has been changed, mostly to avoid lawsuits, but also to be as up-to-date as possible for 2019. Otherwise this is pretty much the same as I mostly used to sometimes submit. Also, whatever used to be in <u>RED</u> ink (from me) is shown here as black ink <u>underscored</u>.]

There is only one good reason to come to the Barkley<u>:</u> to find out if you are an egg…
or a potato.
When you put an egg in boiling water, it gets harder.
But if you put a potato in the same boiling water, you end up with mashed potatoes.
If you are a potato, you might as well stay home.
If you don't know which you are…
It probably won't take too long to find out.

◇◇◇◇◇◇◇◇◇◇◇◇◇◇◇◇◇◇◇◇◇◇◇◇◇◇◇◇◇◇◇◇◇

This is your one last clear opportunity to walk away with your reputation, your skin, your sanity, and your soul intact. Close this file, if it is open on your computer, and deliver any equipment which stored or displayed it to a hazardous waste disposal unit. If it has somehow escaped in hard copy form, incinerate the hard copy, reduce the ashes to molecular fragments, and deliver them in a hermetically sealed container to a hazardous waste disposal unit.

Either that, or mail your entry, and your $1.60 to:

Idiot
XXXX Millsomething Road
Some Place, TN 3XXXX
USA

Overseas entrants should send in your entries also. If you have been selected to run already, send in your entry fee as well as the $1.60. If you are on the weight list, only the $1.60 is necessary. If a slot comes open, and I do not have my $1.60, I will bypass you for the next name on the list. It only takes 4 of those entry fees to buy me a pack of Camels and a Dr Pepper…. And I like my Camels and DP's. Send this stuff in now. It is a pain in the ass to deal with it during the race weekend.
Sweet dreams, and painful training.

◇◇◇◇◇◇◇◇◇◇◇◇◇◇◇◇◇◇◇◇◇◇◇◇◇◇◇◇◇◇◇◇◇

Date: furnished with your acceptance.
Time: announced by a conch shell blast, one hour in advance.
Location: the yellow gate at Icehouse Delirium State Park.

218 Official Entry Form for 2016—filled in

Time Limit: 60 hours for the 100-mile men's race;
40 hours for the 60-mile fun run (women, children, and wimps).
No: GPS, Altimeters, Cell Phones, Pacers, Caching, or Anything else we don't approve.
Your Watch: will be supplied by the race after the conch sounds. It will be set to race time.
Layout: 20-mile loop…. To be repeated 5 times.
Aid: Water drops are possible at 8 and 13 miles each loop. Your car at the start/finish.
Net altitude change: 0 feet (0 meters).
Expected weather: Temperatures between 0- and 85-degrees F. Probable fog, rain, sleet, snow, hail, or high winds. Possibly all of the above. Possibly all within the same loop.
Application fee: $1.60 (non-refundable) and an essay on "Why I should be allowed to run the Barkley" (required before acceptance of entry or to be called from weight list).
Entry fee:
Virgins—a vehicle license plate from your home state or country.
Veterans (prior DNFs)—Overseas runners: an extra-large T-shirt, (with printing) from your home country. North American runners: A pack of Gold Toe white athletic socks. Alumni (see below*)—a pack of Camel Filter Cigarettes (regular).
Pre-race meal: Chicken BBQ. We provide digitally prepared BBQ Chicken & paper plates. Side items are potluck. Bring your own beverages. You will never find chicken like this anywhere else. (The cook works for praise… lavish it on him.)
Awards: After 5 loops, you don't have to go back out.
Requirements: No children; they are too small. No women; they are too soft. No Yankees; we don't want them buried here. No Crimson Tide fans; you can't eat chicken without teeth. No vegans; they provide no nutrition. No wimps, worms, slugs, or weenies, because they don't have what it takes.
How to find Icehouse Delirium: You are kidding, right? If you can't even find the park on your own, then what chance do you think you have during the race?

*The Barkley Marathons 100 Mile Alumni are: John Kelly (Class of '17), Nick Hollon (Class of '13), Travis Wildeboer (Class of '13), Brett Maune ('11, '12), Jared Campbell ('12,'14,'16), John Fegyveresi ('12), J.B. Basham ('10), Andrew Thompson ('09), Brian Robinson ('08), Mike Tilden ('04), Jim Nelson ('04) R.I.P.,

Ted "Cave Dog" **Keizer** ('03), Blake Wood ('01), David Horton ('01), and Mark Williams ('95). [Editor's Note: The one thing in this annual application that can always be counted on is that Ted's surname is always misspelled, which is, of course, ridiculous. One would think the genius that comes up with this stuff could at least correctly spell the names of *all* these magnificent finishers!]

◇◇◇◇◇◇◇◇◇◇◇◇◇◇◇◇◇◇◇◇◇◇◇◇◇◇◇◇◇◇

Written Exam:

1) Explain the excess positrons in the flux of cosmic rays:
Refer to the motion picture trilogy "Back To The Future." It's the flux capacitor that enables time travel in the first place, and any excess positrons might be found in the Posi-

Traction differential unit attached to the DeLorean's rear axle.

2) *What is the meaning of the name of the element Dysprosium?*
It's lanthanide, of course! Everybody knows that Dysprosium (also called Dy66) means lanthanide, in addition to possible other slang expressions for lanthanides, like "rare earths." In recent decades the singular of that expression was the name of a rock band.

3) *What is the closest living relative of the ginkgo biloba?*
I don't know, but they sell it in little plastic bottles at the GNC store. Bodybuilders swear by it. Ultrarunners swear at it. Everybody else just swears at *you*.

4) *Find a positive integer (n) that you can perform these calculations: (for odd numbers 3n + 1) (for even numbers n/2), repeating the calculations with the resulting values indefinitely, and not end up with the sequence 1,4,2,1,4,2,1,4,2...:*
You mean, NOT 1,4,2,1,4,2,1,4,2,1,4,3,1,4,2,1,4,4,1,4,2,1,4...? Well then, the answer is easy. Use whatever fucking integer DOESN'T result in that sequence! (There's probably lots of 'em.)

5) *Translate the Voynich Manuscript into English:*
The Wilfrid M. Voynich Manuscript. (That's in English.) It's named after the Polish-American antiquarian bookseller who acquired it in 1912, believe it or not. The contents of the manuscript—note that the question here does NOT ask for the *contents* to be translated—are indecipherable. The whole whacked-out thing has puzzled so-called scholars (and other Barkley runners) since the 15th or 16th century. Ah, I remember it well. I recall the idiotic monk who wrote it. His name was Friar Assiolith, and he was as nuts as Lazarus is. Today's "Official Barkley Instructions" bear a marked resemblance.

220 Official Entry Form for 2016—filled in

6) When did plate tectonics start?
Whenever the hell Planet Earth started. For other planets, possibly earlier. For still other yet-to-be-banged-out planets, more likely later.

7) What will be your finishing time for the first loop?
A century-and-a-half after the start. Possibly longer if I were to start this year. In previous years, my finish time was less, of course, but not by much. Then too, throughout my many decades of experience here, there only ever has been one finish of one loop once.

Extra Credit:

1) I am thinking of a number between 1 and 100. Name it:
42, which I believe is the answer to everything.

2) How much butter should you use to cook a pound of liver (with onions)?
$\frac{1}{2}$ to $\frac{3}{4}$ stick (lightly salted) or 3 full tubs if the butter is whipped. This is to remind the weight-conscious runner of his own eventual condition after enduring a like fraction, or whole number, of loops.

This Space Accidentally Left Blank

Name: _Richard "Barkley scRitch" Limacher_ Mayan Birthdate: _12/12/12 less 62 years, 9 months, 10 days_

Street: ___Yes, it's a street, as opposed to road, lane, circle, place, avenue, parkway, or back alley_____ Hat Size: __MAX_____

City: ___Yes, same as above. This ain't no town, village, outpost, or 'hood I'm livin' in. This here's a damn **city**._____ Favorite Parasite: __IDSP's superintendent___
State/
Nation/Zip: _Yes, yes, and yes (although ain't much damn "Zip" left anymore)_____
Next of kin: __Orangutan, or possibly Silverback (hair?) Gorilla_____
◇◇◇◇◇◇◇◇◇◇◇◇◇◇◇◇◇◇◇◇◇◇◇◇◇◇◇◇◇◇◇◇◇◇◇

I really <u>DO NOT</u> want to run the Barkley. I have been warned how hard it is. (*Hell, been there, done that.*) I have been warned that I am entirely responsible for my own safety and well-being. I know that I might get hurt out there, or die, or worse (!), but I promise to do everything possible to make my adventure a safe one. I agree to accept the decision of race management officials, should they deem me unfit to continue (*or even to stay alive*), and I also promise to haul my stinking carcass the hell OUT, should I croak and they decide not to bury me here. And I agree to reimburse all expenses, should a search or rescue be required on my behalf. If I am stupid enough to attempt the Barkley, I deserve to be held responsible for any result of that attempt, be it financial, physical, mental, or anything else.

Signed: _____*Electronically, by clicking the "OK" button?*_____
[Where's the damned "OK" button?]

Notarized: _____*Electronically, by clicking the "I'm a witness" button, "can I get a witness?" button, or by scrawling my name with a magic marker across my screen where this here line is, eh?*_____

Read and follow the next instruction, or your entry will be rescinded:

Go to: http://www.usatf.org/usatf/files/92/92fe11bc-4634-4e44-858f-71e03368e080.pdf
Fill out the USATF waiver form, and include it with your entry.
We need this for our insurance!

222 Official Entry Form for 2016—filled in

This Whole Page Intentionally Left Blank

[All righty then, leave the whole-and-entire pissing page *empty!*]

HERE (ON THE NEXT NO-LONGER-BLANK PAGE) IS MY DAMNED ESSAY:

Why I Should (or actually Should Not) Be Allowed To Run The Barkley

Ain't it obvious?

AND WHILE WE'RE ON THE SUBJECT, I'M THINKING SOME NEW CLARIFICATION NEEDS TO BE MADE REGARDING THIS ENTIRE FREAKISH "ENTRY" PROCESS TO BEGIN WITH. FOR INSTANCE, IF *THIS* SPACE (HERE ON THIS VERY ENTRY FORM) IS THE EXACT PLACE FOR ONE'S ENTRY ESSAY TO BE WRITTEN, THEN WHY ARE PEOPLE THINKING IT MUST BE WRITTEN *IN ADVANCE* AND *SUBMITTED ON THE OFFICIAL ENTRY-DAY NIGHT* (SPECIFICALLY AT THE FIRST CLOCK TICK AFTER MIDNIGHT ON THE VERY NEXT DAY)? PEEPS ARE VERY CONFUSED HERE! THE UNDERSTANDING THAT I'VE HAD ALL THESE YEARS IS THE FOLLOWING:

A) ON OFFICIAL ENTRY-DAY NIGHT, YOU SIMPLY E-MAIL YOUR "INTENTION" TO RUN THE BARKLEY; OR, *YOU KNOW*, HUMBLY BESEECH BARKLEY MANAGEMENT TO COUNTENANCE YOUR MISERABLE ENTREATY, AND CONSIDER YOUR BRAZEN INTENT OR REQUEST OR WHATEVER. HELL, IT'S GOOFY FROM THE GET-GO. IN YEARS PAST THE PROCESS WAS SIMPLER. FIRSTLY, "RACE MANAGEMENT" WOULD E-MAIL AN <u>INVITATION</u> *TO* WHOMEVER IT HAD PREVIOUSLY DECIDED WAS EVEN WORTHY TO APPLY; AND SECONDLY, THE RACE ENTRY/APPLICATION FORM (*I.E.*, THIS SHIT ENTRY BLANK RIGHT HERE) WOULD BE INCLUDED IN THAT E-MAILING. THEN B) THOSE SUBMISSIVE SUCKERS—WHO WISHED TO ENTERTAIN SAID INVITATION AND

Official Entry Form for 2016—filled in

ACTUALLY APPLY—WOULD *MAIL* (YES, VIA U.S. MAIL) THEIR FILLED-IN APPLICATION ***PLUS*** THE DOLLAR FIFTY-FIVE, (I BELIEVE THIS COST ONLY INCREASED TO $1.60 DUE TO INFLATION, OR BECAUSE CONFEDERATE CURRENCY WAS BELIEVED TO GO UP IN VALUE A NICKEL) WHICH WAS CONSIDERED THE NON-REFUNDABLE "**APPLICATION FEE**." <u>THIS MAILING, BY THE WAY, WAS SUPPOSED TO BE DELIBERATELY TIMED TO ARRIVE AT THE *IDIOT'S* ADDRESS ON UNION RIDGE WITH HIS NORMAL MAIL ON THE DAY AFTER OFFICIAL ENTRY-DAY NIGHT. HIS NIBS, THE IDIOT, WOULD THEN STACK HIS MAIL IN THE ORDER RECEIVED.</u> (YEAH, RIGHT.) THEN, AFTER FILLING THE RACE'S ALLOTTED "SLOTS," THE REMAINING MAIL WOULD COMPRISE THE (YOU GUESSED IT) "WEIGHT LIST." THE "**ENTRY FEE**" ON THE OTHER HAND—CONSISTING OF A LICENSE PLATE OR WHATEVER THE HELL ELSE WAS REQUIRED FOR ENTERING THE RACE—WOULD BE REQUIRED TO BE SUBMITTED, NATURALLY, **<u>AFTER</u>** ACCEPTANCE!

THAT ENTIRE PROCESS WAS IN EFFECT AT THE TIME I MYSELF FIRST APPLIED (IN 2001, AFTER FINDING AN INVITATION IN MY INBOX). EVER SINCE THEN, THIS GOOFY OVER-RELIANCE ON THE INTERNET HAS FUCKED **EVERYTHING** UP. NOBODY KNOWS *WTF* TO DO ANYMORE. PEOPLE EVEN MAIL IN LICENSE PLATES *BEFORE* THEY'RE ACCEPTED! IT'S GOTTEN SO STUPID GOOFY IN RECENT YEARS, THAT PEEPS THINK SUBMITTING A *HAIKU* IS **REQUIRED** EVEN FOR ACCEPTANCE ON THE BARKLEY E-MAIL LISTSERV! OTHER IDIOTS THINK THEIR RACE ACCEPTANCE ACTUALLY ***DEPENDS ON HOW FAST THEY HIT THE "SEND" BUTTON*** AT MIDNIGHT ON THE OFFICIAL ENTRY-DAY NIGHT, AND THEY *OFTEN* THINK THEY'RE ALSO SUPPOSED TO BE FILLING OUT *THIS* STUPID ENTRY FORM *BEFORE IT'S EVEN BEEN CREATED!* AND THEN (OH GEEZESUS) SOMETIME *AFTERWARDS* (WHENEVER THE HELL *HE* FEELS LIKE IT), RACE MANAGEMENT *FINALLY* CREATES HIS LATEST GOOFY GENIUS ENTRY FORM AND MAKES IT AVAILABLE TO ***EVERYBODY*** WHO HAPPENS TO BE ON THE BARKLEY E-MAIL LISTSERV (OR NOW EVEN ON THE BARKLEY FB PAGE); HENCE, WE HAVE *THIS* ABOMINATION THAT I'M NOW LATE IN FILLING OUT *RIGHT* <spit> *HERE!!!*

THERE IS NO WAY THAT MY SUBMITTING THIS CRAP SHOULD EVEN BE TOLERATED! I HAVEN'T BEEN INVITED! I CANNOT POSSIBLY BE ALLOWED TO FILL OUT THIS PISSANT FORM,

WRITE THIS PHILOSOPHICAL ESSAY, AND APPLY FOR RACE ENTRY WITHOUT FIRST RECEIVING A BLOODY DAMN INVITE!!! (*CAN I?*)

[NO EXTRA CHARGE, BY THE WAY, FOR MY YEARLY EDITING SERVICES. IT'S JUST SO FRUSTRATING—*YA KNOW?*—*NOT* TO BE UNDERSTOOD—*EVER!*—BY ANYONE SOUTH OF THE MASON-DIXON LINE.]

YANKEES *ARE* VALUABLE! WE *ARE* IMPORTANT FOR THE NATION'S LANGUAGE COMPREHENSION, AS WELL AS THE PRESERVATION OF ENGLISH ITELF! ALL POWER TO THE YANKEES! (SCREW THE CUBS AND WHITE SOX.) YOU *WANT* US BURIED THERE! OUR GRAVES BRING *TOURISTS!! AND* THEY *HAVE MONEY!!!* **YOU JOHNNY REBS HAVE NEEDED OUR CASH FOR YOUR RECONSTRUCTION EVER SINCE 1865!!!!**

[HEH. NEVER MIND.]

Printed by Amazon Italia Logistica S.r.l.
Torrazza Piemonte (TO), Italy